Women and Power
on Capitol Hill

WOMEN AND POWER ON CAPITOL HILL

Reconstructing the Congressional Women's Caucus

Irwin N. Gertzog

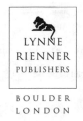

LYNNE
RIENNER
PUBLISHERS

BOULDER
LONDON

Published in the United States of America in 2004 by
Lynne Rienner Publishers, Inc.
1800 30th Street, Boulder, Colorado 80301
www.rienner.com

and in the United Kingdom by
Lynne Rienner Publishers, Inc.
3 Henrietta Street, Covent Garden, London WC2E 8LU

Library of Congress Cataloging-in-Publication Data
Gertzog, Irwin N., 1933–
   Women and power on Capitol Hill : Reconstructing the Congressional
Women's Caucus / by Irwin N. Gertzog.
      p.   cm.
   Includes bibliographical references (p.   ) and index.
   ISBN 1-58826-283-9 (hardcover : alk. paper)
   1. Congressional Caucus for Women's Issues—History. I. Title.
JK1417.G47 2004
328.73'076—dc22   2003020612

British Cataloguing in Publication Data
A Cataloguing in Publication record for this book
is available from the British Library.

Printed and bound in the United States of America

⊗ The paper used in this publication meets the requirements
     of the American National Standard for Permanence of
     Paper for Printed Library Materials Z39.48-1992.

   5 4 3 2 1

To the memory of my parents,
Sadie and Benjamin Gertzog

Contents

Acknowledgments   ix

Introduction: Before and After the "Republican Revolution"   1

1 Origin and Early Years: 1977–1981   7
    Strategic Goals *9*
    Workways *13*
    Policy Goals *14*
    Extending the ERA Time Limit *16*
    Organizational Strains *19*

2 Transformation and Growth: 1982–1992   23
    Membership Change *23*
    Countering the Reagan-Bush Agenda *25*
    Caucus Viability *29*

3 Before the "Republican Revolution": 1993–1994   35
    Inside the Numbers *35*
    Gaining Leverage *37*
    Aspiring to Power in the House *40*
    Promoting the Feminist Agenda *43*
    Tackling the Abortion Issue *50*
    The Unraveling of Bipartisanship *53*

4 The Republicans Take Control: 1995–1996   57
    Consolidating Power *58*
    Abolishing the LSOs *67*
    The Revolutionaries *71*
    The Contract and the Role of Government *74*

5 Coping with Change: 1995–1996   77
    Life as a CMO *77*
    The New Women *86*
    Abortion Rights Redux *92*
    A Tale of Two Sessions *103*
    The Erosion of Strategic Premises *109*

6 Reclaiming the Initiative: 1997–1998   117
    Recruiting New Members *119*
    Reinforcing Bipartisanship *121*
    Strengthening the Caucus Infrastructure *125*
    Promoting Consensus *127*
    Improving Rapport with House
      and Administration Leaders *139*
    Two Contested Elections *143*
    Assessing the Caucus in the 105th Congress *157*

7 Congresswomen and the New Millennium:
   The Future of the Caucus   161
    Recruiting Feminist Cochairs *162*
    Attracting Committed Congresswomen *164*
    Changing the Caucus's Structure *166*
    Finding a Usable Agenda *169*
    Adjusting to Competing Claims on National Resources *171*
    Connecting with the President
      and Congressional Leaders *172*

List of Interviewees   179
Bibliography   181
Index   187
About the Book   197

Acknowledgments

A s is the case for most studies of this kind, the publication of this book is in substantial measure the product of the ideas, the expertise, and the goodwill of many people willing to share their time and thoughts without regard for the credit or benefits they may receive.

The topic of this book emerged out of my conversations with Ruth Mandel and Deborah Walsh of the Eagleton Institute and the Center for American Women and Politics (CAWP). When I decided to undertake the project, they made available to me transcripts compiled by CAWP staff members Debra Dodson and Kathleen Casey, who did a superb job of questioning congresswomen and congressional aides about the role of women in the policymaking process.

Their taped conversations were supplemented by interviews I conducted with congresswomen and staff in 1993 and 1994, and between 1997 and 2003. (The names of representatives and staff who agreed to share their thoughts with the CAWP and with me appear in the List of Interviewees on p. 179.)

When gathering information for this book in Washington, I relied on the guidance and insights of Cindy Hall, first in her capacity as an aide to Congresswoman Constance Morella, and then later, after she had become president of Women's Policy Inc. (WPI). The policy expertise of WPI issue specialist Jennifer Lockwood-Shabat was unusually helpful. On Capitol Hill, I benefited especially from the assistance of Michael Gerber, Kathleen Havey, Cindy Pellegrini, Erin Prangley, Gail Ravnitsky, and two of my former students at Allegheny College, Susan Lexer and Derrick Owens. Anne Womeldorf and Larry Pearl provided me with a home away from home during my visits to Washington.

Two specialists in women and politics, Susan Carroll and Cindy

Simon Rosenthal, gave me helpful advice when the manuscript was ready to be sent to a publisher.

I also thank my wife, Alice, who read chapter drafts and who is my best critic and my best friend.

—Irwin N. Gertzog

Introduction: Before and After the "Republican Revolution"

This book traces the origin, development, and legislative contributions of the Congressional Caucus for Women's Issues (CCWI), and portrays the women who, since 1977, have been instrumental in championing CCWI priorities. It also describes the shifting institutional and political environment within which the caucus has sought to exert influence, and analyzes the tactics and strategies its leaders have devised to adjust to environmental changes.

The most significant of these changes by far occurred after the 1994 election, when, for the first time in forty years, Republicans seized control of the House and eliminated the offices, staffs, and finances of twenty-eight legislative service organizations (LSOs), the Congresswomen's Caucus among them. Denied the resources that had helped make the 103rd Congress (1993–1994) the most successful in CCWI history, caucus leaders scrambled to find alternative means by which to advance their women-friendly agenda. The task was daunting, and the 104th Congress (1995–1996) saw the CCWI falter and almost dissolve. The disparity in CCWI fortunes reflected in the 103rd compared with the 104th Congress could not have been more dramatic, and the consequences of these developments are still being felt in the first decade of the twenty-first century. What follows is an account of these changing fortunes—a description and analysis of how the CCWI carried out its mission before and after the "Republican revolution."

* * *

The 1994 election for the U.S. House of Representatives was the most consequential midterm contest since the end of World War II, arguably

1

since the beginning of the twentieth century. The election ended forty years of Democratic dominance, and it installed a zealous Republican majority determined to enact a conservative agenda, change the culture of Congress, and alter fundamentally the way politics worked in the nation's capital.

The undisputed architect of this "revolution" was Newt Gingrich, a once backbench Georgia maverick who, after years of attacking Democrats, mainstream Republicans, and the House itself, became the leader of his party and Speaker of the House. The new majority seized its responsibilities enthusiastically, energized by the exhilaration of victory and guided by an unprecedented congressional party platform—the Contract with America—to which virtually all Republicans had sworn fealty in the months preceding the election.

For Gingrich and GOP leaders, the Contract was the centerpiece of their dramatic victory and the template for their governance strategy. It provided an agenda for the 104th Congress and served as the cement holding Republicans to a common purpose. It also represented a symbolic embodiment of the claimed Republican mandate. And because its ten "commandments" could be expressed succinctly on an index card, it became a theatrical prop that could be whipped out of jacket pockets and flashed before sympathetic audiences. Essential though the Contract was for mobilizing and motivating the new majority, it was only the first step in the drive to repeal New Deal and Great Society social welfare programs.

To enact the Contract in the promised 100 days, Gingrich and his lieutenants changed House and party rules in order to centralize power within their own hands. At the same time, they stripped the Democratic minority of resources that could be used to delay, dilute, or defeat the majority's initiatives, and they silenced or eviscerated more than a score of partisan and bipartisan LSOs that might stand in their way. These informal House groups were a particularly vulnerable target, and were eliminated soon after the 104th Congress convened.

The LSOs were made up of House members who shared common characteristics—ideological orientations, racial or ethnic backgrounds, regional ties, or constituencies with similar economic interests. Members of each met periodically to explore ideas, common problems, and lawmaking possibilities. They used their groups to raise issues insufficiently addressed by House committees, to develop policy expertise, to obtain voting cues, and to formulate legislative strategies. Among the larger, better-known LSOs were the Democratic Study Group, a collection of liberal and moderate Democrats typically numbering more than

150, the Congressional Black Caucus, the Republican Study Committee, and the Congressional Caucus for Women's Issues.[1]

The LSOs coexisted with a much larger number of another type of informal group—congressional membership organizations (CMOs), as they came to be known beginning in 1995. Among the latter were the Asian Caucus, the Conservative Opportunity Society, the Sportsmen's Caucus, and the Chowder and Marching Society, the last of which was made up of mainstream Republicans.

LSOs and less formal House groups served many of the same purposes for their members, but there were fundamental structural differences between them. Unlike the latter, the LSOs hired staff who were separate and distinct from members' office workers and who furnished research assistance, public relations initiatives, and communication networks. LSO members used funds from their employee allowances to compensate the groups' staffs. And their organizations were given Capitol Hill office space, furnishings, and equipment, in much the same way that members were serviced to run their individual offices. Other informal groups benefited from none of these perquisites.

Over the years, LSOs had been under attack, often because critics believed their use of public funds, space, and equipment was an unwarranted drain on the public treasury. Other complaints grew out of the parochial policy goals they pursued, and their readiness to serve as conduits for special interest lobbyists. The most penetrating criticism of LSOs was that many did not keep accurate records of funds raised and spent. Sometimes the goods and services LSOs purchased smacked of patronage, and had little relevance to members' professional responsibilities or to legitimate congressional objectives.

In spite of charges that they played fast and loose with public funds, LSOs managed to survive and even prosper through the early 1990s. They had been in place for a generation or more, they had become valued components of the House structure, and virtually all boasted memberships that included influential Representatives of one party or the other—and sometimes both. Democratic leaders, who might have viewed these groups as competing centers of power, were nonetheless willing to allow them to be funded. They saw them as instruments for institutionalizing and managing House diversity, and as instrumentalities through which Republican and Democratic backbenchers could blow off steam.

After Republicans seized House control, charges of fiscal profligacy would have been ample justification for reforming or eliminating LSOs. But the new majority also feared that these publicly funded, well-staffed groups had the potential for derailing the Contract with America, and ultimately the Republican revolution. LSOs had championed affirmative action (the Congressional Black Caucus), more robust social and economic reform (the Democratic Study Group), stricter environmental controls on extractive industries (the Environmental and Energy Study Conference), and family and medical leave and abortion rights (the Congressional Caucus for Women's Issues).

Gingrich and other Republicans realized that if these and other LSO issues became salient, alternative agendas would divert attention from the Contract with America, and the narrow Republican majority—the smallest House majority since 1954—would have difficulty passing Contract proposals expeditiously. Consequently, in January 1995, as the 104th Congress got under way, the LSOs were denied their offices, furnishings, and equipment. House rules were changed to stop members from using their salary allowances to pay LSO staffs, and the groups were prevented from charging members fees to support newsletters, information packets, and public relations initiatives.

The LSOs exhibited a variety of responses to the challenge. For the influential Democratic Study Group, the rules changes were a death knell, and some of its staff were hired by the Congressional Quarterly publishing company. Most other LSOs, including the Congressional Black Caucus and the Hispanic Caucus, became CMOs. Their members continued to meet regularly to discuss issues of common interest, establish policy priorities, and map legislative strategies. But as CMOs, they were deprived of permanent, stand-alone staff. Support responsibilities were now shifted to office personnel of Representatives who were named CMO officers. Gone were the research talent, the specialized expertise, and the institutional memories that had made the LSOs important policy entrepreneurs—which is precisely what Contract proponents intended.

These changes were particularly painful for the Congressional Caucus for Women's Issues. The CCWI had risen from a relatively small, obscure coterie of 15 congresswomen and a single staff member in the 1970s to a visible and effective group of more than 40 women, nearly 120 dues-paying men, and a full-time staff of 6 by the mid-1990s. In the 103rd Congress, the caucus had for the first time established task forces on such issues as domestic violence and women's health. And it had worked with Bill and Hillary Clinton to promote a feminist agenda, successfully sponsoring family and medical leave legislation, appropriating hundreds of millions of dollars to finance research on diseases unique to women, and supporting abrogation of many of the anti-abortion rules adopted in the Reagan and Bush years.[2]

These dazzling successes in 1993 and 1994 made reverses in the next two years all the more dramatic. The CCWI went from a resourceful, aggressive, confident advocate for women-friendly policies to an understaffed, reactive, and desperate defender of the status quo. Its members suddenly found themselves working frantically not so much to promote new feminist initiatives but to salvage past legislative gains once thought to be beyond the reach of detractors. The change was so fundamental that it took more than a year for the caucus simply to recover its equilibrium. At this writing, it has yet to regain the full measure of influence it exerted before 1995. Nevertheless, the CCWI never stopped posting legislative milestones in selected policy domains, notably in the field of women's health, and to appreciate fully how it has affected public policy and congressional behavior, its history before as well as after the Republican revolution is worth exploring.

Notes

1. The group called itself the Congresswomen's Caucus when it was created in 1977, but changed its name in 1982 to the Congressional Caucus for Women's Issues after it admitted men as associate members.

2. Unless otherwise indicated, the President Bush referred to in the Introduction and Chapters 1 through 6 is George Herbert Walker Bush, the forty-first president. The President Bush referred to in Chapter 7 is George Walker Bush, the forty-third president.

1 Origin and Early Years: 1977–1981

The Congresswomen's Caucus was formally launched in March 1977, but not before a series of false starts. During the early 1970s, several women Representatives, including Patsy Mink (D–Hawaii), Margaret Heckler (R–Mass.), and Bella Abzug (D–N.Y.), had independently tried to organize women House members. These earlier efforts had been stymied by a combination of obstacles, the most troublesome of which was the reluctance of other congresswomen to join such a group. Those who believed in the utility of such a caucus reasoned that unless all women were members, this legislative service organization (LSO) would not be taken seriously by key decisionmakers inside and outside of Congress. Critics would label the upstart group as "unrepresentative" or a product of "marginal" congresswomen.

Membership of the most senior congresswomen was especially important to organizers, yet three veterans who would have added the most gravitas to a fledgling caucus were the least amenable to affiliation. Convincing someone like Julia Butler Hansen (D–Wash.) to join would have been a major coup, inasmuch as she chaired a subcommittee of the powerful Appropriations Committee and had won the abiding respect of her colleagues. Hansen was sympathetic to the women's movement, but she was an integral part of the prevailing power structure, and she had neither the time nor the need to identify with an informal House group whose durability and purposes were in doubt.

Two other congresswomen who would have given the proposed caucus greater credibility were Edith Green (D–Oreg.) and Leonor Sullivan (D–Mo.). But Green was hostile to the idea of a women's caucus. She had been instrumental in promoting the 1963 Equal Pay Act, which mandated equal pay for equal work; in passing Title IX of the 1972

Education Act, which prohibited gender discrimination in schools; and in prying the Equal Rights Amendment (ERA) out of the House Judiciary Committee, thereby forcing an up-or-down vote on the House floor. But Green believed that a congressional women's caucus would call attention more to divisions within the country than it would address women's needs, and she would have nothing to do with early efforts to create such a group.

Sullivan chaired the Merchant Marine and Fisheries Committee and, like Hansen and Green, was identified with important legislative achievements—particularly in the field of consumer protection. But unlike her two senior colleagues, she was openly contemptuous of the goals of the feminist movement. She was the only woman in the House to vote against the ERA, she urged the House to adopt a dress code that would prohibit women from wearing pant suits, and she insisted on being identified not as "Leonor Sullivan" but as "Mrs. John Sullivan," a preference rooted in her conservative social orientation. Insistence on this traditional form of address may also have been related to her having succeeded her husband in the House after he died, and her desire to perpetuate his memory. Mrs. Sullivan was secretary to the Democratic House Caucus and she agreed to use her access to the party leadership to help Democratic women secure desirable committee assignments. But she refused to countenance forming a women's caucus.

Senior congresswomen were not the only women harboring doubts about the value of a women's group. Junior colleagues questioned whether such an organization could adequately serve a coalition of members whose political interests and constituency demographics differed significantly. They also disagreed about the purposes a women's caucus could serve. Some saw it as exerting a united force to promote unanimously approved agendas, others as a catalyst for processing and refining legislative measures, and still others as simply a forum for exchanging ideas.

Skeptics were unsure about whether concentration on women's issues was a worthwhile or even an appropriate investment of their time. Several feared that their constituents and future election opponents would question the propriety of a caucus devoted exclusively to women's interests. Informal House groups promoting economic, regional, or ideological goals were commonly accepted, and many of these groups already existed in the House. Gender issues, on the other hand, had not yet been given the legitimacy enjoyed by other socioeconomic concerns, and public officials in most jurisdictions risked election defeat if they were branded as "feminists"—a charge that could alienate traditional women as well as men. For congresswomen from competitive districts, the potential risk was especially high.

Reluctance to affiliate with a women's group was deepened by their belief that membership would join them at the hip with one of the most controversial and, in some circles, despised members of the House—Bella Abzug. Abzug was a high-profile advocate of a half dozen hot-button issues, including abortion rights, affirmative action, gay rights, an immediate end to the Vietnam War, and military downsizing. Her stances resonated with her upper–Westside Manhattan constituents, but much of the rest of the United States was deeply conflicted on these issues. Abzug's outspoken advocacy (critics called it strident), her flamboyant style, and her ability to attract national media attention made Representatives from Middle America think twice before agreeing to become a member of any coalition of which she happened to be a part. Congresswomen invited to join a women's caucus in the early 1970s had to weigh the elusive advantages of membership against the prospect of sharing an organization with a woman whose domineering personality, appetite for controversial causes, and radical feminism could become political liabilities.

Consequently, the Congresswomen's Caucus was created only after congresswomen who were seen as standing in its way had left the House. By 1977, the start of the 95th Congress, Hansen, Green, and Sullivan had retired, and Abzug had relinquished her seat to run an unsuccessful campaign for the U.S. Senate. At the same time, two women emerged who had the energy, leadership skills, and motivation to form a congresswomen's caucus—Margaret Heckler (R–Mass.) and Elizabeth Holtzman (D–N.Y.). These congresswomen, working with like-minded colleagues, adopted a series of strategic goals calculated to blunt charges that the group was illegitimate and overcome doubts about its purpose.

Strategic Goals

The most important strategic goal adopted by founders of the Congresswomen's Caucus was to make the group's membership bipartisan. They reasoned that unless both Republican and Democratic women joined the caucus and promoted policies supported by lawmakers in both parties, their fledgling LSO would be dismissed as narrowly partisan and self-serving by colleagues, women's special interest organizations, and the media. Accordingly, Holtzman and Heckler established a leadership structure institutionalizing cooperation between members of the two parties. They created Democratic and Republican "cochair" positions, and ensured that at least one congresswoman from each party would fill the four remaining Executive Committee positions—treasurer and three at-large members. Heckler's decision to serve as GOP cochair was expected to help persuade outnumbered House Republicans that the new group would not become an instrument of the Democrats' liberal wing.

A second strategic goal was to make the caucus as inclusive and as representative as possible. All congresswomen were urged to join, and those selected for the Executive Committee posts collectively spoke for a broad cross section of women. Holtzman and Heckler had the confidence of major economic groups, inasmuch as they respectively enjoyed the confidence of labor unions and the business community. Shirley Chisholm (D–N.Y.), the first African American woman elected to Congress, was chosen as an at-large member, thereby assuring observers that the caucus would not confine its attention to the needs of middle-class, white women.

Barbara Mikulski (D–Md.) was also an at-large member. The Maryland Democrat had established excellent rapport with leaders of prominent women's organizations, groups that for years had been urging formation of a women's caucus through which they could try to affect policy decisions. She also had the respect of Speaker Thomas "Tip" O'Neill and other House power brokers. Yvonne Braithwaite Burke (D–Calif.) and Shirley Pettis (R–Calif.) rounded out the caucus leadership. Burke, a black lawyer from Los Angeles (and the first woman to give birth while serving in Congress), was named treasurer. Pettis had succeeded her husband in office after he was killed in a plane crash and, while not a part of the GOP power structure, was nonetheless considered a reliable conservative who took her cues from Republican leaders.

A third goal was to accommodate the diverse views congresswomen held about women's roles in society, and to help them realize their disparate objectives. To meet these objectives, caucus leaders agreed to honor members' policy differences, even if it meant diluting the group's impact on the legislative agenda. They vowed to be what one founder called a "pluralistic" group. She added, "We don't have commonly shared ideas about what women should be, and, consequently, do not expect or require a united front on all issues." Members were determined to search for consensus on policies affecting women, but acknowledged that they would not find one on all issues. Each congresswoman would decide for herself whether to support other congresswomen on an issue-by-issue basis. And leaders adopted a "unanimity rule," assuring members that no action would be taken in the name of the caucus unless it had the support of each and every one of them.

The issue of abortion was treated differently, with organizers agreeing to keep this most controversial of social issues off the caucus agenda. Holtzman was pro-choice, Heckler pro-life. They believed that taking abortion off the table would enhance their membership drive and obviate the prospect of having the caucus bogged down on a fractious, intractable issue. Eliminating this source of contention would make it easier for liberals, moderates, and conservatives to find common cause on other matters. In the meantime, individual members could promote their pro-choice or pro-life preferences independently.

A fourth strategic goal was to erase all doubt about the purposes the caucus would fulfill. Some believed that a women's caucus should use its numbers in concerted efforts to influence the character and fate of legislation. The model for this vision was the Congressional Black Caucus (CBC), an LSO whose members acted in a highly disciplined, united fashion, collectively throwing their weight behind legislative measures to exert leverage and produce outcomes helpful to their constituents. But the CBC was made up entirely of Democrats whose constituencies tended to be overwhelmingly black, and for whom broad consensus, if not unanimity, on issues was relatively easy to achieve. The Congresswomen's Caucus, by contrast, was a more diverse group, and prospects of its being a player in the deals brokered by coalition builders were unrealistic.

Nevertheless, there were several purposes the Congresswomen's Caucus could serve. One was as a catalyst and facilitator. Members were encouraged to air their priorities, discuss pending measures, and propose new initiatives. While doing so, they could benefit from the positive reinforcement of other congresswomen, enlist cosponsors, receive pointers on how to improve their product, gain insights about how better to market the product, be alerted to unintended consequences of their initiatives, and develop a parliamentary strategy best suited to securing congressional approval. By working with a group of sympathetic colleagues, congresswomen could more effectively (and more confidently) promote their women's agenda.

Another service the caucus could provide was that of a repository and incubator for ideas that had not yet obtained conventional acceptance, but could one day ripen. By keeping these ideas alive, their emergence in a digestible form at a propitious moment became more likely. With staff to help provide a clearinghouse and an institutional memory, the caucus would be in a position to salvage, store, and resurrect feminist proposals that Congress had initially been unwilling to take seriously. Finally, on policies attracting broad membership consensus, the caucus could also play an advocacy role.

A fifth goal of the Congresswomen's Caucus was to maintain good relations with House leaders, particularly majority Democrats. They informed Speaker Tip O'Neill of their plans, were awarded LSO status, and encountered no resistance to using room H-235 in the Capitol for weekly meetings. The space had been set aside for congresswomen in 1962, and although its official name was the "Congresswomen's Suite," it was used occasionally for meetings of other groups. After formation of the Congresswomen's Caucus, it was made available to women members only. This suite is a few steps away from the House floor and across the hall from the Speaker's "working offices." It was renamed the "Corinne 'Lindy' Boggs Congressional Women's Reading Room" in 1990, in part to honor a much-loved member prior to her retirement, in part to discourage covetous House leaders from one day claiming this desirable space as their own.

The caucus also was able to persuade House leaders to make available an office on the top floor of the Rayburn building. Room 2471 was among the least conspicuous facilities in the marble-laden, cavernous House office building, but it served the group's purposes well. It became caucus headquarters, housing its executive director. By the mid-1980s, it accommodated a full-time staff of five and a steady stream of college interns. (It was this space—together with its furnishings—that, no longer under the protection of a succession of Democratic leaders, was expropriated after the "Republican revolution.")

A final strategic goal was that of establishing rapport with the newly installed Carter administration. Caucus leaders were interested not only in promoting legislation designed to help women, but also in ensuring that statutes already on the books would be administered in a woman-friendly way. A good working relationship with Carter appointees meant that congresswomen would obtain direct access to White House and cabinet officials. These contacts would allow them to press their requests for new legislation, oversee executive agency behavior, encourage administration studies addressing women's unmet needs, and urge appointments of more women to executive and judicial branch vacancies.

The extent to which these six goals have been realized over the years has affected the amount of influence the caucus exerted in the House. When its efforts were genuinely bipartisan, when its membership was inclusive, when its agenda was broadly supported by members, when its financial, staffing, and physical resources were abundant, and when the support of House leaders and the White House was solid, then its organizational integrity was secure and its policy agenda was viable. All of these conditions were in place in 1993–1994, when the Congresswomen's Caucus was at its most effective.

In 1995, following the Republican revolution, the caucus had all but lost its bipartisan coloration. A large percentage of Republican women refused to join, while others were members in name only. At the same time, the highly controversial abortion issue came to dominate deliberations in the Congresswomen's Caucus. And after financial, physical, and staff resources evaporated, House leaders ignored the group. In the meantime, a sympathetic administration was too busy coming to terms with a hostile Republican Congress to pay attention to the caucus's policy goals.

The contrast between the caucus's vitality in the 103rd Congress and its weakness in the 104th could not have been starker. The differences will be described in Chapters 3–5. Suffice it to say here that the nature of the strategic goals initially established and the extent to which they are realized continue to affect the caucus's influence.

Workways

The first formal meeting of the Congresswomen's Caucus was held on April 19, 1977, in H-235, when four congresswomen discussed the high incidence of domestic violence, contemplating remedies Congress could prescribe. During the remainder of the 95th Congress, the caucus met weekly when the House was in session, with an average of nine of the fifteen members attending. Holtzman and Heckler alternated as chairs, and discussions were informal and wide-ranging. Members broached pressing issues, shared concerns about problems women faced, requested support or cosponsorship of legislative proposals, and speculated about parliamentary strategies they might employ.

Formal votes were rarely taken at these meetings, with members usually reaching consensus on how to advance their agenda. Individual congresswomen volunteered to take the lead in contacting party or committee leaders, calling the White House, or working with caucus staff to draft a letter or a press release. These loosely structured exchanges characterized almost all of the meetings during the early years of the caucus, and even after written agendas were prepared in subsequent years, freewheeling give-and-take has been the predominant mode of discourse.

During the first two years of its operation, the caucus invited a dozen members of the Carter administration to attend its meetings. Guests made short presentations about women-related programs they were administering, and responded to questions. Sessions with secretaries of commerce and labor focused on opportunities for women in business and in the labor force. The secretary of the Department of Health, Education, and Welfare (a department about to spin off a separate education portfolio) was asked about circumscribed opportunities for women in higher education, the limited amount of research being conducted on breast cancer and osteoporosis, and programs designed to assist women and children on welfare. And the director of the Office of Management and Budget was periodically quizzed about the impact the president's proposed budget would have on working women, poor women, aged women, minority women, divorced women, and widows.

Guest appearances became a staple of caucus meetings in 1977 and 1978. They were well attended, and the face-time congresswomen spent with key decisionmakers rivaled any enjoyed by House colleagues. These sessions continued during the 96th Congress, the last two years of the Carter administration, but at a reduced rate. They were largely discontinued in the Reagan years, partially resuscitated during the Bush administration, and fully restored after Clinton became president. They all but disappeared after the election of George W. Bush. The ebb and flow of these interactions continues to be influenced primarily by how much the caucus and its agenda are valued by the administration.

Growth in the size of caucus staff allowed its members to undertake more ambitious legislative and public relations initiatives. The group's executive director played a critical role in coordinating caucus meetings and following up on proposals growing out of these meetings. The director also kept members apprised of the status of legislation, relevant upcoming events, and new research findings generated by caucus staff and outside specialists. She was responsible for helping the cochairs poll the membership to determine the extent to which a proposed caucus action—a letter to the president, a press release, explicit endorsement of a bill—had the support of rank-and-file congresswomen.

Policy Goals

Several weeks before the first caucus meeting, Barbara Mikulski sent a questionnaire to the other seventeen women House members asking them to identify women's issues worthy of caucus attention in the 95th

Congress. Thirteen responded. Leading the list of priorities was the need to provide more high-level jobs for women in the federal government. Other frequently mentioned goals were a less discriminatory social security system, improved health care, increased availability of child care, and help for displaced homemakers—women abandoned by husbands and left with scant financial resources and no marketable skills.

During the next five years, caucus members struggled to make these and other issues part of the congressional agenda. The tactics they adopted during the late 1970s, while not always successful, were serviceable enough to warrant continued use into the 1990s. One approach was to focus upon a feminist policy that had already received legislative sanction and to call for more vigorous enforcement of its provisions. Title IX of the 1972 Education Act, a measure forbidding gender discrimination in education, is a case in point. Caucus members argued that the statute's goals were not being achieved quickly enough and asked the administration for more conscientious enforcement.

A second tactic was to extend the benefits of laws affecting one group of women to women in similar but legally exempted circumstances. After the caucus helped push through a law providing former wives of Foreign Services officers with pro rata shares of their former husbands' pensions in divorce settlements, it worked to promote the same benefits for women who had been divorced by military and civil service personnel.

A third tactic was to bundle legislative proposals dealing with related subjects under a single rubric and introduce it as an omnibus bill. This practice allowed each caucus member to add one or more legislative priorities to a caucus-sponsored measure, thereby enlarging the stake each had in the package and increasing the likelihood that at least some of the items in the grab bag would be enacted. One such measure was labeled the Economic Equity Act. It was introduced soon after the caucus was established, with variations offered in every Congress thereafter through 1996. Another package of bills, the Women's Health Equity Act, appeared first in 1990 and it, too, took on a life of its own. In any given year, only a few of the act's components received congressional attention. But more and more were adopted over time, and the caucus retained within its institutional memory versions of unsuccessful proposals, poised to resubmit them in subsequent Congresses until they were enacted as ideas whose time had come or until caucus objectives had been achieved through other means.[1]

A typical Economic Equity Act included a score or more of items, including assistance for women in business, improved social security benefits, prohibitions on discrimination against women in the work-force, more entitlement aid for poor women, increased opportunities for women in the military, and financial incentives for women contemplating specialization in math and science. Caucus members were also interested in finding ways to help women who were fulfilling traditional responsibilities. They maintained that such women were at a disadvantage because, while willingly performing tasks mandated by cultural norms, women suffered inasmuch as society assigned no monetary value to the tasks they performed. When women were divorced or widowed, neither the social security system nor private pension systems compensated them to a degree commensurate with their familial contributions. Many were poorly served in divorce courts as well.

One other tactic caucus members employed was to seize on a dramatic development or revelation to promote a feminist cause. An administration study documenting the high incidence of spousal abuse sparked a spate of measures to help battered victims and impose stiffer penalties on batterers. When the Treasury Department announced it was minting a new silver dollar, caucus members successfully urged that the coin bear the image of suffragist Susan B. Anthony. And after defense attorneys in high-profile rape cases asked rape victims about their prior sexual history, the caucus rallied around rape shield legislation prohibiting that line of questioning in federal courts.

During these early years, caucus-sponsored bills were aired in committee hearings, and a few, like the one creating the Susan B. Anthony silver dollar, were enacted into law. But most caucus proposals were given little serious attention by leaders of the standing committees, and while their reintroduction in each Congress became a ritual, most were regularly relegated to the back burner. According to Congresswoman Pat Schroeder (D–Colo.), "The women in Congress had to wage virtually every battle alone, whether we were fighting for female pages (there were none) or a place where we could pee. . . . There were men's bathrooms right off the main floor of the House, but the ladies room was at the end of the earth" (Schroeder 1997, p. 31). The most important exception to this pattern was the caucus's successful drive to extend the time period during which the Equal Rights Amendment could be approved by the states.

Extending the ERA Time Limit

Congress passed the Equal Rights Amendment in March 1972, fifty years after the measure was first introduced. The vote was overwhelming—354 to 24 in the House, 84 to 8 in the Senate. But the size of these margins belied both the intensity of the half-century struggle and the fact that the resolution reached the House floor only after a discharge petition freed it from the grasp of an antagonistic Judiciary Committee chairman.[2] Now the measure was in the hands of state legislatures, three-quarters of which had to approve it within a seven-year period before it could be added to the Constitution.

The states' initial reaction was overwhelmingly positive. Before the year ended, twenty-two had approved the amendment. Eight more followed suit in 1973, bringing the total to thirty, eight shy of the number needed for ratification. But succeeding years saw a decline in ERA momentum, as more conservative legislatures—mainly in the South and West—began routinely voting the measure down. Between 1974 and 1977, five more states were added to the list, but proponents became increasingly uncertain about which three of the remaining fifteen would help them reach the thirty-eight-state threshold.

Organizations opposing the ERA were growing in number, size, and influence, and they were successfully promoting arguments that state legislators and their constituents found compelling. Claims that the amendment would send women into combat, that it would lead to unisex bathrooms, and that it would give constitutional permanence to the reproductive rights conferred by *Roe v. Wade* swelled the ranks of ERA critics (Mansbridge 1986). To complicate matters, four state legislatures had rejected the amendment after having initially voted for it, and observers were in doubt about whether Congress would consider the first or the second of these actions controlling.

With time running out, caucus leaders decided to try to extend the period during which states could consider the ERA. In October 1977, caucus cochair Elizabeth Holtzman introduced a resolution extending the March 1979 deadline by seven years. Sponsors of the measure maintained that since their proposal did not affect the substance of the amendment, merely the span of years during which it could be considered, majority votes in the House and Senate, rather than the two-thirds majority normally needed to pass constitutional amendments, would be enough to extend the time limit. They also argued that Congress should ignore state actions to rescind their initial approval of the ERA, and recognize earlier adoption of the amendment as binding.

Caucus members were under no illusions about the difficulties they faced. House Democratic leaders pledged their cooperation, but advised Holtzman that chances of passage in the form she preferred were dim. There was no precedent for extending the time period for state consideration of a constitutional amendment, and opponents were determined to require passage of the extension by a two-thirds vote. They also asserted that if states were given more time to consider the amendment, a state's right to reverse earlier approval of the measure during the expanded time period should be recognized as well.

To get the measure out of the House Judiciary Committee, a panel on which she sat, Holtzman was forced to compromise on the length of the extension. Seven years was adjudged too long, even by some ERA supporters, and the committee shortened the proposed time span to three years and three months—which set the expiration date at June 30, 1982. On the other hand, the committee recommended that a simple majority vote be sufficient for the resolution's passage. It also refused to acknowledge the right of states that had passed the ERA to reverse that decision during the expanded time frame.

This generally positive outcome for ERA proponents was, in large measure, a product of caucus efforts. Holtzman, Heckler, Mikulski, Gladys Spellman (D–Md.), and Pat Schroeder helped mobilize women's groups all over the country, meeting with their leaders on Capitol Hill and urging supporters to write or call key Representatives. Caucus members conferred with women's delegations three and four times a week in their own offices and their Rayburn building headquarters. Representatives of the National Organization for Women and the National Women's Political Caucus were joined in Judiciary Committee hearings by the heads of less politically oriented organizations, like the Young Women's Christian Association and the Girl Scouts of America. And at this first stage of the deliberation process, they prevailed.

But the Judiciary Committee version evoked strong protests from ERA critics, who promised to defeat if not seriously weaken it when it came to the floor for debate. For a time it appeared as if the opposition would succeed. Sentiment seemed to be running in favor of requiring a two-thirds vote and of allowing states to rescind previous ERA approval. Caucus leaders responded by conducting an intensive lobbying campaign among House and Senate colleagues. They began another round of meetings among themselves and with supporters, identifying lawmakers who could be converted to their cause, and who could be reached by White House or interest group appeals. When a congressman advised them that constituency opinion made it impossible for him to vote for the ERA, they acknowledged this political necessity, but asked for his vote against amendments that would weaken the measure, suggesting that the vote against final passage would give him the political cover he needed.

Ultimately, their tactics worked. Amendments to require a two-thirds vote and allow rescissions were defeated, and the extension was passed—230 to 189 in the House, 60 to 36 in the Senate. All but one of the eighteen congresswomen voted in favor of the amendment, with the lone dissenter "paired" against it. The closest call was on the rescission amendment. A switch of sixteen would have given states explicit authority to reverse prior approval of the amendment. Thirty-four Representatives who voted against ERA extension also voted against allowing state legislatures to rescind earlier ERA approval. Almost all had been lobbied actively by caucus members.

The resolution's adoption represented the most significant caucus achievement in its early years. It had forced the House to make the ERA part of the legislative agenda even though party leaders had little appetite for a battle that was unprecedented and likely to fail. Moreover, it had built a winning coalition and devised a legislative strategy to allow the coalition to work its will. Largely through caucus efforts, a probable defeat turned into a signal victory, no small achievement for an organization barely a year old. But in the end, the caucus's legislative victory proved to be hollow. Not a single additional state legislature approved the ERA during the extension period, and on June 30, 1982, the proposed amendment died.

Organizational Strains

The caucus's organizational integrity during these early years was fragile. Obstacles to achieving strategic and policy goals surfaced soon after its formation, and they recurred intermittently even after the group gained greater stability. Most troublesome were challenges to enroll all congresswomen, to achieve fiscal viability, and to establish a reputation for bipartisanship. Threats to all three of these organizational imperatives forced caucus leaders to limit their policy agenda.

Not all congresswomen were predisposed to join the caucus, and concessions were made to attract members. Fifteen of eighteen joined in 1977, with the skeptics among them reassured that no document would be distributed under the caucus's imprimatur unless it had the unanimous support of the membership. They were also advised that annual dues requirements ($50) and expected contributions from clerk-hire allowances ($2,500) could be understood as discretionary.

Retirements and election defeats in 1978 meant that six caucus members would not return for the 96th Congress. However, the midterm election produced three new congresswomen—Democrats Beverly Byron (Md.) and Geraldine Ferraro (N.Y.), and Republican Olympia Snowe (Maine). Cochairs Holtzman and Heckler, together with Lindy Boggs (D–La.), met with the three first-termers and later with the three women who had not joined the caucus in the preceding Congress—Republicans Marjorie Holt (Md.) and Virginia Smith (Nebr.), and Democrat Marilyn Lloyd (Tenn.). Each of the six subsequently affiliated with the caucus. This meant that all fifteen congresswomen serving in 1979 and 1980 were caucus members and that the goal of total inclusivity had been reached.

But this achievement came at significant cost. The unanimity rule led to inordinate amounts of time being devoted to persuading hesitant members that proposals cleared by the cochairs were worthy of caucus sponsorship. It forced the group to water down and limit caucus-sponsored initiatives, and even benign legislative measures, press releases, and letters to the president were delayed by nitpicking disagreements over wording and tone. In the meantime, proposals having majority but not unanimous support were denied organizational authorship. Before long, the percentage of members attending meetings fell off sharply, and many fewer members of the Carter administration were invited to these weekly sessions. The decision by Holtzman to cut back on her caucus activities while campaigning for a Senate seat in the 1980 election further slowed the group's momentum.

Lax enforcement of members' financial responsibilities threatened timely compensation of staff. Betty Dooley, the group's first executive director, and her immediate successors, Susan Scanlan and Ann Charnley Smith, struggled with limited resources to coordinate caucus activities. In 1980, Smith worked with the caucus cochairs to devise a remedy for the problem. She inaugurated a biweekly newsletter, *Update,* which was designed to provide timely information on the status of legislation affecting women, information until then unavailable in a single, easily accessible source. The newsletter summarized bills salient to the caucus, announced pending hearings, reported federal regulations adopted by government agencies, and presented special reports on issues that had ripened in recent months.

But *Update*'s raison d'être was more financial than informational. The publication was free of charge to caucus members, but other Representatives, along with Senators and interest groups tracking women's issues, paid an annual subscription fee of $125. Corporate subscriptions were priced at $1,000. By mid-1981, the newsletter had generated revenue that, together with contributions from congresswomen who met their financial obligations, was enough to cover staff costs.

In the 97th Congress, problems associated with inclusivity were accompanied by caucus difficulties maintaining a bipartisan image. The 1980 election saw the addition of four moderate Republican congress-women, all of whom the cochairs believed could be induced to affiliate. Three of the four had received campaign support from women's groups, and each represented a constituency whose demographics would not normally threaten a Republican incumbent interested in women's issues. Heckler and Schroeder, who had replaced Holtzman as the Democratic cochair, were optimistic when they began recruiting the four first-termers after the 97th Congress convened.

But all four rejected the cochairs' overtures. They explained that adjusting to legislative and representational responsibilities would leave them little time for caucus activities and, further, that they were not sure an annual contribution of $2,500 from clerk-hire allowances was worth the benefits caucus membership conferred. One GOP first-termer also volunteered that gender might not be an appropriate criterion for evaluating legislative proposals inasmuch as all policies ultimately affect both men and women. But the four women could not help but have been influenced by the election of a conservative Republican president. Ronald Reagan left no doubt about where he stood on most issues—he strenuously opposed the Equal Rights Amendment, for example, asserting that equality for women could be obtained through other means—and new congressional Republicans, regardless of their gender, tended to withhold commitments that could conceivably put them at odds with the White House.

Decisions by the four to decline membership was a blow to the reputation of the caucus, and especially galling to Heckler. The Massachusetts Republican was often torn between the conservative orthodoxy of her party and the progressive orientations of most caucus activists. She had hoped that the addition of the new GOP congresswomen would bolster the bipartisan character of the organization and help her steer a moderate course. The prospect of recruiting Republican reinforcements, therefore, was enormously appealing, and when none of the four signed on, she was deeply disappointed.

By the summer of 1981, frustrations of the cochairs and the Executive Committee became intolerable. After examining the new administration's budget proposals, they had concluded that Reagan's policies would wreak havoc on women who were least able to help themselves. The White House was proposing cuts in food stamps, Aid to Families with Dependent Children, Medicaid, the Social Security Minimum Benefits program (three-quarters of whose beneficiaries were women), the

Women, Infants, and Children program, and the Legal Services Corporation (two-thirds of whose clients were poor women).

But criticism of the Reagan administration in the name of the caucus was impossible. The unanimity rule allowed the opposition of a single caucus member to block it. Delays necessitated by requiring all caucus members to sign off on proposals were just as obstructive. As a result, those wishing to speak out against the administration were forced to act either individually or through the collective voices of smaller combinations of congresswomen. The cochairs gave up trying to meet regularly, partly because of poor attendance, and most of their invitations to cabinet and other Reagan advisers were either refused or ignored. A session with Social Security Administrator John Svahn became acrimonious and, from the caucus's perspective, counterproductive.

And then, in July 1981, the Executive Committee decided to end the inertia. First, it repealed the unanimity rule, thereby allowing initiatives to go forward with less than full caucus concurrence. Second, it imposed a seventy-two-hour time limit on how long members could delay a proposed caucus action by withholding approval. Finally, the committee voted to require, rather than simply "urge," $2,500 annual contributions. The response was immediate and predictable. The four most conservative members of the caucus, two Democrats and two Republicans, resigned. Their departure permitted remaining members to be more aggressive in promoting a feminist agenda, and consensus on most issues became routine.

Having sacrificed inclusiveness and size for greater homogeneity and fiscal integrity, the caucus was now poised to adopt a more comprehensive agenda and to articulate its goals more forcefully during the remainder of the 97th Congress. But in the fall of 1981, the House Administration Committee adopted new rules governing the operations of LSOs, and the caucus was forced to change both its fundraising procedures and its criteria for determining who could join its ranks.

Notes

1. Kingdon (1995) offers a seminal discussion of "an idea whose time has come."

2. The Democratic chair of the Judiciary Committee, Emanuel Celler of New York, adamantly opposed the proposed amendment, and had it not been for the efforts of Martha Griffiths (D–Mich.) and other pro-ERA members, it would have been bottled up indefinitely.

2 Transformation and Growth: 1982–1992

Membership Change

The 1981 House rules-change altered the ways in which legislative service organizations (LSOs) could raise funds to pay their staff and meet other costs. Under the old guidelines, these groups could occupy space in House office buildings, use office supplies and equipment, and raise funds from sources inside Congress (members' contributions from their clerk-hire allowances) and outside Congress (donations and subscription fees from interest groups). Under the new rules, LSOs could continue to depend on public office space and furnishings, but only if they stopped accepting funds from outside sources.

For the Congresswomen's Caucus this meant that if it wished to continue operating on Capitol Hill—using the Rayburn office and all its furnishings—it would have to end its reliance on *Update* subscriptions paid for by private interest groups. Elimination of this source of funding would once again threaten the group's financial viability inasmuch as contributions from fewer than a dozen members could not sustain a staff. Consequently, the caucus was faced with a dilemma: move its staff operations out of public space on Capitol Hill and continue to benefit from interest group subscription fees, or keep its Rayburn Building quarters and furnishings and retain a token staff. The former would affect the quality of the interaction between staff and members. The latter would sap the group of its vitality, and some members feared the caucus would have to be abandoned. Faced with a Hobson's choice, the caucus decided to open its membership to congressmen. *Update* subscription payments from men willing to join the group would replace revenue contributed by interest groups. Congressmen would pay annual dues as well.

Ever since the caucus had been launched, members had intermittently discussed the virtues of admitting men. They acknowledged that some congressmen were more ardent feminists than some congresswomen, and that the former could do more to help achieve caucus goals because more of them were close to the House's centers of power. But some feared that congressmen would try to take over the organization if admitted and use it for their own purposes. Skeptics also pointed out that an open invitation to congressmen would possibly attract colleagues who would try to trade on their affiliation while actively opposing policy goals congresswomen considered sacrosanct.

These arguments became academic when the caucus bowed to fiscal necessity and opened its doors to congressmen. The new recruits did not have the same standing as congresswomen, however. They were considered "associate" members and, as such, were ineligible to vote for caucus officers or on policy. They were also barred from positions on the Executive Committee.[1] According to Cochair Pat Schroeder, "When men were admitted to the Caucus, . . . we basically said 'we'll tell you what the issues are. Have a nice day'" (Schroeder 1997, p. 30). The new male members were not billed the full $2,500 annual subscription costs for *Update,* the sum paid by congresswomen. Instead, they were assessed $600, a figure later raised to $900 when women's dues were reduced to $1,800.

The change in membership required a change in the name of the caucus as well, and on March 2, 1982, the Congresswomen's Caucus was renamed the Congressional Caucus for Women's Issues (CCWI). Within two weeks, 66 congressmen affiliated, and the number reached 100 before year's end. Among the more illustrious newcomers was House Speaker Tip O'Neill, a colleague whose "associate" membership congresswomen were quick to point out when they sought new members after each election. It helped that O'Neill was the most approachable of House leaders. Schroeder later observed, "I rarely needed a formal appointment with him. He was always schlepping through the cloakroom, stopping to chat and smoking a cigar" (Schroeder 1997, p. 206).

Precipitate growth in membership toward the end of the 97th Congress was followed by incremental growth in subsequent years. By 1992, all Democratic women and two-thirds of Republican women were members of the group (see Table 2.1). The small number of Republican women in the House during this period tends to exaggerate the percentage-point changes revealed in the table. Nonetheless, that the membership of Republican congresswomen went from three of nine in 1984 to six of nine in 1992 suggests that the caucus's attraction to GOP women

Table 2.1 Caucus Membership, 98th–103rd Congresses (1983–1994)

Congress	% of Democrats		% of Republicans		% of House	
	Female	Male	Female	Male	Female	Male
98th (1983–1984)	85%	42%	33%	5%	64%	28%
	(11)	(107)	(3)	(8)	(14)	(115)
99th (1985–1986)	83%	39%	36%	6%	61%	24%
	(10)	(94)	(4)	(5)	(14)	(99)
100th (1987–1988)	92%	33%	55%	7%	74%	23%
	(11)	(83)	(6)	(12)	(17)	(95)
101st (1989–1990)	93%	42%	55%	8%	77%	28%
	(14)	(102)	(6)	(13)	(20)	(115)
102nd (1991–1992)	100%	53%	67%	8%	89%	35%
	(19)	(130)	(6)	(13)	(25)	(143)
103rd (1993–1994)	97%	49%	58%	3%	87%	30%
	(35)	(111)	(7)	(5)	(42)	(116)

Source: Congressional Caucus for Women's Issues 1983–1994.

was stronger than the antifeminist signals sent out by a Republican-controlled White House.

Growth in the percentage of Democratic congressmen, albeit irregular, is also evident. The early rush to affiliation by these Representatives was followed by little change in their proportions until 1992, when more than one-half (53 percent) in the 102nd Congress were associate members. Unwillingness of Republican congressmen to join is perhaps the most significant pattern revealed in the table. Fewer than one in ten affiliated during this period, a proportion that reflects not only the failure of feminist issues to resonate with Republican congressmen, but also the dangers the feminist agenda would face if these men ever became a House majority.

Countering the Reagan-Bush Agenda

The caucus's augmented numbers did little to head off the Reagan-Bush assault on landmark gains women had made during the preceding twenty years. Actions taken by the Reagan administration between 1981 and 1988 had the effect of rolling back feminist achievements in such areas as affirmative action, educational equity, social welfare, and family planning. The White House proved to be resourceful in crafting legislation, issuing executive orders, and making administrative and judicial appointments that had the effect of restricting women's socioeconomic opportunities to those available in the years just after World War II.

Affirmative action and equal employment programs were among President Reagan's prime targets. The Justice Department filed a series of Supreme Court briefs supporting narrow interpretations of affirmative action legislation and judicial rulings, and sought to reopen affirmative action consent decrees entered into by more than fifty cities and counties in order to dilute or end these negotiated settlements. At the same time, Reagan appointees on the Federal Communications Commission (FCC) voted to abandon affirmative action guidelines when awarding broadcast licenses, in one case forcing a woman to relinquish a license granted her by an earlier FCC ruling. The president fired critics on the Civil Rights Commission, replacing them with conservative allies. And his appointee to chair the Equal Employment Opportunities Commission, future Supreme Court Justice Clarence Thomas, abandoned use of numerical guidelines and timetables to help settle employment discrimination cases, which resulted in the resolution of fewer discrimination claims.

The administration's attack on Title IX of the Education Act, legislation prohibiting gender discrimination in education, led to both an important Supreme Court decision and a Civil Rights Act overturning that decision. During the Carter years, Pennsylvania's Grove City College denied that it discriminated against women, but refused to sign a pledge to that effect, a requirement of the law. The college claimed that inasmuch as it was not the beneficiary of federal funds, except as they were made available to students in the form of tuition loans and grants, Title IX strictures did not apply to Grove City. The Carter administration thought otherwise and advised the college to either formally affirm its nondiscrimination policy or risk the loss of the federal funds students used to pay tuition.

Grove City challenged the ruling, and the case had not yet been decided on appeal when Ronald Reagan became president. His Justice Department abandoned its predecessor's position and sided with the college. It now argued that since none of the institution's programs benefited from federal assistance, it was not affected by Title IX requirements. Federal funds supporting student tuition, asserted the Justice Department, were benefits conferred directly on students, not the college, and therefore should not be construed as federal aid to Grove City.

The Supreme Court's decision, *Grove City v. Bell* (1983), gave a narrow interpretation to Title IX. It held that federally supported tuition payments made the college subject to Title IX. But the Court went on to say that the legislation's reach extended only to those programs supported by the funds, which in a case of tuition support meant the admissions program. Since no financial aid went, for example, to its academic programs, the college was under no obligation to abide by the Education Act when organizing and administering its curriculum. CCWI members were outraged by the decision and successfully promoted the Civil Rights Act of 1991 to overturn it

During this period, the caucus battled scores of administration attempts to cut back women-friendly social welfare programs, including social security benefits and aid to new mothers and their children. A troubling proposal offered by the Office of Management and Budget (OMB) threatened to eliminate standard census questions dealing with housing, employment, and social services. The ostensible justification for paring down the questionnaire was to expedite administration of the 1990 census and, as a result, save money. Caucus members charged that the OMB was motivated not by financial considerations but by a political agenda. They argued that if these socioeconomic data were not collected, there would be no information base upon which to build a case for improving and expanding programs to address housing, employment, and welfare needs. Within weeks, the OMB backed off and most of the disputed census questions were restored.

Even though the caucus took no official position on abortion, it supported family planning, and during the Reagan-Bush years it was embroiled in more than a dozen battles to preserve programs whose purpose was to help women and their spouses prevent unwanted pregnancies. Federally supported family planning clinics were serving on the front line of these efforts, using trained medical and social service personnel to counsel clients. The Reagan administration threatened their counseling routines when the Department of Health and Human Services declared that private clinics—many of which were run by Planned Parenthood—mentioning "abortion" as a family planning option for pregnant women would be denied federal funds. Caucus members and other critics labeled the prohibition a "gag rule."

A similar directive, referred to as the "Mexico City policy," denied U.S. financial assistance to international family planning agencies that funded or otherwise encouraged abortions, even when the bulk of an agency's resources were devoted to promoting and administering practices having nothing to do with abortion. The caucus added its weight to efforts to overturn the "gag rule" through a friend-of-the-court brief in a case before the U.S. Supreme Court, and it distributed a "Dear Colleague" letter to other House members calling for abandonment of the Mexico City policy. Neither effort succeeded, and repeal of both rulings did not occur until President Clinton annulled them by executive order in 1993.

Caucus frustrations did not end with the election of a "kinder, gentler" president, George Herbert Walker Bush. Officials in the new administration were more sympathetic to the caucus than Reagan advisers had been, and dozens attended caucus meetings between 1989 and 1992. These years also saw fewer attacks on past feminist gains. But the new president was just as antagonistic to family planning proposals that could be interpreted as countenancing abortion, and his administration was almost as tight-fisted when distributing funds supporting programs promoting gender equity. Nevertheless, the caucus could claim credit for helping to authorize a $10.5 billion block grant for child care development to help states improve the accessibility and quality of child care and help low-income families pay for such care. It could also claim credit for making it more difficult for noncustodial parents to avoid child support payments. And the Small Business Administration was authorized to help women and minority entrepreneurs obtain low-interest loans.

But most caucus successes were recorded on matters that required little or no money, that were at the margins of its agenda, or that restored gains that women made in the 1960s and 1970s but that had been undermined later by the administration or the federal courts. Thus the group persuaded Congress to proclaim a National Women's History Week; to approve placing a statue of the first woman House member, Jeannette Rankin, in the Capitol Rotunda; to authorize $500,000 to help designate the residence of Alice Paul, a radical suffragist and feminist, a National Historic Site; and to create a commission to study the "glass ceiling"—attitudinal and economic barriers preventing women from rising beyond middle management positions in the workplace regardless of their talents or quality of performance. The 1991 Civil Rights Act passed, but it sparked a bitter battle in Congress and within the administration, and placed a huge burden on caucus resources. Rather than conferring new rights on women and minorities, however, the act overturned court decisions that had made proof of discrimination in the workplace more difficult to establish than had once been the case.

Some of the caucus's greatest disappointments were suffered in the area of women's health. President Bush vetoed a bill that would have made permanent a then temporary Office of Research on Women's Health in the National Institutes of Health (NIH), a proposal caught up in a dispute over fetal tissue research. More disturbing was his veto of the Family and Medical Leave Act (FMLA), even though he had promised to support such a measure during the 1988 election campaign. The proposed law required larger companies to offer twelve weeks of unpaid leave to employees who were parents of newborn, newly adopted, or seriously ill children, or who were needed to care for an incapacitated family member. The bill applied to men as well as to women, and seniority and other employment benefits were protected during their absence. In spite of strenuous opposition from much of the business community, it passed both the House and the Senate on two separate occasions. The presidential vetoes were devastating to caucus morale, and most members concluded that the FMLA would never see the light of day as long as George Herbert Walker Bush was in the White House.

Caucus Viability

Even during these frustrating years, however, caucus members harbored little doubt about the viability of their organization. They understood that few House caucuses had clout sufficient to win major battles on their own, and that it often took a decade or more before the political climate was favorable enough for passage of groundbreaking measures. Legislative losses—even terrible losses—in one Congress could be redeemed in a later Congress. This mixture of realism and hope characterized the mind-set of most caucus members during the 1980s and early 1990s, and it was recognized, as well, by the group's cochairs, Democrat Pat Schroeder and Republican Olympia Snowe.

The partnership between these two leaders was as harmonious as any that had obtained between caucus cochairs. The two had vastly different personal and political styles. Schroeder was an uninhibited, often combative woman, the kind of feminist traditional men loved to hate. One commentator remarked: "She goes out of her way to alienate men. She enjoys giving it to the good old boys" (*Rocky Mountain News,* January 24, 1994). Snowe was no less of a feminist, but she was more diplomatic and managed to make her points without upsetting men she privately considered Neanderthals. These differences were not enough to undermine their shared emotional commitment to feminist goals and their determination to make Congress address neglected issues central to women's lives. The monthly meetings they alternately chaired were well attended, and they supervised an experienced caucus staff—numbering six full-time administrative and policy specialists by 1990—who conducted research, published the *Update* newsletter, communicated with representatives of women's groups, and drafted policy proposals, "Dear Colleague" letters, and press releases.

At the same time, they clung to the strategic goals adopted in 1977. A bipartisan approach to policy objectives was woven through the group's procedures. All bill endorsements and strategic options were considered by the Executive Committee. If the two cochairs agreed on how to proceed, their decision was usually approved by the committee. This approval was a signal for the staff to set in motion a caucus-sponsored "action," an event that could take the form of a press release, a "Dear Colleague" letter, testimony before a committee, an invitation to meet with the caucus, or an endorsement of legislation. In the absence of cochair or Executive Committee approval, no action could be taken in the name of the caucus. The cochairs and staff often negotiated one-on-one with members to learn what, if any, changes could be made to gain their consent. But nothing of importance could bear the caucus's imprimatur unless it had bipartisan support.

Securing the membership of all congresswomen continued to be a caucus priority, but Schroeder had an easier time recruiting fellow Democrats than Snowe had persuading Republicans to join. There were never fewer than 80 percent of women Democrats in the caucus, with all nineteen affiliated in 1991. Snowe's task was more difficult because more women in her party were unprepared to associate themselves with a women's agenda; because Republican congresswomen who joined risked losing leverage with antifeminist Republican men, many of whom were ranking members of committees and gatekeepers to leadership positions; and because they believed that affiliation with the caucus would all too often put them at odds with first the Reagan and then the Bush White House. That there were so few Republican congresswomen made their affiliation all that more visible. Nonetheless, an increasing proportion of Republican women concluded that the risks were worth taking, and by 1991 two-thirds had become members.

The cochairs continued to accommodate the diversity in members' legislative and gender orientations, while at the same time maintaining an embargo on the abortion issue. Each congresswoman was encouraged to promote priorities she believed best served women, with the understanding that not all caucus members would support or even agree with her. The unanimity rule was no longer in place, and most decisions to take an action were negotiated by the cochairs, in consultation with their respective partisan constituencies.

Thus the omnibus economic and health equity bills introduced in each Congress were ideal vehicles for promoting collective, even if not fully integrated goals. Each caucus member was invited to attach one or more provisions to a catchall bill and then articulate support for the entire measure even though it contained sections about which they were unenthusiastic. The absence of a unifying, central theme connecting these proposals was not necessarily a disadvantage. The bill's many subjects fell within the jurisdiction of different committees, and consequently each would be considered on the basis of its own merits. Moreover, caucus members did not expect all components of the package to be given a committee hearing, let alone consideration by the full House. But they knew that proposals unaddressed in one Congress would reappear in the reintroduced omnibus bill in the next Congress.

The Executive Committee's decision to keep abortion off the table also contributed to the caucus's continued viability—not only because it prevented fissures within the group from surfacing, but also because it allowed the members to invest their time, energy, and emotion into working on less controversial, more attainable goals. The issue intruded into caucus deliberations only when broad family planning programs at home and abroad were threatened by abortion opponents. Most pro-life advocates believed it was more important to stop the use of federal funds to underwrite abortions and abortion counseling than it was to continue financial aid to national and international agencies whose abortion services were only a part of a broad range of family planning services. As has been noted, caucus efforts to end the "gag rule" and the Mexico City policy were unavailing during the Reagan-Bush years.

The group's permanent staff played a key role in keeping the caucus focused on its principal purposes—those of catalyst, facilitator, repository, incubator, and advocate. Caucus meetings were used to air and refine members' priorities, and mobilize support for them. They also provided a venue in which to devise legislative strategies designed to enact agenda items into law. In the meantime, the caucus continued to serve as an incubator for feminist initiatives upon which no national or congressional consensus had yet formed. Staff research and recurring articles in *Update* kept ideas alive long after their legislative shelf life in a given Congress had expired.

Caucus ties to the House Democratic leadership remained reasonably strong, with many veteran congressmen, including party leaders and committee chairs, retaining their associate membership in the organization. Their support of the CCWI often went beyond lip service and marginally improved House receptivity to caucus proposals. Moreover, the status of the caucus as an LSO remained unchallenged, its facilities and resources on Capitol Hill were kept intact, and Democratic leaders, with help from CCWI members, were able to fend off serious threats to the independence of all LSOs.

Caucus relations with the White House during this period were not nearly as good as they had been in the Carter years. Carter aides went out of their way to accommodate caucus requests, taking some of their unorthodox ideas seriously. Reagan advisers, on the other hand, ignored the CCWI. Reagan never met with the caucus after taking office, in spite of repeated requests from the coleaders, and even though he met with the Black and Hispanic Caucuses. Nancy Reagan lunched with the group, but not before calls from the White House made clear that she expected no policy issues to be raised. Schroeder remembers going to the White House with a gold ERA pin in her lapel and being asked to take it off (Schroeder 1997, p. 74).

President Bush also refused to meet with CCWI leaders, failing on several occasions to return phone calls, but his aides regularly accepted invitations to attend CCWI meetings. Officials holding health-related portfolios—NIH director Bernadine Healy, Surgeon General Antonia Novello, and Health and Human Services secretary Louis Sullivan— were particularly attentive to the CCWI's interests. They also helped mobilize administration support for several provisions in the Women's Health Equity Act. But they opposed research on fetal tissue and on the abortion pill RU-486, and they were either unwilling or unable to protect family planning programs from attacks by pro-life members of Congress and by a president who believed that even a hint of softness on abortion would jeopardize his 1992 reelection.

Sustained realization of its strategic goals was not the only reason the caucus retained its viability. Membership satisfaction was another. In spite of their frustrations, congresswomen enjoyed palpable advantages from affiliation with the CCWI. For one thing, they became better informed about women's issues. Meetings among themselves and with cabinet officials allowed them to exchange specialized information economically. Administration officials provided current data on scores of women-related programs they oversaw, and sent caucus members additional material when discussions pointed up information gaps and ambiguities. Ideas members exchanged with one another, often touching on measures being considered by their respective committees, were also valuable. These exchanges provided an early warning signal about proposals in the pipeline, a perspective on breaking developments, and an assessment of the consequences legislative proposals could have for women. The bipartisan character of these meetings also allowed participants to learn about attitudes "on the other side of the aisle."

Apart from generating specialized information at relatively low cost, the caucus provided a forum for members to articulate their political and personal priorities. Meetings gave congresswomen an opportunity to express policy preferences among colleagues who were generally supportive, and before cabinet members who were in a position to promote them in the executive branch. Participants often acted as sounding boards, making constructive suggestions, signing on as cosponsors of proposed legislation, and brainstorming to introduce fresh ideas and reinvigorate neglected ones. Caucus meetings also promoted networking among members and their staffs, while at the same time allowing attendees to vent their frustrations.

By affiliating with a group and pooling collective resources, members were able to reduce pressures on them to speak on behalf of all women on matters about which they had only modest expertise—or none at all. Before the caucus was created, each congresswoman was expected to provide congressmen with the "women's point of view" on all manner of issues when they found themselves the lone woman in a deliberative setting. They faced a frustrating task, because men's expectations required them to have at their disposal more information covering a wider range of legislative concerns than was humanly possible. Involvement with the caucus encouraged women to adopt a process that had been institutionalized in the House for decades—namely the division and specialization of labor. Each caucus member began to focus on two or three women's issues, often chosen because the issues were within the subject-matter jurisdiction of her committees. Congresswomen began to rely on one another to a greater extent than they did in the past, referring questions on matters outside their expertise to other caucus members and their staffs.

Affiliation with the caucus helped members improve their rapport with women's groups in their constituencies. The House has never had a standing committee specializing on diverse issues directly affecting women, as it has had committees focusing, for example, on farmers and veterans. As a result, there was no policy-shaping congressional agency to which Representatives could point when persuading women constituents that their needs were being addressed. After the caucus was formed, affiliation allowed members credibly to claim that they were committed to issues of concern to women. It was in improving their representative image more than in any other respect that men capitalized on their associate membership in the caucus. Their $900 subscriptions to *Update* entitled them to 100 copies of the publication for distribution to constituents and interest groups within their districts.

Congress is a social as well as a political institution, and many members derive emotional satisfaction from interacting with members of the groups they choose to join. In the past, women had few opportunities to establish close personal ties with other women. The caucus partially filled this void. Its meetings provided an agency for conviviality and mutual social support. The sense of community members experienced offered a respite from the frantic pace they ran each day. Thus congresswomen derived personal satisfaction from their membership in the group, with the single-sex character of its Executive Committee not the least appealing quality. Said one member in an interview: "The major benefits of the Caucus are cultural in nature. Women meet with other women in an all-female setting, and you don't have to explain what you mean when you say something. Everyone present 'gets it' the first time."

The usages of the caucus as an instrument for generating information and ideas, for allowing members to articulate their priorities in a sympathetic forum, for dividing the workload more equitably, for improving their image as women's representatives, and for providing social and emotional support helped it retain its organizational vitality during a time when it was struggling simply to hold on to gains made before 1981. It experienced some successes in women's health, particularly in the Bush years, and they, too, provided reasons for caucus leaders and rank and file to conclude that membership was worth the financial and political costs.

Motivating many of these women was the hope that favorable political circumstances would one day come together and the caucus would emerge as a powerful engine moving women's issues on to the national agenda, forcing Congress to address concerns it had so far successfully dodged. And with the 1992 election, they thought their time had come.

Note

1. After men were admitted, the Executive Committee was reconstituted to include all women members, not simply the cochairs, the treasurer, and the three at-large members.

3 Before the "Republican Revolution": 1993–1994

The 103rd Congress witnessed unparalleled success for the Congressional Caucus for Women's Issues. The 1992 election sent twenty-four new women to the House, twenty-two of whom joined the organization. These women brought with them a more diverse range of social experiences than any previous group of fledgling congresswomen. Several secured key committee appointments, and some senior caucus members, exploiting the dramatic rise in women members, prevailed on party leaders to gain choice assignments of their own.

Leverage at the committee level and with the new administration led to significant policy triumphs. During the 103rd Congress, sixty-six caucus-sponsored measures were passed, nearly as many as had been adopted in the preceding ten years. Some broke new ground in the fields of domestic violence, health, education, and employment. At the same time, the caucus changed its bylaws to limit cochairs to a single, two-year term, and abandoned its neutrality on the abortion issue. The first decision did not always serve the caucus well. The second had a profound impact on the organization after the "Republican revolution."

Inside the Numbers

The 1992 election produced unprecedented increases in the number of women serving in Congress. Women Senators went from two to six, dramatic growth in that, until then, no more than two women had ever served in the upper chamber simultaneously. The influx of women Representatives was also remarkable. The twenty-four new congresswomen increased the number of women in the House by almost 70 percent.[1] All twenty-one of the new Democratic and one of the three Republican women affiliated with the CCWI, bringing the membership of the Executive Committee to forty-two.[2] At the same time, few of the ninety new congressmen joined the caucus. The House Bank and Post Office scandals made some of them unwilling to use office allowances to pay the membership fees of legislative service organizations (LSOs). They planned to turn back a portion of these funds to the federal treasury and head off future charges of fiscal profligacy. Consequently, when female membership grew from 25 to 42, male membership dropped to 116 from 143 (see Table 2.1).

Almost as noteworthy as the number of new congresswomen was their diversity. Five African American women joined the three already serving in the House. Two new Latina Democrats were elected, and they became the first Hispanic congresswomen to join the caucus. Democrat Carrie Meek, a black congresswoman from Florida, was a granddaughter of a slave and had once worked as a cleaning woman. Lynn Woolsey (D–Calif.) had been a welfare mother before going back to school and entering politics. And the addition of these twenty-four new women to the twenty-four returning congresswomen meant that twenty-seven states from all sections of the country were now represented in the House by at least one woman.

The forty-eight women breached the 10 percent threshold of House membership, and by all accounts fundamentally changed the House atmosphere. Pink, red, fuchsia, and salmon-colored suits and dresses were now liberally sprinkled among the dour garb of congressmen. The bright colors made the women appear more numerous than they were and prompted one veteran congressman to admonish caucus cochair Pat Schroeder: "Look what you've done. The place looks like a shopping center," which prompted Schroeder to wonder whether there was a shopping center he patronized where 90 percent of the shoppers were men (Schroeder 1997, p. 122).

The first-term African American women brought a new dimension to the largely white, male House. All were seasoned politicians, and they readily affiliated with the caucus. One remarked, "Women's issues are almost like African American issues. You automatically support them without thinking about it." Another said: "I'm an African American. If someone brought in legislation to reinstate slavery, I would fight it tooth and nail. Well, it's the same with women's issues. . . . It's more or less a given that women's issues are a part of my agenda."

Accordingly, the new black women coalesced around issues touching the lives of minority women and rallied behind President Clinton's nominations of black women to the executive and judicial branches. Cynthia McKinney (D–Ga.), the youngest of the new black women, claimed, "We're shaking up the place. If one of the godfathers says you can't do this, my next question is 'why not?' And who are you to say we can't?" North Carolina's Eva Clayton, who was elected president of Democratic first-termers for the first session of the 103rd Congress, articulated a similar view: "We'll stand up quicker [to protect our rights]. I think the traditions of society have not inhibited us as much [as they have others]. There are just some indignities you are not conditioned to take" (*Washington Post,* August 2, 1993).

Caucus affiliation of the twenty-two new women resulted in crowded Executive Committee meetings, making them clamorous affairs, with members often competing with one another for colleagues' attention. The disadvantages of disorder at early meetings were offset by the heady exhilaration caucus members experienced in the company of a record number of women—a number that most had concluded before the 1992 election was beyond their reach in the foreseeable future. The atmosphere was electric as they proposed new policy initiatives, plotted parliamentary tactics, and explored strategies calculated to promote feminist goals. After lively meetings among themselves or with administration aides, many congresswomen reconvened in small groups in the House corridors to expand on arguments aired moments before. The satisfaction, the sheer joy, the buzz of excitement and laughter exhibited in one of these minimeetings prompted one observer to remark that the congresswomen sounded like a bunch of "giggly high school girls."

Gaining Leverage

Election of a president sympathetic to caucus priorities was central to its success. Also important was improved rapport CCWI members established with the Democratic leaders, as well as the choice committee assignments many of them secured. Caucus leaders established issue-specific task forces, thereby permitting a more economical division of labor in an organization whose size now rivaled that of a standing House committee. And before long, some senior caucus members set their sights on party leadership positions.

President Clinton met with the CCWI shortly after he took office— the first time in twelve years a chief executive had done so. He spent two hours discussing issues affecting women and children, exhibiting a better understanding of these matters than any of his predecessors, and giving more time and attention to the women's agenda than any had anticipated (Schroeder 1997, p. 82). In the months that followed, the caucus met with scores of presidential advisers, and phone calls to the White House and executive agencies were reliably returned—a practice all but unknown during the Reagan years. The president's approval of the Family and Medical Leave Act, and his issuance of a series of pro-choice executive orders, were early down payments on assurances he had given the caucus.

Hillary Clinton also met with the group. One month after her husband's inauguration, she came to Capitol Hill to discuss health care reform. Conversations with the congresswomen were not confined to health care, however, even though it was the centerpiece of the president's agenda. Violence against women, reproductive rights, and increased federal support for research on osteoporosis and breast cancer were also discussed. The meeting was the first held with a president's spouse since the substance-free luncheon with Nancy Reagan in the early 1980s. Later, the first lady's staff conferred regularly with congresswomen, and Pat Schroeder credited the caucus's stunning success in the 103rd Congress to the "Hillary factor": "We could not have designed a better advocate for women's issues than Hillary Rodham Clinton" (Schroeder 1997, p. 84). When the first session of the 103rd Congress ended, the Colorado Democrat stated that the first lady's influence and popularity had given women "more clout" than they had exerted for some time (*Minneapolis Star Tribune,* December 12, 1993).

Capitalizing on augmented numbers, caucus members began to demand more from House leaders. Their assertiveness was expressed first during the committee assignment process, when more than one-half of the twenty-four first-termers listed the Appropriations Committee, the Ways and Means Committee, or the Budget Committee as their first choice—not because they expected to secure positions on these panels but because they believed that, even if they failed, similar requests in subsequent Congresses would be given greater weight (Gertzog 1995, p. 222). Two first-term Democrats, Lynn Woolsey and Carrie Meek, gained appointments respectively to the Budget and Appropriations Committees. Three other fledgling Democrats won assignments to the coveted Energy and Commerce Committee. In the meantime, three veteran congresswomen won seats on the Appropriations Committee, bringing the total number of women members to a record high of seven.

The sharp increase in the number of caucus members ensured representation of at least one congresswoman on every House committee.

This allowed women's perspectives and experiences to find expression on virtually every issue raised in the House. Although no woman chaired a House committee, several headed key subcommittees, and Patricia Schroeder and Marilyn Lloyd used these positions on the Armed Services Committee to help secure $20 million for a Women's Health Research Center in the Department of Defense, and to repeal a prohibition on women's service on combat ships (Angle 1994).

The enhanced size of the caucus had consequences for the group's structure as well. Soon after the 103rd Congress convened, the CCWI Executive Committee created five task forces, each focusing on an important agenda item, and each chaired by a congresswoman possessing the relevant expertise. Louise Slaughter (D–N.Y.) was tapped to lead the task force on women's health, and Patsy Mink (D–Hawaii) chaired a task force on economic and educational equity. Constance Morella (R–Md.) was task force leader on violence against women, and Nita Lowey (D–N.Y.) was named to lead a task force on reproductive rights. Maxine Waters (D–Calif.) helped establish and direct a task force on caucus bylaws, believing that the size and potential influence of the CCWI required more formal rules governing leadership selection and succession. She also believed that the women chosen as cochairs should reflect the caucus's ideological and demographic diversity. Later, two additional task forces were created, one focusing on older women, the other on children, youth, and families.

These subgroups performed some of the responsibilities of House subcommittees, although without the all-important staff, budget, and institutional forum. Nonetheless, they allowed caucus members and their personal staffs to concentrate on a bounded, manageable range of problems facing women. The task forces also provided additional leadership opportunities for congresswomen, some of whom had been inclined earlier to view themselves as generalists in the field of women's issues, often working on the margins of several unrelated feminist policies. Now their task force agendas often dominated Executive Committee discussions.

The CCWI's decision to adopt a pro-choice position represented an important change in its strategic goals. After years of keeping the issue off the table, the caucus, swollen with more than a score of new women who knew nothing about the organization's origins, created a task force on reproductive rights. The life of the new subgroup would be brief, but for four years it gave no quarter in protecting a woman's right to choose, and doggedly tried to fend off attacks from pro-life proponents. Abandonment of official neutrality on the issue would come back to haunt the caucus in the 104th Congress.

Aspiring to Power in the House

The CCWI's visibility and influence were reinforced in the 103rd Congress when three of its more active members—Connecticut Democrat Barbara Kennelly, New York Democrat Louise Slaughter, and New York Republican Susan Molinari—decided to seek party leadership positions. Kennelly had already won the respect of fellow Democrats, gaining a seat on the Ways and Means and Budget Committees, and working her way up through the party whip system to an appointment as one of four chief deputy whips. She was regularly consulted by Democratic leaders, and was frequently asked what position the caucus had taken on pending legislation. In 1991, Kennelly ran for vice chair of her party, compiling a respectable vote total while losing to California's Vic Fazio. In November 1993 she announced she would run for vice chair again when Fazio was required by term limits to relinquish the post.

Several months later, Slaughter publicly declared that she, too, would seek the vice chair position, and ultimately the contest was fought out between the two congresswomen. A Kentuckian by birth, Slaughter moved to New York and represented residents of the Rochester region, first in the state legislature and then in the House. In 1989, she was handpicked by House Speaker Tom Foley to serve on the House Rules Committee, only the third Democratic woman ever appointed to this strategically important panel, and like Kennelly she served on the Budget Committee. The battle between the two feminists forced Democratic Caucus members to make a difficult choice, and ultimately the more senior, better-connected Kennelly eked out a 93–90 victory to become the first Democratic woman vice chair.

Susan Molinari announced she would run for Republican vice chair in June 1994. Molinari had succeeded her father, Guy Molinari, in the House after he had been elected borough president of Staten Island, New York City's most Republican enclave. She had previously been elected to the city council, and had served in that body as her party's sole representative. Although an outspoken feminist, and ardently pro-choice, Molinari generally avoided identification with women's issues during her early years on the council. She believed that as the lone Republican she should exhibit interest in a wider range of issues, including such bread-and-butter concerns as road maintenance as well as waste disposal in the waters that wash Staten Island shores.

She later regretted shying away from women's issues, noting that "they are the very issues that voters most need women in politics to care about because the men won't touch them" (Molinari 1998, p. 63).

Immediately after her election to the city council, she had decided to ask the elections board to change the language instructing voters how to "write in" the name of a candidate not printed on the ballot. The instructions referred to such a candidate as "he." She acknowledged that this politically incorrect locution was small potatoes, especially when compared with the truly gross inequities contained in New York's election laws. But she said that the slight to women "stuck in her craw," and she planned to send out a press release announcing her complaint to the elections board.

Her advisers demurred, however, and urged her not to go public on this kind of issue so soon after her election, lest she be marginalized by friend and foe alike as a single-issue feminist. Molinari abandoned the effort, but later concluded that she had been mistaken to do so. "It's not just language," she said. "It's child care, and abortion, and violence against women programs, and child abuse. And too many women, myself included, get scared away from them by handlers who don't have a clue" (Molinari 1998, p. 63).

When she was elected to the House in 1989, she was determined never to distance herself from women's issues again. She joined the CCWI early in her first term and later noted, "One of the joys of my first years in Congress was the easy cooperation between Democratic and Republican women active in the Women's Caucus" (Molinari 1998, p. 92). Her spirited defense of a woman's right to choose prompted some of the more conservative members of her party to label her "Bella Abzug without the hat."

Molinari's attachment to the CCWI had begun to wear thin by 1994, when she decided to seek her party's fifth highest ranking House position. Part of the disaffection can be explained by the CCWI's increasingly partisan orientation in the 103rd Congress. More important was Molinari's belief that she could not be elected to high party office as a thirty-six-year-old moderate unless she persuaded senior conservatives that she was a team player and that she was flexible enough to modify or mask some of the socially progressive, feminist positions she had already articulated. Her marriage to Congressman Bill Paxon in July 1994 affected her behavior as well, inasmuch as Paxon was the chair of the Republican Congressional Campaign Committee and a principal tribune for the party's conservative socioeconomic platform. Accordingly, Molinari distanced herself from the caucus, retaining nominal membership.

When the New Yorker announced her candidacy for Republican vice chair—days before her marriage to Paxon—she entered a race that her leading Republican opponent, Florida's Cliff Stearns, had begun the previous November. This meant that she had to play catch-up, and she saw her "road to victory" as "paved with the IOUs I could collect by helping Republican candidates all over the country" (Molinari 1998, p. 160). Earlier, she had sought and won seats on the House Commerce Committee and Republican Committee on Committees because they both provided opportunities for placing Republicans in her debt. She also contributed campaign funds to a number of GOP candidates, and accompanied her husband from one congressional district to another, meeting with House candidates, speaking on their behalf, and playing an especially supportive role for Republican aspirants who also happened to be women.

By election day Molinari had barnstormed in eighty-four House districts, promoting the candidacies of some conservative pro-life men who were running against liberal or moderate pro-choice women. She later explained these efforts as necessary for becoming vice chair. She also said that she had no choice but to support the objectives of her husband (Molinari 1998, p. 142). Some of her caucus colleagues deplored her support of the Contract with America, and she was labeled a "femi-Newtie"(Molinari 1998, p. 186). Molinari defeated Stearns and became the first Republican CCWI member who was also part of her party's top leadership.[3] After her victory, she assured the caucus that, as a member of the GOP hierarchy, she was now in a better position to promote women's issues.

The power plays by the three women reflected palpable attitudinal changes about the leadership potential of women in the House. Interviews in 1978 with thirteen of the eighteen congresswomen and a dozen randomly selected congressmen revealed that few anticipated selection of a woman for important leadership positions in the foreseeable future. Congressmen based their judgments on the small number of women then serving in the House, a belief that virtually all were "unqualified" for responsible party posts, and a conviction that too many of their colleagues were unwilling to take their legislative and political cues from a woman—any woman.

Congresswomen interviewed at the time were not much more optimistic about their own leadership prospects. They noted that women generally did not seek out these power positions, concentrating on policy concerns and constituent relations instead. They also pointed out that few had enough seniority to be taken seriously, and that, as in so many other pursuits, a woman would have to be twice as good as competing congressmen to pull it off. One Republican congresswoman was especially pessimistic: "Women will never get anywhere in the Republican party because the men in the House in my party cannot conceive of the prospect of sharing power with a woman and taking directions from her" (Gertzog 1995, p. 113).

Interviews with House members fifteen years later revealed a sharp reversal in expectations. More than three-quarters of the dozen men and twenty-eight of the thirty-three women venturing a guess believed that chances were good to excellent that a woman would be in a top leadership position of one or both parties by the beginning of the next millennium. Whereas congressmen interviewed in 1978 went out of their way to disparage the political skills of the women with whom they served, naming names, in 1993 their successors mentioned the names of women who *could* become party whip or floor leader or even Speaker. Kennelly, Slaughter, Nancy Pelosi, Nancy Johnson, and Jennifer Dunn were among those singled out. Attitudes toward women colleagues had changed substantially, said one congressman, and if at least one woman were not elected to a top position, he added, "it will not be because of gender" (Gertzog 1995, p. 117).

A large majority of the congresswomen in the 103rd Congress agreed. Much of their optimism was based on the unprecedented numbers then in Congress, and the belief that the percentage of women in the House would only grow. They also underlined the appealing personal qualities and political skills possessed by their colleagues, and maintained that many would be outstanding lawmakers in the twenty-first century even if they did not emerge atop of the party hierarchy. And one GOP woman predicted, with remarkable prescience, that the women in her party could receive the recognition they deserve in the next Congress, the 104th, when Republicans gained control of the House.

Thus, augmented numbers of congresswomen with more polished political skills produced a large talent pool, out of which able women leaders could emerge. These developments fed the ambitions of women like Kennelly, Slaughter, and Molinari, and gave credibility to their aspirations for party leadership positions. The 1992 election also increased the legitimacy of the feminist agenda, and CCWI leaders seized their unprecedented opportunities.

Promoting the Feminist Agenda

The 103rd Congress produced more legislation addressing the needs of women and their children than any Congress in history. During the first session alone, thirty bills promoting the feminist agenda were passed, three times the number of such measures approved in the combined first sessions of the 101st and 102nd Congresses. At the end of the year, CCWI cochair Pat Schroeder said that the caucus has "never had such a productive year" (*Washington Post,* December 3, 1993), and her Republican counterpart, Olympia Snowe, remarked: "For families with new babies or elderly parents who need care, for women who are afraid to walk down to their cars at night, for all who fear that breast cancer will deprive them of a mother, sister or daughter, this Congress has made a difference" (*USA Today,* December 3, 1993).

By the time the 103rd Congress adjourned in October 1994, sixty-six measures endorsed by the caucus had been adopted (*Houston Chronicle,* November 23, 1994). Democratic majority leader Richard Gephardt remarked that the caucus had made a "big impact" on the House's legislative record. He added, "They've brought a lot of idealism and energy to issues important to them." And one British observer noted: "Not only has the long ignored Congressional Caucus for Women's Issues seen its family-oriented agenda take centre stage, but women lawmakers also have made a difference on a broad range of other issues, from initiating institutional reforms to providing decisive votes on the top issues of the current Congress" (*The Independent,* [London] October 6, 1994).

The political influence exerted by the caucus in the 103rd Congress was not exhibited solely or even principally in the bloc of votes members could deliver for endorsed legislation. To be sure, the votes of forty-two women sometimes made the difference between success and failure. They helped provide the margin needed to pass an assault weapons ban when only 46 percent of congressmen supported the measure (*USA Today,* November 7, 1994) But the caucus was most effective in shaping the agenda indirectly by raising problems and legitimating arguments that past, male-dominated Congresses had either dismissed or ignored. There were now more congresswomen who could recount instances of discrimination and humiliation suffered on the job. More of them could recall private struggles with health problems encountered by their families, including breast or ovarian cancer, osteoporosis, and eating disorders. As principal caregivers in their homes, they could provide intimate, firsthand accounts of the anguish and guilt they felt trying to find a way to care for ill children and parents while continuing to earn a living. Marge Roukema pointed out, "Families are thrown into crisis when serious illness strikes. I know. When my son Todd was stricken with leukemia and needed home care, I was free to remain at home. But what about the millions of mothers who work? I don't think you would have a man plead for family leave the way I did" (*USA Today,* May 4, 1993).

These accounts were very different from those offered by generations of congressmen whose experience in fighting hot and cold war, and in conducting financial and commercial transactions, defined what was relevant and therefore what was irrelevant to the business of Congress. The sheer weight of these women's' testimonies in committees and on the House floor shifted the terms of the ongoing national debate about what was and what was not a legitimate national concern. This is what Pat Schroeder may have had in mind when, at the close of the 103rd Congress, she said: "While the number of measures passed in this Congress is historic, . . . the other story is the one behind the numbers: the cooperation among congresswomen, their persistence in working to bring legislation important to women to the House floor, and their political savvy in making this a record-setting Congress" (*Update,* September–October 1994).

The Ripening of the Social Agenda

The most substantial gains made by the caucus were in social policy. The 103rd Congress adopted more than a score of measures dealing with women's health, education, battered women, and problems facing mothers and their children. Most of the bills enacted had been in the caucus memory bank for as long as a decade. They had been introduced in the 1980s, ignored by the Reagan and Bush administrations, denied a place on the agenda by sympathetic but realistic Democratic House leaders, and recycled for the next Congress—when they would suffer a similar fate.

Among the first bills passed by 103rd Congress in 1993 was the Family and Medical Leave Act (FMLA). Initially introduced by Pat Schroeder in 1985, the measure sought to allow both women and men to take unpaid leave from their jobs immediately before and after they became new parents without fear of losing their employment and collateral benefits. The proposal languished in committee for several years. In the meantime, its language was changed to allow leave during the illness of family members. These added benefits appealed to a broader range of House and Senate members, and the FMLA passed Congress twice during the Bush administration. Twice President Bush vetoed it.

President Clinton was on record as supporting the legislation, and when 87 percent of congresswomen and 58 percent of congressmen approved it in the weeks following his inauguration, he enthusiastically signed it. The new law gave workers in businesses with more than fifty employees the opportunity to take up to twelve weeks of unpaid leave each year to care for a newborn or newly adopted child, to minister to a seriously ill family member, or to recover from serious illness, without losing their jobs or health benefits. Later, the president approved a related caucus-supported measure allowing federal employees to either receive donated annual leave from coworkers or voluntarily donate leave time to a "leave bank" to be used for family or medical emergencies.

Although the president's comprehensive health care reform package was never enacted, a half dozen new laws addressing women's health needs did pass. These measures had their roots in the Women's Health Equity Act, the omnibus bill introduced initially in 1990. It had been inspired by a General Accounting Office report revealing that women were routinely excluded from government-sponsored clinical studies of maladies ranging from heart disease to the overuse of prescription drugs. The findings of these studies, many conducted by the National Institutes of Health (NIH), were considered by investigators to be applicable to women as well as men, even though not a single woman had participated in the experiments. When caucus members learned that the tests had been limited to men, they "went ballistic," as one congresswoman put it, and drafted a package of measures that would prevent women's unreasonable exclusion from future clinical tests.

The CCWI reintroduced a Women's Health Equity bill in the 103rd Congress, and several of its thirty-two provisions were incorporated in the 1993 National Institutes of Health Revitalization Act. One section of the measure strengthened and codified NIH policy requiring the inclusion of women and minorities in clinical research. Other provisions authorized an additional $400 million for basic and clinical research on breast and ovarian cancer. The same act required the National Institute on Aging to conduct research on women's aging process, with particular emphasis on menopause, and it authorized $40 million for research on osteoporosis.

Congress also reauthorized the 1990 Centers for Disease Control (CDC) Breast and Cervical Cancer Mortality Prevention Act, legislation to provide mammograms and pap smears for low-income women. Other language extended the agency's responsibility for reducing the incidence of sexually transmitted diseases. Later, a Department of Defense (DOD) reauthorization bill provided for delivery of primary and preventive health care services to women at military hospitals and clinics, and established a DOD clearinghouse to gather information and conduct research on the health care needs of women in the military. Health concerns of women veterans were also recognized with the creation of a Women's Center in the Department of Veterans Affairs (VA). The center was authorized to distribute information on VA programs for women, conduct research and outreach activities, and monitor complaints. The caucus suffered a setback when Senate-approved language to provide women veterans with prenatal and postpartum care, as well as delivery services, was defeated in the House by pro-life leaders who feared that these pregnancy provisions would be construed so as to permit abortions at VA facilities.

Congress approved a half dozen CCWI-sponsored measures to help mothers, would-be mothers, and their children. One created a new entitlement program to allow states to provide free vaccines to Medicaid-eligible children, Native American children, and children who lacked health insurance. Another helped establish three satellite health centers for mothers and infants in the District of Columbia, while a third allowed nurse-midwives to be reimbursed by states with Medicaid funds even when their services fell outside of the maternity cycle. Other provisions permitted the NIH to create three contraceptive and two infertility research centers. Thus, much of the health agenda the caucus had put together in the late 1980s and early 1990s was enacted by a Congress whose policy frame of reference and priorities had been altered by women members.

The same was true in a related area—physical abuse of women. During the closing weeks of the 103rd Congress, the Violence Against Women Act (VAWA) was passed as part of the administration's crime prevention bill. Under VAWA, $1.62 billion was authorized over a six-year period to create rape crisis centers and women's shelters, to require restitution to victims in sex offense cases, to expand rape shield laws, and to train judges unaccustomed to hearing complaints brought against men who regularly battered spouses and companions. The new law made it easier to prosecute batterers who stalk women across state lines, and it allowed victims to prove by a preponderance of the evidence that crimes against them were not random—motivated, instead, by an animus toward the victims' gender.

The Crime Control Act modified federal rules of evidence to allow previous acts of violence to be introduced as evidence in the trial of someone charged with sexual assault or child molestation. It also granted $30 million to help officials in rural areas investigate and prosecute domestic violence and child abuse. The act increased penalties for hate crimes in which the victim was targeted because of race, gender, religion, or sexual orientation. And safeguards were established to protect the confidentiality of information kept by state motor vehicle bureaus, which could be used by stalkers and other criminals to find intended victims. The new law also gave victims of a federal crime of violence or sexual abuse the right to address the court prior to the sentencing of a defendant, and it restricted gun purchases by persons guilty of domestic abuse.

Legislation promoting equality for women in education was also enacted. More money was authorized to monitor sex discrimination in federally funded education programs, and to develop innovative curricula to promote gender equity. One section of the 1994 Elementary and Secondary Education Act authorized teacher training in gender-equitable teaching methods, while another encouraged both the recruitment of women teachers in math and science and gender-neutral strategies in teaching these subjects. In the meantime, the position of special assistant for gender equity was created in the Department of Education.

Laws were passed to discourage pregnant and parenting teens from dropping out of school, and funds were made available through the Safe and Drug-Free Schools Act for both sexual harassment and child abuse prevention programs. Statistical studies completed by the National Center for Education Statistics were required to cross-tabulate data by sex, as well as by race and socioeconomic status. Additional legislation directed colleges receiving federal funds to disclose participation and funding rates for men's and women's athletic programs.

The caucus's deep commitment to Head Start helped expand the program's reach to a larger number of children, and embedded in the School to Work Opportunities Act were provisions stipulating that young women should be given opportunities to receive training for high-skill, nontraditional jobs. In the meantime, the president's high-priority Goals 2000: Educate America Act was edited to include gender-equity language to ensure that the needs of girls and women were met. The law also authorized the Office of Educational Research and Information in the Department of Education to analyze and report its data by sex whenever possible.

Promoting Economic Equity

The caucus's Economic Equity bill contained thirty provisions addressing the concerns of women in the workplace. Portions of the measure affected women running small businesses, divorced mothers with young children, women in the military, and women working on Capitol Hill. For businesswomen, one measure established a permanent Office of

Women's Business Ownership within the Small Business Administration (SBA) and allocated $4 million for training and assistance to women interested in launching or expanding a business enterprise. One provision of the SBA reauthorization required federal agencies to establish a 5 percent goal for contracting with women-owned businesses.

The Economic Equity Act made it easier for a single parent to collect payments for child support. A federal registry for reporting child support orders was created to streamline the collection process, and new procedures were put in place to establish the paternity of children entitled to financial support. Congress also enacted legislation requiring states to impose criminal penalties on deadbeat parents, and to expand medical coverage children receive from noncustodial parents. Two additional child support provisions were part of the Bankruptcy Reform Act. The new law required the courts to rank child support obligations as a priority debt to be paid when individuals declare bankruptcy, and it made it more difficult for a divorced person claiming bankruptcy to make a former spouse liable for the outstanding debt.

Other legislation required persons applying for Small Business Administration loans to certify that they were not in violation of a child support order. Two additional measures established procedures for background checks of child care providers, and allocated $48 million in fiscal 1994 to fund state programs helping children in troubled families. The Special Supplemental Food Program for women, infants, and children (WIC) expedited the process by which pregnant women and new mothers receive WIC nutritional services.

Women in the military received a boost when the Department of Defense reauthorization bill removed remaining statutory limitations on women serving on combat ships—restrictions that affected their earning capacities. The same measure required the Air Force, Navy, and Marines to adopt an Equal Employment Opportunity Complaint program already being implemented by the Army. Under the program, claims of gender- or race-based discrimination had to be investigated by officers outside the complainant's direct chain of command.

Legislation calculated to promote status and pay equity for women working on Capitol Hill was also passed. The Congressional Employees Fairness Act was sponsored by the caucus cochairs and by Washington, D.C., delegate Eleanor Holmes Norton. It authorized collection of information about pay scales and employment practices by House members, while controlling for sex and race. Those conducting these studies were instructed to publish annual reports and to compare each year's findings with figures compiled for previous years.

The success of all of these social and economic bills should not be confused with the amount of clout the caucus was able to exert in the 103rd Congress. Some would almost certainly have passed even without the support of women affiliated with the caucus. A better measure of the organization's influence is the number of issues the new laws addressed that had languished, unattended, in House committees. The power of the caucus could not be measured solely by the number of wins and losses on roll call votes, but by the fact that floor votes on some issues were conducted at all. Feminist values and the language of feminist legislative discourse were given a legitimacy that until 1993 they had lacked.

Groundbreaking though many of the women-friendly measures were, however, they were often obscured by the recurring, bitter battles caucus members fought over a woman's right to choose.

Tackling the Abortion Issue

One of the CCWI's most important and fateful decisions in the 103rd Congress was to abandon formal neutrality on the abortion issue. It was no secret that most members were pro-choice and that they actively championed women's reproductive rights in the House. But caucus leaders and staff avoided group identification with what was arguably the most volatile domestic issue facing the country, and no official caucus statement took a position on the subject. The 1992 election cracked this facade of neutrality.

That all twenty-four newly elected women were pro-choice, and that twenty-two of them joined the caucus, helped trigger the change. Before the new Congress convened, the twenty-four met to determine the legislative issues upon which they could make common cause. Four were selected. Among them were support for the Family and Medical Leave Act, full funding for Head Start, and the application of federal sexual harassment prohibitions to congressional offices. The fourth was endorsement of the Freedom of Choice Act (FOCA), a measure unsuccessfully promoted in previous Congresses to codify the Supreme Court's 1973 *Roe v. Wade* decision. During the Reagan and Bush administrations, feminists were concerned that new justices appointed to the Court would produce a pro-life majority and overturn the landmark decision. Their fears were partly realized when the *Webster v. Reproductive Health Services* (1989) and *Planned Parenthood v. Casey* (1992) decisions upheld state actions to limit women's accessibility to abortion services. Concerned that this whittling away of reproductive rights would end with the evisceration of *Roe v. Wade,* pro-choice House members were determined to give the decision the legitimacy of a congressionally approved statute.

The pro-choice first-term women further skewed an already lopsided balance between pro-choice and pro-life CCWI members. Overwhelmingly Democratic, and unaware (or dismissive) of the group's past neutrality on the issue, most newcomers simply assumed that reproductive rights would be a part of the CCWI's agenda. Their numbers and the strength of their commitment to abortion rights made it easier for CCWI veterans who had been impatient with the caucus's past position on the issue to abandon one of the group's strategic premises. Some veteran congresswomen demurred, but their doubts could not withstand the momentum generated by new members, and their reservations were ignored.

When the caucus decided to create task forces on issues central to its mission, reproductive rights, together with women's health, women in the workplace, and violence against women, was given a prominence that until then had been denied it. During the CCWI's initial meeting in January 1993, Louise Slaughter formally moved to make abortion rights part of the CCWI's agenda. No objection was heard, and Nita Lowey was named to head the pro-choice task force. Slaughter later explained the reason for the unanimity: "Some women who objected so violently in the past are gone" (Glasser 1993). One first-term Democrat said she was shocked, not by the decision, but by the revelation that the caucus had not been pro-choice all along. She recalled:

> When I was first elected in 1992 and attended the first Caucus meeting in 1993, a vote was held to make the Caucus pro-choice. I was stunned. What in the world has the Women's Caucus been doing all these years. I thought that's what they had been doing. I could have fallen off the face of the earth. I think it happened because we had so many new recruits, all of whom were pro-choice. But I really feel for the [Caucus] pioneers who were there for so many years. It's tough now; it must have been incredibly tough then.

Caucus members were triumphant when President Clinton highlighted the importance of women's right to choose by targeting the issue in his first official acts as president. Days after being sworn in, he issued a half dozen executive orders reversing a decade of abortion restrictions imposed by the Reagan and Bush administrations. The new president repealed the ban on abortion counseling at federally funded clinics (the so-called gag rule), and eased the policy on abortions in military hospitals. He also reversed a Reagan administration's prohibition on aid to international family planning programs that permitted abortion-related practices.

At a White House ceremony, the president lifted restrictions on federal financing of research using fetal tissue, and directed federal regulators to reassess whether the abortion pill RU-486 was safe and effective. The executive orders were issued on the day that a throng of 75,000 pro-life advocates, who had come to Washington on the twentieth anniversary of *Roe v. Wade,* were demanding that the Court decision be overturned.

Encouraged by the administration's initiatives on the issue, CCWI leaders began to work closely with the White House to define and promote an abortion rights agenda. During the 103rd Congress, the caucus threw its weight behind proposals to restore abortion coverage to federal employees and dependents under their health benefits program, and to make abortions available to women in federal prisons, a service eliminated in 1983. The group also worked to lift a 1988 ban on municipally funded Medicaid abortions for District of Columbia women. And a provision was inserted into the 1994 Foreign Operations Appropriation bill to restore the U.S. contribution to the United Nations Fund for Population Activities, an allocation that had been blocked each year since 1985. All of these measures became law.

Even though 77 percent of congresswomen voted to defeat the Hyde Amendment—a provision passed each year to prohibit the use of federal funds to finance abortions for women entitled to Medicaid—the measure passed 255–178. Nevertheless, pro-choice forces managed to help make abortions more accessible to poor women, allowing those who had been victims of rape or incest, as well as those whose lives were endangered by their pregnancy, to pay for abortions with Medicaid funds. Violence and deaths at abortion clinics gave the Clinton administration and the caucus the leverage to pass the Freedom of Access to Clinic Entrances Act, making it a federal crime to intentionally injure, intimidate, or interfere with someone who is obtaining or providing reproductive health services. The president signed the bitterly contested measure in May 1994.

But some CCWI-sponsored abortion measures failed. The Freedom of Choice Act was passed by both House and Senate committees, but further action was blocked when opponents announced they were prepared to offer scores of damaging amendments when the measure came to the floor for debate. In May 1993, Lowey had sent Hillary Clinton a letter signed by thirty-three CCWI women urging that a comprehensive reproductive health care benefit be part of the administration's health reform package. But when the centerpiece of the president's domestic program failed, the CCWI-supported provision died with it.

The CCWI's about-face on the abortion issue, and the aggressive role played by Lowey's task force, were not lost on pro-life supporters inside and outside the House. For years they had been suspicious of CCWI neutrality. Cochairs Schroeder and Snowe were among the most outspoken champions of reproductive rights, and their leadership on this issue persuaded many that the group was pro-choice from top to bottom. The caucus's 1993 decision to adopt a pro-choice stance ended all doubts about where it stood on the issue, and when a pro-life Republican leadership assumed power in the 104th Congress, it had one more reason to undermine the CCWI's viability.

The Unraveling of Bipartisanship

The dramatic increase in the number of Democratic CCWI members and their unmistakable dominance in group activities induced many of them to come to believe that what was good for the Democratic Party was good for the CCWI. Appointments of women to top administration positions, including attorney general, reinforced the view. Republican members began to feel uncomfortable with the invective Democratic women directed against Republican House leaders. Now that their party controlled the White House for the first time in twelve years, Democratic congresswomen vented an accumulation of bottled-up frustrations

Looking back on the 103rd Congress, Susan Molinari observed: "The tragedy of women's politics within the House was how frequently we were divided not by ideology, but by pure partisanship, by the pressures and politics from within our own caucuses" (Molinari 1998, p. 95). The New York City Republican believed that the Democratic president was also at fault, recalling, "After Clinton was elected, the Women's Caucus became increasingly partisan, making any cooperation, and thus gains for women, more difficult" (Molinari 1998, p. 99).

Relations between Republican and Democratic women were further strained when partisan differences led to personal animosities. A Ways and Means Committee hearing on health care in March 1994 witnessed a dispute between California Democrat Pete Stark and Nancy Johnson over health care reform, during which Stark asked the Connecticut Republican, whose husband is a physician, if she had acquired her claimed expertise through "pillow talk." Stark apologized for his remark later that day, but Republican women Representatives circulated a letter criticizing him for his sexist comments, and observed that when Hillary Clinton had appeared before the committee to discuss the administration's health care bill, no one suggested that she had derived her knowledge of the subject from "pillow talk."

The letter was signed by thirty-five Republicans, eleven women and twenty-four men. Democratic women were accused of applying a double standard by failing to sign the letter, and Ohio's Deborah Pryce, who was not a CCWI member, asserted that the women on the other side of the aisle would have been appalled if the remark had been made by a Republican congressman. Some Democrats considered endorsing the statement, but found the reference to Hillary Clinton too partisan. Later, Johnson registered regret that no Democratic women had signed on, but Pat Schroeder and other Democratic women said that they had never even heard about the letter (Foerstel 1994).

Molinari complained that she had received no support from Democratic women on a bill that would require colleges to inform student rape victims of their right to go to the police. The bill required annual reports documenting the incidence of campus crime so that prospective students and their parents, in assessing colleges, could compare the potential dangers present at each. These Democrats, she said, were overly concerned about offending the committee chair, who opposed these measures (Molinari 1998, p. 96). She also blasted the caucus for allowing the abortion issue to become "center stage" and using it as a litmus test for blocking CCWI admission of Republican congressmen who had generally supported their party's pro-life platform. She later recalled: "Little by little, even while I remained active on women's issues, I moved out of the caucus. I was no more interested in spending time with women who bashed men than with men who bashed women. I was no more inclined to use my time fighting Republican-haters than I was to use it fighting women-haters" (Molinari 1998, p. 100).

GOP Congresswomen Nancy Johnson and Tillie Fowler (Fla.) also concluded that the caucus had become too partisan. But Republicans were not the only CCWI members to question the group's efficacy. Democrats who believed that the CCWI was not sufficiently single-minded and forceful also complained. Eva Clayton observed that the women were "not as unified" as she had hoped they would be, and although she acknowledged that "in the final analysis that may not be unhealthy, it does mean that you're not going to be as effective as you could be." And Barbara Kennelly concluded that the increase in women's membership meant that the time was ripe to form a separate, Democratic women's caucus. "We should start one next year," she said (*Christian Science Monitor,* July 30, 1993). Friction between black Democratic women and some white Republican women also eroded CCWI solidarity. A senior Democratic congresswoman remarked in an interview:

> The new women of color brought different concerns to the table, and it strained the bipartisan community. These women made Republican women a little uncomfortable because they were very outspoken and very clear about what our agenda should be. It really wasn't that their agenda was all that much different than what the Caucus had stood for in the past. It was just that they were a little aggressive in asserting it . . . and they were willing to attack some of the Caucus members, asking "How come you're hiding on this issue?"

One of the new black congresswomen offered her own perspective on conflicts within the House:

> If I didn't represent what I am, then I wouldn't be true to myself and true to the people who elected me. They elected me because I am an African American woman who has a certain set of life experiences that differentiate me from the typical member of Congress. Therefore, I bring that to the institution, and the institution is changed and enhanced because of the difference I bring. So if I try to blend in and become one of them, then that is a disservice to the people who support me.

These partisan divisions were not helped by a CCWI decision to change its bylaws and require a two-year limit on the service of its cochairs. As has been noted, the change was sparked by Maxine Waters, who rightly believed that term limits would give more women an opportunity to serve as cochair. But another African American congresswoman stated her support for the change more bluntly. She said in a confidential interview: "Pat Schroeder and Olympia Snowe are white ladies who ran the caucus like their little personal tea party. They set the agenda, they called the meetings, they had the staff. And even though both of them had the proper attitude and desire to do right, there was not very much input we could make."

The bylaws change meant that Snowe and Schroeder would be stepping down after a decade of providing much of the glue holding the caucus together. They would be replaced in the 104th Congress by Constance Morella and Nita Lowey, women who had the highest regard for one another and who were committed to a feminist agenda. But they had no experience in running the caucus. And when the CCWI lost its space, its furnishings, and its permanent staff early in 1995, it became apparent that the practice of rotating cochairs would impede the group's ability to make smooth transitions from one Congress to the next.

Notes

1. The largest increment of nonincumbent women sent to the House in a single election before 1992 was six, in 1974.

2. The two first-term Republican women declining to join the CCWI were Jennifer Dunn (Wash.) and Deborah Pryce (Ohio). This figure excludes District of Columbia delegate Eleanor Holmes Norton, who was a nonvoting member of the House and who was elected caucus cochair in the 105th Congress. The number fell to forty-one when first-term Missouri Democrat Pat Danner resigned from the caucus in mid-1994.

3. Lynn Martin of Illinois had held the position from 1985 to 1989, but Martin never joined the caucus. Nancy Johnson's 1992 candidacy for GOP vice chair had been unsuccessful.

4 The Republicans Take Control: 1995–1996

The 1994 elections produced a fundamental change in the House's composition, leadership, policy orientation, and political culture. The new majority chose as their leaders conservatives who had spent their congressional lives excoriating liberal-leaning Democrats, antagonists whom they believed had been conspicuously uncaring about the frustrations of a "permanent" Republican minority. Although past Democratic leaders had consulted their GOP opposite numbers regularly—compromising occasionally when they needed Republican votes—GOP priorities were largely ignored.

Leading the Republican charge was the man nearly everyone believed was responsible for the election outcome—Newt Gingrich. For many, Gingrich was arguably the most charismatic figure to emerge on the Washington scene since Ronald Reagan. Moreover, he was able to persuade many Americans that the 1994 election constituted a continuation of a conservative revolution begun by the former president. For him, the stunning GOP triumph was the product of an ongoing party realignment that would culminate in the election of a Republican president and even larger Republican congressional majorities in 1996. He believed that a change in the way people thought about government would accompany the realignment and vowed he would "reinvent" government. Gingrich began the process by changing the culture of the House itself.

An admirer of the parliamentary form of government, especially as embodied in the leadership of former British prime ministers Winston Churchill and Margaret Thatcher, Gingrich sought to use the Republican House majority to institutionalize and capitalize on partisan differences. For forty years, Republican leaders had grudgingly acknowledged that

57

they had no choice but to cooperate with Democratic majorities. Gingrich believed this was a failed strategy. He insisted that Republicans had received little of value for their willingness to compromise. Indeed, the appearance of bipartisanship had given the voters no basis for distinguishing between the parties—thereby perpetuating Democratic majorities. He would replace the House's modus operandi of lawmaking through deliberation with one of campaigning through partisan confrontation, magnifying the issues that divided the two parties. On the day the Republican-led House was sworn in, the new Speaker vowed he would not compromise the conservative principles that now constituted his party's mandate. And he encouraged his rank and file to sacrifice constituency concerns in the interests of party advantage.

The content of the mandate was embedded in the Contract with America, a series of ten broad policy proposals virtually all GOP House candidates had endorsed in the weeks preceding the election. They included constitutional amendments to require a balanced budget and term limits for members of Congress, changes in the fiscal relationship between state and federal governments, tort reform, a streamlined national security policy, a fundamental restructuring of tax policies, and a revamping of social security, welfare, and criminal justice programs.

To achieve these goals within the promised 100 days, Gingrich and his lieutenants had to control virtually every aspect of the legislative process. This meant reshaping the rules by which the House conducted its business, controlling the composition, scheduling, deliberations, and recommendations of House committees, and ensuring that floor debate and roll call votes would result in predetermined outcomes. It also meant preventing the emergence of competing agendas, whether from the White House, the Democrats in Congress, or legislative service organizations (LSOs), and Gingrich moved quickly to monopolize power.

Consolidating Power

In the weeks immediately following the election, the Speaker-designate laid the groundwork for his revolution. Among the objectives claiming his attention, three were particularly important. Gingrich wanted above all to exercise undisputed control over the policy agenda. He had promised that the ten items in the Contract would be addressed during the first 100 days, and that the House committees responsible for processing agenda items would move with more than ordinary speed.

Second, Republican leaders had to acknowledge their debt to the seventy-three first-termers to whom they believed they owed their majority. The fledgling lawmakers made up the second largest group of majority party newcomers since the end of World War II, and their loyalty had to be cultivated and reinforced. All but eight represented districts held by Democrats in the 103rd Congress, and they required House recognition adequate to vouchsafe their reelection. Gingrich scheduled weekly lunches with them, and made a point of meeting one-on-one to listen to their concerns. The Speaker saw to it that most received committee assignments compatible with district needs, and he reserved appointments to the chamber's most powerful panels for those likely to face stiff reelection challenges. A total of twenty-four were assigned to the five most influential committees, one of whom, Enid Greene Waldholtz (R–Utah), was appointed to the Rules Committee, the first Republican newcomer to receive that plum since 1915.

Third, Gingrich sought to capitalize on the devastating defeat dealt to the Democrats and undermine their ability to challenge Republican control of the agenda. Because the GOP majority was smaller than any commanded by either party since 1954, Republicans had to be highly cohesive if they were to prevail on controversial items, and Democrats had to be denied opportunities to offer policy options attractive to Republicans who were less imbued with revolutionary fervor. Failure by Democrats to present viable policy alternatives would augur well for Republicans in the next round of House elections. The GOP would be well positioned to improve on its tenuous majority, discredit a hapless opposition, and create a national political climate conducive to recapturing the White House.

To secure these objectives, Gingrich first had to alter House and party rules that could be employed to threaten his hegemony. Control of the standing committees was crucial to his success, and he moved quickly to override the seniority claims of Republican veterans whom he believed could not effectively advance the party's policy goals. Fifth-ranking Bob Livingston of Louisiana was tapped to head the Appropriations Committee, and when the more senior John Myers of Indiana threatened to challenge the decision, he was told that he would be denied a subcommittee chair if he persisted. Myers backed off. California's Carlos Moorhead, a twenty-two-year veteran whose seniority would ordinarily entitle him to chair either the Commerce or the Judiciary Committee, was denied both, presumably because he would not be a reliable, energetic proponent of the Contract.

Gingrich persuaded his party to impose a three-term limit on how long a member could chair a committee, while simultaneously imposing an eight-year limit on his own tenure. Accelerated turnover of chairs meant that junior Republicans loyal to the Speaker would accede to top committee positions more rapidly. The four-term restriction on the Speaker's tenure meant that if the Republicans maintained their majority over the next three elections and Gingrich served out his four terms as Speaker, he would be able to control selection of a new cohort of committee chairs two years before he himself would have to relinquish the Speakership, thereby increasing the likelihood that the committees would continue to harvest the fruits of the revolution in the post-Gingrich era. Republicans agreed to these proposals, partly because they believed they would never have gained control of the House without Gingrich, partly because a number of first-termers had made term limits for committee chairs a plank in their campaign platforms, partly because no Republican was forced to give up a position of power he or she had formerly occupied, and partly because a cohesive freshmen class would empower both the class and the leaders from whom they planned to take their cues (Barnett 1999, p. 62).

Gingrich also altered the means by which Republicans filled committee vacancies. He eliminated the long-standing Committee on Committees and replaced it with a "Steering Committee," a title that implied policymaking as well as committee assignment responsibilities. The Committee on Committees had been made up of senior Republicans from the largest states and regional representatives, together with a handful of party leaders. State and regional delegates cast weighted votes whose magnitude was determined by the number of Republican-controlled House districts within the areas they represented. Thus, the California representative cast twenty-two votes, 11 percent of the total. Party leaders, by contrast, accounted for 6 percent.

Under the new system, a total of thirty-one votes would be distributed among Steering Committee members, with the Speaker's vote valued at six, and nine other GOP leaders casting ten more—a majority of the total votes. This meant that no Republican could be appointed to a committee without the approval of at least some party leaders. The change permitted Gingrich to secure valuable assignments for vulnerable first-termers and for his loyalists, one of whose roles would be to prod hesitant chairs to act expeditiously and force them to stay on the Republican message. An aide to the Speaker remarked, "We reconfigured [the committee] to give Newt absolute power" (Drew 1996, p. 37).

Gingrich's willingness to violate the seniority system and his command of the assignment process allowed him to threaten Republicans with loss of seniority, removal as chair of a committee or subcommittee, or removal from a committee altogether if they failed to support the leadership. Before the new Congress convened, he demanded written assurances from all committee chairs and from the thirteen "cardinals" chairing Appropriations subcommittees that they would support the Contract with America. He told some rank-and-file members they were granted one chance to deviate from the party line. A second "mistake" would exact denial of a place on a conference committee or a task force (Drew 1996, p. 57).

Later, he advised some wavering Republicans on the Agriculture Committee that he would remove them from the panel, and even recruit primary opponents to run against them in the next election, if they continued to ignore leadership voting cues (Drew 1996, p. 180). As the new Congress worked its will, the Speaker further placed his stamp on the committee process by establishing timetables each panel was to follow, controlling the size and character of committee staffs, and determining the amount of money available to each committee to conduct its business, all the while monitoring committee compliance.

But Gingrich was prepared to circumvent committees if he believed they were going off course or dragging their feet. He formed a Speaker's Advisory Group (SAG) made up of his closest confidants to consider the entire range of issues facing the new majority. This group approved appointment of Republican task forces to study and make policy recommendations on issues cutting across committee jurisdictions (Drew 1996, p. 37). When suspicious of the direction a committee was taking, Gingrich created a task force to consider independently the legislative measure in question and generate a proposal he believed would be more in keeping with preferences of the rank and file—particularly GOP first- and second-termers.

The SAG also settled disputes about whether proposed legislation was consistent with the GOP mandate. Bills sent to committees sometimes arrived with an injunction against language changes. When some were, in fact, modified, party leaders ignored the committee-approved version and restored the original language. Judiciary chair Henry Hyde, whose committee was responsible for considering one-half of the items in the Contract, referred to himself as the "subchairman," often clearing committee decisions with party leaders. Later, one Republican complained, "Being a Chairman in the Newt Congress means not being in the room when deals are done" (Cook 1996).

Like Democratic leaders before him, Gingrich made extensive use of the Rules Committee as an instrument for shaping the measures reported for debate. Because committees were working at breakneck speed, often holding cursory hearings (or none at all), and because measures emerging from them were frequently loaded down with ill-considered, technically flawed provisions, the legislative product was vulnerable to challenge during floor debate. Consequently, Gingrich and his lieutenants freely altered committee-approved language and sent the revised measures to a generally accommodating if not compliant Rules Committee. The Rules Committee, in turn, had more than the usual number of opportunities to be creative.

During the 100 days, Gingrich allowed and even encouraged members to attach riders to hastily approved appropriations bills. Many were directed against policies considered too liberal by recent GOP arrivals, and the House defunded or limited programs authorized only weeks earlier. In this way, restrictions were imposed on abortions, and environmental regulations—and some social programs—were vitiated. Most of the riders were later dropped by the Senate, vetoed by the president, or subsequently defeated in the House. But they proved to be a useful instrument by which Gingrich satisfied the goals of his more revolutionary supporters when committees were apparently not doing their bidding.

Most new Republicans were staunchly conservative on economic issues, and they had sworn to cut federal spending for welfare and other entitlement programs. They were also determined to reduce the size and intrusiveness of the Washington bureaucracy, and to cut taxes. GOP first-termers were socially conservative as well, eager to end abortion, promote prayer in public school, allow use of federal funds for private and church-related schools, and reverse the growing acceptance of unconventional sexual orientations. Gingrich made it clear that he, too, supported these goals, but persuaded his revolutionaries to delay introduction of their social agenda until after the economic and political objectives in the Contract were realized (Rae 1998, p. 9). Predisposed to support the Speaker, the new members agreed, and they exhibited unusual party cohesion in the early months of the 104th Congress. During the first session, a majority of one party voted against a majority of the other party on more than seven of ten roll calls, and the mean party unity score for Republicans rose to 93 percent (Owens 1996).

Destruction of Democratic influence in the House was arguably Gingrich's most successful initiative. Already shell-shocked and demoralized by the suddenness and magnitude of their loss, Democrats were further weakened by significant changes in the House's structure and procedures. Without consulting Democrats, the new majority eliminated three standing committees, all of which served predominantly Democratic constituencies. Gone was the Committee on Merchant Marine and

Fisheries, a panel of special interest to mostly Democratic coastal districts. At the same time, responsibilities of the District of Columbia and Post Office and Civil Service Committees were shifted to the Government Reform and Oversight Committee (known until then as the Government Operations Committee), which meant that D.C. residents, postal workers, and other federal government employees would have less direct access to House decisionmaking. They could no longer count on the undivided attention of House panels enjoying a monopoly on matters affecting them.

A committee name-change dealt a blow to another Democratic constituency when the term "Labor" was deleted from the title of a committee known until then as Education and Labor. The panel was renamed Economic and Educational Opportunity. At the same time, overwhelmingly Democratic large cities lost both recognition and political clout when the Committee on Banking, Currency, and Urban Affairs became the Committee on Banking and Financial Services. Barbara-Rose Collins (D–Mich.), a central-city black congresswoman who had been a member of the committee, remarked: "As soon as I saw the change, I knew I would no longer be able to help the people I represented." These and other name changes, she said, were designed to reflect the priorities of the new majority, but by adopting them before informing Democratic leaders, Republicans were also displaying contempt for the new minority.

The Republican drive to cut government spending included proposed reductions in the size of House office and committee staffs. Ultimately the number of positions allocated to House members to staff Washington and district offices remained unchanged, in spite of a freshmen-led effort to cut them. But committee staffs were cut by one-third. And while, in principle, both parties would suffer, Republicans could anticipate large net increases in most committee staff at the same time that Democrats experienced devastating losses.

The reasons for this asymmetric outcome were rooted in grossly unequal allocation of staff resources that had obtained in past years. For example, in the 103rd Congress, 82 of the 100 Ways and Means Committee staff were Democratic appointees. In the 104th, the total staff size was cut to 75, with 50 to be appointed by Republicans. As a result, 57 Democratic appointees lost their jobs while Republicans were able to add 32 new aides. Loss of Democratic staff support was particularly debilitating because of the sweeping policy proposals their diminished ranks would be forced to confront and because of the procedural shortcuts the new majority would later adopt to process legislation.

Bills embodying Contract goals were rushed through committee and onto the floor, often with no hearings. There was little opportunity for effective dissent and even many Republicans were not fully aware of the implications of the measures they were approving. Proposed constitutional amendments received less attention than ordinary laws had in the past, and many of the bills debated had never received committee approval. A GOP leader later remarked: "[The opposition] was still off-balance from the surprising election returns . . . and we needed to change the terms of the debate definitively before [they] . . . could be effective in the minority" (Molinari 1998, p. 180). One Democratic Judiciary Committee aide observed:

> We'd have a one-day hearing on a constitutional amendment and then we'd be voting on it in the full committee the next day. . . . We didn't have the votes to try to change things we saw as egregious errors, not necessarily policy differences, but things we thought were ill-conceived. . . . We would point things out saying, "This just doesn't work" or "I don't think this is what you intended to do," or "There are problems here that you are not accounting for." And very often they replied "Sorry, we can't worry about that now. The Senate will fix it."

Circumvention of traditional procedures deprived backbench Republicans, as well as Democrats, of their best chance to influence policy. One reason for the haste was to meet the 100-day timetable for passage of the Contract. Another was to prevent Democrats from organizing a national opposition to a menu of ten priorities that most Americans had never heard of when they cast ballots in the 1994 election (*New York Times,* November 10, 1994). One first-term Democrat commented on the treatment Democrats on her committee received from the committee chair: "The Chairman was really a gentleman, but the ranking member was not allowed to get anything passed. Nothing. And many times we weren't even recognized to speak. That was the atmosphere. The whole atmosphere was, 'We've got to get even. After 40 years we've got to show these people.'"

Republicans adopted two other practices that put Democrats at a disadvantage. First, they eliminated proxy voting, an arrangement whereby majority party committee members delegated to their committee chair the authority to cast their votes in the event that they were not present for committee roll call votes. For years, Democratic House members had given blanket approval to chairs to cast proxy votes, and many intracommittee disputes were decided by Democrats who were not present. The new Republican leadership banned the practice, required members to be present if they wanted their votes to count, and ordered that committee attendance and the "yeas and nays" be recorded.

This policy affected Republicans as well as Democrats, and the former were just as inconvenienced as the latter as they hurried back and forth between the committees to which they were assigned and between committee meeting rooms and the House floor. Members suffered from a work overload as demands on their time mounted, and they were sometimes expected to be in two (or three) places at the same time (Drew 1996, p. 99). But Democrats were especially inconvenienced because they did not control House and committee agendas, and because they were working with diminished committee staffs. Their efforts to rebut and offer substitutes to Republican measures were hampered by insufficient time, expertise, and opportunity.

Gingrich also ordered that the fifteen-minute time period during which members were required to arrive on the House floor to vote—after the sounding of bells signaling a roll call—be strictly enforced, albeit with a two-minute grace period. This rule was put in place after the House, years earlier, had adopted electronic voting, but Democratic leaders had been casual about observing it. They allowed more time for members to arrive on the floor, and used the added minutes to persuade wavering rank and file to support party positions. Believing that Republicans would be more cohesive than the Democrats, but mindful of his narrow majority, Gingrich was determined to give the Democratic leaders less time to switch votes within either their or his party and thereby reverse what would otherwise be a GOP victory (Drew 1996, p. 148).

But the most pervasive threat to Democratic leverage was the exclusion of their leaders from decisionmaking councils. When Democrats dominated the House, they sought frequently to hammer out bipartisan compromises, with leaders of the two parties conferring regularly, and with committee chairs and ranking minority members working together closely. On many if not most issues, Democrats imposed their will on a frustrated minority, but bipartisanship was a strategic premise even if not always realized.

By contrast, Gingrich arrogated power to himself in a manner rarely seen in the twentieth century. And he delighted in rubbing salt in Democrats' wounds. Phone calls to the Speaker from minority leader Richard Gephardt went unreturned, and Gingrich strongly urged Republican committee and subcommittee chairs not to work with or consult their Democratic opposite numbers. When committee chairs and Republican moderates were invited to the White House to meet with the president, they were told by Gingrich to reject all such invitations, at least through the first 100 days (Drew 1996, p. 61).

Driven by his belief that "politics is bloodless war," Gingrich had come to despise the Democrats and to treat them as mortal adversaries. He rejected the norm of "collegiality" that had often, even if not always, characterized the relationship between the two House parties, and he viewed congressional politics as a zero-sum game. To win, you had to destroy rather than placate or accommodate the opposition.

The implications of these developments for the effectiveness and even survival of the Congressional Caucus for Women's Issues were far-reaching. Forced to work on the margins of political power even under the best of circumstances, the CCWI would now have to try to promote its agenda under conditions more problematical than even during the Reagan era. This bipartisan organization would have to adjust to a House in which partisanship has become the defining imperative. It would have to work with a House leadership that had replaced accommodation and cooperation with confrontation and vilification. It would have to come to terms with a monolithic power structure that had replaced one allowing for multiple access points.

Caucus leaders' efforts would be further complicated by their need to appeal to a large group of new Republicans whose commitment to a conservative agenda was as strong as any exhibited in recent years, whose collective experience in legislative settings was minimal, whose impatience with compromise and the give-and-take of the bargaining process became famous, and whose contempt for the federal government and its programs was unabaiting. And they would have to try to inspire CCWI members and promote the feminist agenda while the Republican legislative schedule was extracting every ounce of intellectual and emotional energy from members who also had constituency, committee, and personal demands to worry about.

Thus the portents were not favorable for an informal House group that was most successful when a bipartisan spirit of accommodation and civility prevailed, when majority party leaders and committees were willing to take seriously a smorgasbord of relatively inexpensive, progressive proposals that expanded the role of the federal government, when pragmatic rather than ideological values suffused House debate, and when members were prepared to subordinate partisan necessity to constituency interests and problem solving. Caucus prospects became bleaker still when the new majority eliminated legislative service organizations.

Abolishing the LSOs

A month before the new Congress convened, Republican leaders decided to rid the House of legislative service organizations. The decision did not require a vote of the full House inasmuch as regulation of LSOs had been delegated to the House Administration Committee, and especially to the committee chair. For years, Democrats had exercised a virtual monopoly on accreditation of new LSOs, on their funding, accounting, and reporting procedures, and on the ground rules under which they operated. From the time North Carolina's Charlie Rose became committee chair, he had brooked little interference in the supervision of the House groups.

In January 1995 the committee's name was changed to House Oversight, and Rose was replaced by Republican William Thomas of California, who now commanded a five-to-three GOP majority on the panel. Among the other Republicans on the committee was Pat Roberts of Kansas, a strident critic of the LSOs who had devoted more than a decade trying to impose stricter regulations on their activities and financing. Just weeks into the new Congress, the committee formally stripped the LSOs of the office space assigned them on Capitol Hill. It also barred House members from pooling portions of their annual $557,400 clerk-hire funds to pay LSO staffs, and from using part of their $122,500 office expense allowance to pay for LSO equipment and supplies.

Denied space, staff, and equipment, the LSOs officially passed from the scene, although Thomas assured their members they could reorganize as congressional membership organizations (CMOs)—joining more than 100 informal House groups operating without direct benefit of public funds. Members could continue to meet regularly in House space to discuss business, but coordination of group activities was expected to be carried out by the personal office staff of members who occupied CMO leadership positions.

Even for some Democrats, the change was long overdue—although many favored fundamental reform to outright elimination. Reports of LSO financial abuses had surfaced regularly. Collectively they had spent $35 million in the preceding decade and, according to Roberts, more than $7.7 million had never been accounted for. Moreover, financial reporting deadlines were chronically ignored (Love 1994). Receipts for $10,000 in petty cash controlled by the Congressional Black Caucus could not be found, for example, and Gingrich remarked that the sloppiness of LSO accounting procedures was another "scandal waiting to explode." He and other critics compared the irregularities to the Bank and Post Office scandals that had earlier embarrassed the Democratic leadership and cost scores of Republicans, as well as Democrats, their House seats (*Atlanta Constitution,* December 7, 1994). Some LSOs used funds allotted to them to cover food and entertainment expenditures that the offices of individual members were not allowed to spend. The New York State LSO, for example, spent $1,620 on three lunches in the spring of 1993, and $2,646 on gifts for retiring House members and staff (Jacoby 1993b).

Critics also claimed that LSOs promoted the interests of parochial elements within the society rather than helping Congress foster a broader vision for the country as a whole. "LSOs are specialization run amok," said one former congressman. They take "solution-seeking away from the committees and put it in the hands of advocacy groups," thereby serving as "outsider's inside groups" (*New York Times,* December 7, 1994). Some Republican ire was directed against LSO staff members, who over the years had aggressively resisted restrictions on CCWI activities, and against Rose, who was seen as high-handed and excessively partisan. They believed the North Carolinian had too often ignored Republican recommendations to reform the LSOs, and that some of his decisions were arbitrary. In 1993 he approved formation of three LSOs devoted to social issues—hunger; narcotics abuse; and children, youth, and families—but claimed budgetary constraints a year later when denying accreditation to three other potential LSOs to which he was less sympathetic—constitutional issues; national defense; and terrorism and unconventional warfare (Jacoby 1994e).

But the most serious charge leveled against LSOs concerned the intimate ties nine of them had to nonprofit "foundations." These outside organizations bore names similar to the caucuses, their boards of directors were made up of caucus members, but spending by the foundations was not subject to congressional control. They raised money from foreign as well as domestic sources, and their funds were often spent to hire staff and underwrite travel, entertainment, and campaign costs of House members in ways that, if the caucuses had spent them, would have violated House rules (Jacoby 1993d).

During the Gulf War, for example, the Congressional Human Rights Caucus held a hearing on Iraqi atrocities in Kuwait at the same time that its affiliated Congressional Human Rights Foundation was taking $50,000 from a front group for the Kuwaiti government (Jacoby 1994a). The subcommittee on Africa, on which several members of the Congressional

Black Caucus served, approved a nonbinding resolution recognizing a claim to the presidency by a Nigerian political leader who funneled tens of thousands in contributions to the Congressional Black Caucus Foundation. The Foundation's board of directors included eleven members of the House caucus, one of whom was the board chair (Jacoby 1993c). And members of the Congressional Hispanic Caucus served on the board of the Congressional Hispanic Caucus Institute when the latter asked corporations for a $15,000 fee to join its "Congressional Circle." One benefit of membership was private luncheons with Hispanic Representatives (*Roll Call,* July 29, 1993).

Some steps had been taken to end these abuses. In July 1993 the House Administration Committee adopted new regulations to improve oversight of LSOs. They were placed under the supervision of the House Finance Office (HFO), eliminating extracongressional individual bank accounts, and all expenses would have to be documented when reimbursement vouchers were submitted to the HFO. They could not spend more than $2,500 annually on food and beverages, and they would have to submit annual budget and activity reports to the Administration Committee chair. The reports would have to affirm that the LSO provided its members with "bona fide research and/or legislative service or assistance" before it could be recertified. In the meantime, the full House approved a measure sponsored by CCWI member Jan Meyers (R–Kans.) to give LSO staff the same fringe benefits enjoyed by members' office staffs, including coverage under the Federal Employment Retirement system. The staff would now be paid through the House Finance Office.

But the changes did little to regulate the relationship between the LSOs and their companion foundations. Republican demands that the full Administration Committee, not just the chair, approve budget requests were rejected by Chairman Rose and committee Democrats, as was a proposal for random audits of LSO books by the General Accounting Office. Measures to require recertification of LSOs every two years, to prohibit them from affiliating with outside foundations, and to prevent outside organizations from adopting names similar to their companion LSOs were also defeated.

Even if these reforms had been adopted, chances are that the LSOs would have been eliminated as soon as they were no longer under Democratic (and Rose's) protection. Their potential threat to the Republican agenda, the blatant abuses that had by then become common knowledge, and the possibility of future scandal were persuasive reasons to terminate them forthwith. Critics also claimed that LSO elimination would result in ninety-six fewer staff to pay, sixteen more offices on Capitol Hill that would become available for more worthwhile purposes, and $5.5 million in savings derived from the sale of a building then housing LSOs (*New York Times,* December 7, 1994). To a phalanx of first-term revolutionaries obsessed with the need to cut spending, these prospects were irresistible.

Defenders of the LSOs fought a losing battle to preserve them. Black, Hispanic, and women House members interpreted the decision as an assault on diversity in Congress, and, according to the head of the Black Caucus, as an attempt to disempower their constituencies "through racial, ethnic, and gender cleansing." Under the new rules, these groups would have difficulty developing and articulating policy positions at odds with those presented by House committees that had traditionally treated them as "other." The ranking Democrat on the Appropriations Committee, David Obey, charged that eliminating the Democratic Study Group (DSG) would give the majority party a monopoly on legislative information in the 104th Congress. He said, "I don't have a problem with centralized power within an institution, but centralizing information is a very dangerous thing. It invites manipulation of information by committees, it invites rationing of information" (Love 1994).

Supporters of the CCWI were no less vocal. Outgoing CCWI cochair Pat Schroeder said, "It is ironic that one of the first initiatives of the new Republican leadership . . . is to abolish the one organization that exists to give women a stronger voice in the policy process." Republican Olympia Snowe, who was also relinquishing her leadership role in the caucus, was more circumspect inasmuch as her party had at long last gained control of the House. Nonetheless, in remarks some considered a eulogy, she said, "The legislative changes pushed by women members of Congress touched the lives of every woman and her family in the country through expanded research on women's health, better protection against domestic violence and sexual assault, and improved economic opportunities for women" (*St. Louis Post Dispatch,* December 28, 1994).

Schroeder took particular issue with Pat Roberts's charge that LSOs spent public funds irresponsibly, eating and drinking their way through public relations events at the expense of the U.S. Treasury. Roberts had told a reporter that elimination of the LSOs would mean there would be "no more laughing and chortling, no more passing the goodies out behind closed doors." Schroeder's rejoinder noted that the CCWI, whose membership totaled 160, had spent $162.50 during the first fifteen months of the 103rd Congress. "By comparison," she told Roberts, "your office spent $1,521.17, almost 10 times what the CCWI spent" (*Chicago Tribune,* January 8, 1995). Incoming Democratic cochair Nita Lowey tried to put the best face on the diminution of CCWI resources: "They can abolish our Caucus, but they cannot ignore our agenda" (*New York Times,* December 7, 1994). In the 104th Congress, the Republican majority demonstrated how unprophetic she could be.

The Revolutionaries

Not all GOP freshmen in the 104th Congress explicitly targeted the feminist agenda, but their priorities, intensity, and political heft combined to threaten the CCWI's past achievements and to block new initiatives at almost every turn. First, they had strength in numbers. The seventy-three new Republicans elected in 1994 made up the largest class of majority party newcomers since 1974, when seventy-five Democratic first-termers came to Washington following the Watergate scandal. Second, because sixty-five of the seventy-three had either defeated Democratic incumbents or captured a seat vacated by a Democrat, and because no Republican House or Senate incumbent had been defeated, GOP freshmen considered partisan combat to be part of their mandate.

Third, they were politically inexperienced. Nearly 60 percent were under the age of forty-five, and while more than 60 percent had served in federal, state, or local office (Rae 1998, p. 66), only 42 percent had been elected to their offices—compared with 62 percent of the holdover Republicans. Among those with political experience, eighteen had been members of lawmaking bodies, but only seven had been part of a Republican majority responsible for running and controlling a legislature (Fenno 1997, p. 23). The inexperience of so many was not coincidental. Newt Gingrich had succeeded in recruiting business-oriented political amateurs who were determined to cut spending and taxes, and get government off the backs of entrepreneurs. The combative Georgian was not interested in attracting candidates skilled in political negotiation and compromise. Instead, he wanted conservatives who had the courage of their convictions, who were idealists, and who would reject pragmatic solutions (Barnett 1999, p. 137).

Fourth, the new group developed an affinity with the forty-three Republicans initially elected to the House in 1992 (Drew 1996, p. 27). While many of the latter were more politically experienced and less radical than the 104th Republican class, they were collectively more conservative than the House members they had replaced (Donovan 1994), and they shared the ideological and policy predilections of the Republicans who came after them. Most members of both classes were committed to internal reform and the restructuring of government priorities.

In fact, GOP first-termers in 1993 had perhaps unwittingly given Washington a taste of what it could expect two years later. In the weeks following the 1992 election, for example, their votes had been pivotal in electing Texan Dick Armey as chair of the Republican Conference, defeating California moderate Jerry Lewis. They had also helped establish a six-year limit on how long a Republican could serve as ranking member of a standing committee (Donovan 1992). And most had favored constitutional amendments requiring a balanced budget and a line-item veto for presidents (Duncan 1992). John Linder of Georgia, who was later handpicked by Gingrich to chair the National Republican Congressional Campaign Committee, remarked at the time, "We've moved the Republican Conference to the right" (Donovan 1992).

Together, the freshman and sophomore Republican classes made up one-half of their party's House membership in the 104th Congress, and while there was considerable diversity between and among the two classes, common political experiences trumped whatever differences divided them. They had developed their political sensibilities during the Reagan administration, many had been inspired to run by Newt Gingrich, and almost all believed in the wisdom embodied in the Contract with America.

Finally, freshmen class members shared a strong sense of community. They bonded with one another because their candidacies had emerged out of common policy orientations and because they were critical of how Washington was addressing the country's problems. They had campaigned using similar national themes, even before they pledged fidelity to the Contract, and the euphoria triggered by their historic political victory, together with a conscious awareness of their extraordinary collective achievement, reinforced the sense of mission they brought to Washington. Feelings of community and common cause were buttressed, in turn, by their treatment as "a unique collectivity" by the press and by their colleagues (Barnett 1999, p. 62).

For the CCWI, this large collection of cohesive, politically inexperienced Reagan conservatives committed to a Contract whose clauses ignored or subverted most of the caucus's goals was devastating. According to a caucus member, one of the most consequential attributes of the new class was its legislative and representative inexperience. She said:

Many new members come from vocations which did not require them to deal with people who are different from themselves; people who have different perspectives, different experiences, and different backgrounds, and they bring a tunnel vision to the legislative process. Another casualty is the personal relationships that usually develop between members after they come to the Hill. Throughout the 104th Congress, they never established the bi-partisan links that help build consensus and make good legislation possible.

Even some veteran Republicans viewed their new colleagues as an insulated, sometimes arrogant group. One remarked, "[For them] there is no other way but their way. Their lack of sophistication is a big problem. They don't realize you have to form a majority" (Drew 1996, p. 174).

No single postelection event presaged the unyielding ideological mind-set of the revolutionaries more than their rejection of an invitation from Harvard's Kennedy School of Government to attend a week-long policy orientation in Cambridge. The decision had important symbolic, as well as practical consequences. For years, freshmen members of both parties had journeyed to Cambridge a month after their election to hear specialists in domestic and foreign policy discuss issues the new Congress was likely to address. The speakers were normally academics and advisers to previous administrations, who together provided some ideological balance.

After the 1992 election, three conservative organizations—the Heritage Foundation, the Free Congress Foundation, and the Family Research Council—joined forces to sponsor an alternative set of seminars in Annapolis. The three-day event overlapped with the Harvard orientation, but it was possible for freshmen to attend the Annapolis meetings and later participate in most of the Kennedy School sessions. GOP whip Newt Gingrich and other party leaders had made it clear that Republican freshmen were expected to attend policy sessions sponsored by the conservative groups, and thirty-five of the forty-six did so. Six of the thirty-five then joined sixty-nine Democrats in attending the Harvard program. In Annapolis, they heard from a string of uniformly conservative speakers, with Congressmen Charles Stenholm of Texas the only Democratic participant. In Cambridge, House Democrat Lee Hamilton and such liberal academics as John Kenneth Galbraith and Robert Reich were joined by Reagan economic adviser Martin Feldstein, former education secretary Lamar Alexander, and Bush national security aide Condoleezza Rice (Jacoby 1994b).

Following the 1994 election, the Heritage Foundation and its two cosponsors scheduled another series of orientation sessions, inviting all newly elected House members. Sixty Republicans traveled to the Baltimore meetings, and although two Democrats said they would attend, neither appeared (*New York Times,* December 11, 1994). Speakers were again limited to conservative policy specialists, and included Jack Kemp, Lamar Alexander, Ralph Reed, Jeane Kirkpatrick, William Bennett, and Rush Limbaugh. In the meantime, the Kennedy School, having once again planned an orientation, canceled it after receiving only a handful of acceptances.

As a consequence, freshmen of both parties were denied early exposure to a range of policy perspectives from which their predecessors had benefited, and the cancellation reinforced beliefs held by Republican revolutionaries in the rightness of their cause and in the sea change that was taking place in American politics. So deep was the gulf between the parties that even traditionally bipartisan administrative briefings given by the Capitol Police and the House Clerk's Office were offered separately to Democrats and Republicans.

The Contract and the Role of Government

The threat to CCWI priorities was not limited to the language of the Contract. The document's dangers were implied in subjects unmentioned, as well as those spelled out. Almost all of the ten items addressed political and legal reform (term limits, unfunded mandates, the line-item veto, tort reform, criminal justice, reduced government regulation) or economic issues (a balanced budget amendment, tax reform). Only two, social security and welfare reform, dealt directly with social issues, but not in ways calculated to further CCWI goals. And yet, it had been social issues that most occupied the caucus's attention in recent years, whether it was women's health, the safety and care of children, education, special problems of the aging, or sexual discrimination and harassment. Omission of these and other women-friendly proposals was deliberate. Susan Molinari later recalled:

> I believed more women's issues should be included [in the Contract], especially a provision for more access to day care for all Americans. I argued that such a provision would be a concrete demonstration of the value that we placed on families . . . but we could not agree on how to fund it. In the end, I lost that and a number of other battles to the argument that singling out women's issues, or children's issues, or any

other sub-group's issues would defeat the point of the Contract. I
bowed to the consensus that we should concentrate on reforms that
would affect every American. (Molinari 1998, p. 179)

After the new Congress convened, the Contract's generalities were
translated into concrete fiscal and programmatic options, and it soon
became clear that caucus-supported social goals were to be sacrificed
on the altar of the Contract's political and economic objectives. Threatened were Head Start, school lunches, and the Special Supplemental
Nutrition Program for Women, Infants, and Children. All would be
placed in block grants to the states, where they could be vitiated. Also
under attack were financial support for job training, and summer jobs
for low-income youth; funds for home heating assistance to the poor;
the Department of Education; the national service program; financial
aid for domestic and international family planning programs; federal
spending on health and low-cost housing; and civil rights and affirmative action protections in the workplace—all of which had been high
CCWI priorities for a decade or more.

Efforts to strengthen or even sustain these social policies generally
failed. Three-quarters of Contract-inspired cost-cutting measures were
reported out of committee in the form prescribed by Republican leaders (Owen 1996). During the first 100 days, not a single amendment
promoting expanded health care, education, job training, or women's
rights and opportunities was passed (Drew 1996, p. 180), with freshmen
roll call support of their GOP leaders averaging 97 percent (Curren
1995). The first-termers remained more reliable supporters of party
leaders than nonfreshmen during the remainder of the first session
(Conway and DeGregorio 1998). Their membership on the Republican
"Theme Team," a group selected by GOP leaders to publicize the
party's message, was out of proportion to their numbers in the Republican majority (60 percent of the team were freshmen). And six of the top
ten team members delivering daily, Contract-related, one-minute
speeches were first-termers (Conway and DeGregorio 1998).

Perhaps the most pervasive and insidious threat to CCWI goals was
embedded in the contempt GOP freshmen had for Congress, for the federal government generally, and for national policies that restricted state
and local government discretion. From the moment congresswomen created their caucus in 1977, virtually all of its efforts had been devoted
to giving Congress and the federal government more, rather than less,
responsibility in helping women improve the quality of their lives.
Whether the issue was raising more money to help impoverished

women, forcing schools and businesses to treat women and men equally, or promoting such new initiatives as family and medical leave, CCWI proposals increased the presence and reach of the federal government.

Now Washington was overwhelmed by House neophytes whose missionary zeal, cohesiveness, and antigovernment bias threatened policies that CCWI leaders believed had been settled years ago. Looking back on 1995, one GOP member of the 104th freshmen class later said that when he arrived in the nation's capital he saw the city as "a world filled with power, money and sex . . . all the evil spirits," and he was determined "not to become a part of Washington." He saw Congress as "a bunch of greedy, egotistical members who were out of touch" (Doherty and Katz 1998). Anti-Washington outsiders like this freshman considered the concept of "effective government programs" to be an oxymoron.

For many of this freshman's peers, House rules, procedures, and norms were obstacles that had to be overcome in order to realize partisan and policy objectives. They assumed that the committee system and committee specialization were used to circumvent the popular will. Republican task forces, an active Theme Team, and formation of such informal subgroups as the New Federalists and the Conservative Action Team were effective antidotes to what they believed were retrogressive committee practices. This view extended to members' dealings with constituents. One congressman, George Radanovich of California, stopped responding directly to the content of constituent mail, replying instead with a form letter railing against the costliness of the average member's mail operation (Chappie 1996).

Many said they had no plans to move their families to Washington, promising to leave the Capital as soon as their jobs were done, and several imposed term limits on their House tenure. Some looked askance at the everyday courtesies and deference they received from Capitol Hill staff. Steven Shaddegg of Arizona remarked that he "refused to go through the door before my staff. . . . I'm going to do everything I can to resist those trappings of power because I think they corrupt you" (*New York Times*, December 11, 1994).

5 Coping with Change: 1995–1996

Life as a CMO

Legislative service organizations (LSOs) were eliminated as the 104th Congress got under way. They were advised that they had until January 30, 1995, to stop spending money and move out of their quarters, and were given until March 30 to pay all outstanding bills. Most of the twenty-eight affected groups, including the Congressional Caucus for Women's Issues, reorganized as congressional membership organizations (CMOs).[1] Four were disbanded, including the Environmental and Energy Study Conference, which became a private organization. The Congressional Hunger Caucus was absorbed by the House Democratic Caucus, and the Republican Study Committee was shut down, its research responsibilities transferred to the House Republican Conference (*Washington Post,* March 23, 1995).

The Democratic Study Group (DSG) succumbed, following a last-minute struggle to survive. In the 103rd Congress, the DSG had employed eighteen staffers on a budget of $1 million. About 250 House members received its fact sheets, legislative schedules, and special reports, paying $4,200 annually from their office expense accounts for the privilege (Jacoby 1993a). More than thirty-five of those availing themselves of the DSG's highly regarded services were Republicans, a circumstance that vexed GOP leaders. In December 1993, Republican Conference chair Richard Armey had written to GOP subscribers pointing out that they were providing the opposition with $158,900 annually to underwrite special reports that regularly attacked Republican policies. This constituted nearly 12 percent of the DSG's revenue. He asked them to drop their subscriptions and rely instead on *Republican Digest,* a periodical that would not cost them a dime (Burger 1993).

Faced with the loss of staff, space, and equipment, the DSG improvised means to stay afloat. Its staff established DSG Publications, a private, nonprofit company that would continue to produce daily and weekly reports on proposed legislation and pending floor action. An annual subscription price of $5,000 was established, a sum that would be used to sustain the service and replace House members' clerk-hire money formerly used to pay its staff. Subscriptions were to be paid out of members' office expense accounts, accounts normally used to pay for newspapers, magazines, and other periodicals that Representatives believed would improve performance of their official duties.

But when, at the end of January, 120 Representatives asked the House Finance Office to pay the $5,000 subscriptions to DSG Publications, House Oversight Committee chair William Thomas intervened and ruled that House members could not pay more than $500 from official funds for new publications, unless it could be shown that fledgling publications charging more than that sum could be sustained independent of House members' subscriptions (*Washington Post,* March 23, 1995). The ruling destroyed the DSG's financial base, and the thirty-five-year-old organization expired. Its staff accepted a buyout from Congressional Quarterly Inc., and a dozen were hired by the company. In the meantime, the Democratic Caucus assumed some of the DSG's research and reporting activities (Kahn 1995).

The House Ethics Committee, too, prevented former LSOs from salvaging some of their perquisites. Four months into the new Congress, it ruled that House members could not raise funds on behalf of private, nonprofit foundations they had founded or controlled unless the organizations conducted activities entirely unrelated to members' official duties (Love 1995a). Money raising for traditional charities was not affected, but the new guideline meant that the foundations with which LSOs like the Black and Hispanic Caucuses had once been linked could no longer depend on House members' financing (Love 1995d).

Savings produced by the change were difficult to document. Dues and subscriptions supporting LSOs had varied from $25 for the Congressional Automotive Caucus, to $200 for the Rural Caucus, to as much as $35,000 for membership in the Republican Study Committee (Jacoby 1994d). Many members simply channeled clerk-hire and office funds once used to support LSOs into salary increases for their staff and subscriptions to other publications. Some said they planned to return the unspent sums to the Treasury. The claimed windfall savings varied, depending on the number of LSOs to which members belonged and the sum each charged. Democratic leader Richard Gephardt "saved" $13,000 in funds he would otherwise have distributed among ten LSOs, while incoming Republican cochair of the CCWI, Constance Morella, had to decide how to distribute $18,000 once contributed to LSOs (Love 1995e).

The alleged advantages of doing away with LSOs were lost on Morella and other CCWI leaders. As soon as word spread about their imminent demise, the Maryland Republican asked Republican women to lobby the GOP transition team and leaders to preserve the CCWI, whatever the fate of other LSOs (Jacoby 1994c). She argued that the CCWI, unlike some other groups, had managed its funds responsibly, that its expenditures always conformed with House rules, that in 1981 it had severed ties with a foundation created by its members, and that, unlike some of the other LSOs, it was a bipartisan organization with Democratic and Republican cochairs who tried to cooperate fully with leaders in both parties. Some GOP women noted that weakening the caucus was the wrong message to send when their party was having difficulty attracting women voters.

For several weeks the CCWI twisted in the wind, with more sanguine members hoping these arguments would prevail. But Chairman Thomas and his Oversight Committee could not be moved, and as the new Congress convened, CCWI sponsors gave up the ghost. The caucus dismissed its staff, ended the practice of conferring associate membership on congressmen—their dues and subscription payments no longer readily accessible—moved out of its suite of offices in the Rayburn Building, and reconstituted itself as a CMO. Lesley Primmer, the staff director, moved quickly to establish an office in private quarters and created Women's Policy Inc. (WPI), a nonprofit research organization devoted to providing information and legislative analysis on issues facing women and their families (*Washington Post,* March 23, 1995). Office space was provided free of charge by the American College of Obstetricians and Gynecologists in its quarters two miles from the Capitol, and by year's end WPI was publishing *The Source,* a weekly summary of congressional actions affecting women, and the more comprehensive periodical, *Quarterly Update.* Both publications were furnished to subscribers for $495 a year, a sum chosen because it fell just under the $500 Oversight Committee limit.

Shortly thereafter, CCWI leaders asked the House Ethics Committee for an advisory opinion about whether congresswomen could help raise money for WPI without violating the committee's prohibition on fundraising by LSO members whose organizations were linked to private, nonprofit foundations. The committee concluded that since no member of the CCWI had had a role in WPI's incorporation, and inasmuch as new cochairs Morella and Lowey were the only congresswomen on WPI's five-member board of directors, congresswomen affiliated with the new CMO could participate in WPI's fundraising efforts (Love 1995d). Similar requests by the Black and Hispanic Caucuses were denied.

Publications produced by WPI eventually met some CCWI needs, but months passed before it was up and running. And even then, many CCWI members refused to subscribe, deciding they had better use for the $495. WPI's location was an important drawback, with the two miles separating their downtown office and Capitol Hill translating into light years in intellectual and emotional support. More important, Ethics Committee rulings made it impossible for the small WPI staff to coordinate CCWI activities, to take the follow-up action needed to implement a CCWI initiative, and to consult regularly with the cochairs.

The loss of the half dozen Rayburn Building professionals was devastating. The staff had given continuity to the CCWI as its leaders and members arrived and then passed from the scene. The caucus had never been a highly cohesive, well-coordinated group of congresswomen prepared to act in lockstep. The cochairs were not so much coordinators as reference points for caucus members, the House, the media, and women's special interest groups. They articulated their vision for the CCWI and for American women, while at the same time providing the sound bites attaching meaning to unfolding events. Caucus members could invoke its name and reputation to build, proclaim, and exploit a consensus. They often acted as individual entrepreneurs specializing in subjects bounded by their committee responsibilities, all the while relying on the half dozen professional staffers to provide the research, the continuity, and the organizational ballast needed to promote the feminist agenda. Elimination of the LSOs changed all that.

The staff's departure created a vacuum in CCWI operations that lasted for months and that was never completely filled. Some of the responsibilities were assumed by staff members in the offices of the two cochairs, Cindy Hall for Morella, Sharon Levin for Lowey. From all reports, they rose to the occasion and did a splendid job, meeting each Monday with the staff liaisons from CCWI members' offices, and implementing cochair decisions. Said one liaison:

> The staffers in Lowey and Morella's offices were great. They seemed to know everything. I called them when I had a question about any

women's issue and they gave me great background. They were a great resource. They tracked legislation and knew what was happening all over the Hill. They drafted testimony and circulated letters for members to sign. They did a great job even though they were terribly overworked. They were inspiring.

But even the principals acknowledged that there were tasks they could not adequately address or perform in a timely way. One Democratic congresswoman lamented the consequences of the change:

> The defunding had a major impact, as it did on all LSOs. The research and information we were deprived of was considerable. It was not only the absence of research, but the ability to distribute findings in an integrated way, in a way that would be useful, was undermined; as was the ability to use that information to promote your own priorities. The message just doesn't get out.

Some of the broader implications of these developments were revealed in the observations of another staffer:

> Abolition of the LSOs meant you don't have a staff structure, you don't have funding, you don't have an office, and everything the Caucus staff is doing is now done by the staff of the co-chairs. And that has a big impact. In a member's office, there are eight or nine people. Everything these people have to do for the Caucus is on top of everything else they have to do every day—meet with constituents, meet with lobbyists, answer mail, track legislation on the floor, introduce legislation, review it for co-sponsorship, prepare for committee markups and everything else that goes on each day. The staff the Caucus lost was able to devote full time and energy to Caucus business without having to worry about matters that come up in members' personal offices.

A woman who had once been a member of the CCWI staff remarked:

> Perhaps the most important loss associated with moving the staff off the Hill is the loss in continuity, in a sense of history and Caucus tradition. In the past, staff who worked for Caucus members would often call and ask, "What did my boss do on this issue the last time it came up?" It's more difficult to answer that question now than when the Caucus staff was on the Hill with its files intact and accessible. We controlled the records up through the 103rd Congress. We knew which advocacy groups were involved with previous legislation. We knew who the contact people were. When we moved off the Hill some information was lost and now it is less accessible.

Changes in the partisan and ideological complexion of the House, together with the diminution in CCWI resources, vitiated the caucus's task forces. Several possessed no Republican cochairs, as GOP congresswomen assumed key leadership and committee positions within the new majority. Others fell into disuse because they were responsible for matters unlikely to be addressed by Republican power brokers. Limited staff resources meant that the caucus leadership could not effectively encourage already overworked task force leaders to develop an agenda.

Loss of LSO status also meant that the CCWI would be denied the nominal support of the 120 male auxiliary members. Asked to join the caucus out of financial necessity, these congressmen, almost all of them Democrats, often lent more than their names to CCWI causes. Several had occupied influential committee positions, and they had often been prevailed upon to insert women-friendly language into the bills they were considering. They could now pay WPI $495 for *The Source,* and about a dozen subscribed. But few former auxiliary members exerted much leverage in the 104th Congress.

Rank-and-file CCWI members had little time or opportunity to ponder the plight of the caucus. Many Democratic women were too busy fending off Republican attacks on landmark New Deal and Great Society legislation. "We were under siege," said one congresswoman, "and there was simply no time to think about the Women's Caucus." In the past, congresswomen would receive calls from CCWI staff urging them to testify before a House committee or to hurry to the House floor to defend CCWI priorities in an unfolding debate. This task now fell to the overburdened people working in cochair offices.

At the same time, several congresswomen were scrambling to secure new committee assignments to replace those they had lost when the Republican majority adjusted committee ratios. For them, women's interests could not be given much attention when their own congressional influence was hanging in the balance. Attendance at CCWI meetings fell off. Said one previously active member, "We try to get together . . . but the availability of information and the staff support are gone. It's just not the same."

The drop-off was partly due to a downgrading in the perceived value of the organization. Many were not persuaded that their attendance would mean much for either their own legislative aspirations or for realizing feminist goals. Newcomers had no idea that the CCWI had sometimes made a difference, especially in the 103rd Congress, and its frustrations in the 104th gave them no reason to think they had joined an organization with political heft.

Several Black Caucus members were among the missing, some-times because CCWI activities conflicted with events sponsored by the Congressional Black Caucus, but also because, like the newcomers, they were not sure why they should attend. One second-termer remarked in retrospect that the 104th Congress represented two of the worst years of her life, and that the "racism and gender bias" she had encountered all of her life was poisoned further by the "mean-spirited-ness" of the debate and the tyranny of the schedule imposed by the majority party. Being active in the caucus, she implied, would not change the things that needed to be changed.

Even some veteran Democrats became less involved in CCWI activities. They concluded that losing House control to conservative revolutionaries meant that the feminist agenda had become irrelevant. As a result, they devoted less energy to CCWI-related activities and more to work in their committees. One longtime Republican CCWI member remarked midway through the 104th Congress, "My impression is that in the 104th Congress, the Caucus is generally a small group of Democratic women meeting and maybe Connie Morella."

The caucus was fortunate to have Morella as a cochair, not least because, with Olympia Snowe's election to the Senate, there were few experienced Republican women left who were willing to serve in that position. But Morella's record in the House placed her among the most liberal of Republicans. This limited her ability to reach out to other Republican women, and few were available to give her the moral and political support any leader would need in a purportedly bipartisan CMO. As a consequence, with the Democrats marginalized and the Republicans otherwise engaged, on most issues "the Caucus was noth-ing more than a lot of 'background noise,'" according to one Republi-can staffer.

The disengagement of Republican CCWI members was a result of several developments, the most important being the elevation of some of them to key committee and leadership positions. Jan Meyers and Nancy Johnson were named chairs of committees, and Susan Molinari was elected vice chair of the Republican Conference. Molinari also became chair of a subcommittee, as did Marge Roukema and Morella. Johnson secured a subcommittee chairmanship on the Ways and Means Committee, and she was the second ranking Republican on the influen-tial subcommittee on health. One veteran GOP congresswomen regret-fully explained her party's estrangement from the CCWI in this way: "The senior Republican members didn't have the time, and the first term-ers didn't join. We just didn't have the guns. Susan was in the leadership.

Jan and Nancy were tied up in committee work. There were too few of us, so we did not participate to the extent that it would have been healthy."

Several GOP women may not have been active in the CCWI even if their House responsibilities had been less compelling. They had been little more than nominal members, joining because Olympia Snowe had asked them to, but keeping the organization at arm's length. One GOP moderate remarked: "I haven't been awfully active in the Caucus. Technically I'm a member, but I have not been greatly involved in it. I see no real advantage to being a member. I have not worked on its agenda or fashioned my own agenda after the CCWI agenda." Some Republican women were unwilling to identify closely with the CCWI because, historically, the men in their party were unsympathetic to "women's issues." This indifference, if not hostility, was reflected in how few GOP men had joined the caucus as auxiliary members after 1981, and by Republican failure to address explicitly even a single CCWI priority in the Contract with America.

The increased distance Republican women placed between themselves and the caucus dovetailed with the designs of Newt Gingrich. The new Speaker sought actively to weaken the bonds GOP women had established with women Democrats, and to integrate them more fully into the Republican Party. Accordingly, he encouraged selection of Molinari and Jennifer Dunn to secondary party leadership positions. Gender was also a factor in his decision not to eliminate the Small Business Committee, a step he seriously considered, before concluding that by scrapping the panel Jan Meyers would not become one of the few Republican women ever to chair a standing committee of the House. And he scored a first by setting aside a room just off the House floor to allow Susan Molinari to breast-feed her infant daughter.

Gingrich strengthened his rapport with Republican women by meeting with them periodically to hear their priorities and, in turn, inform them about emerging developments. One reason Republican women had attended CCWI meetings in the past was to learn from Democratic women what majority party leaders were contemplating. Regular sessions with the Speaker, whose influence approached that of the president in 1995, made participation in the caucus less compelling.

Looking back on the 104th Congress, one lobbyist observed in an interview:

> Democratic women tend to be representative of the "women's groups," and they're quite proud of it, and they are not afraid of being type-cast as representatives of those groups. By contrast, . . . Republican women

are probably concerned about being type-cast by their male colleagues. . . . What there doesn't yet seem to be is a comfort zone
within the Republican party with the fact that women look at issues
differently than men.

But one moderate Republican congresswomen who valued her many
years of CCWI membership looked at the differences between women
in the two parties as resting on a fundamental disagreement about the
role government should play in addressing feminist concerns. She
defended her party's record in the 104th Congress, observing:

> I think Republican women feel a greater responsibility to attend to the
> issues of economic opportunity for women. The Democratic women
> tended to look at social services for women. That's important, but if
> these social services end up disempowering women, then they are a
> negative in their lives. You have not done them a service; you've done
> them a disservice. The Republican women have been trying to turn
> that around, to look at service to women as a lever to empower them
> to fulfill their own potential. So we were very instrumental, very
> instrumental . . . on welfare reform to leverage [women's] indepen-
> dence. . . . We have really refocused the Congress's attention on
> women's access to credit, women's access to training for their own
> business development—all those services that provide economic
> opportunity that young men tend to get from their fathers or their
> father's friends or the guys at Rotary. . . . Republican women have
> really focused on economic equality and opportunity for women, both
> in terms of welfare services and day care and earned income tax
> credit, . . . [a]nd in terms of small business issues and family issues
> in the military. I think we have done extremely responsible work and
> work that wasn't as popular in preceding Congresses.

Defunding of other LSOs also affected the CCWI. From time to
time its staff had worked with the staffs of the Black and Hispanic Caucuses as well as the Human Rights and Hunger Caucuses to promote
common interests. That so many congresswomen were members of one
or more of these other groups facilitated cooperation among them.
Elimination of LSO permanent staffs curtailed the CCWI's ability to
establish alliances with other members on legislation whose appeal both
included and transcended feminist goals.

Predictably, it took months for legislation formerly championed by
the CCWI to be introduced, and much of it languished in committee.
The caucus failed to introduce a Women's Health Equity Act (WHEA),
or a Women's Economic Equity Act (WEEA), until well into the second
session. Minutes of caucus meetings reveal the tortuous path these

measures followed before they saw the light of day. The April 1995 minutes noted that the WHEA would be introduced "this spring." Later notations scheduled the measure for the summer. In October, the minutes announced that the bill would appear in the fall. In December, the Caucus hoped to introduce the WHEA and the WEEA early in 1996. Ultimately, the former appeared in March, the latter in June. And many proposals that did not fall under the health or economic rubrics and that addressed less tractable women's concerns were simply neglected by overworked CCWI members and their staffs.

Organizational ground rules also fell victim to loss of a permanent staff. Bylaws approved by the caucus at the tail end of the 103rd Congress led to biennial rotation of the caucus cochairs, and appointment of Democratic and Republican vice chairs. But most of the new procedural changes were never implemented, partly because there was no staff director in place on Capitol Hill prodding the organization to live up to bylaw requirements. Consequently, annual meetings of the caucus open to the public, although called for by the new document, were never convened. Few required annual reports by the cochairs and by task forces were submitted. Minutes of monthly Executive Committee meetings were mandated, and while they were prepared regularly through much of 1995, they were increasingly neglected during the second session. And the requirement that meetings take place with a quorum of one-third of the members present was routinely ignored. With the exception of meetings featuring administration guest speakers, fewer than one-third of the members typically showed up.

Chances are, the CCWI agenda would have fared badly even if the LSOs had not been eliminated. Commitment to the Contract with America by the new Republican majority left little room for other legislative initiatives. True, the CCWI was more robust than most other defunded LSOs. Its cochairs continued single-mindedly to promote its causes. And the staffs of CCWI rank and file took it upon themselves to meet weekly to discuss feminist goals, to consider legislative initiatives, and to try to maintain the momentum established by earlier caucuses. But their efforts were inhibited significantly, not only by the GOP House control but also by the ardor, the energy, and the ideological commitment of the new Republican women.

The New Women

The 1994 election sent eleven new women to the House, seven Republicans and four Democrats. Caucus leaders invited them to join the

CCWI, and all four Democrats and a single Republican, New York's Sue Kelly, accepted. That the remaining Republican congresswomen declined the offer came as no surprise. Several were militantly antifeminist, and their postelection comments signaled their antagonism toward all that the caucus stood for. Several presented conservative commentator Rush Limbaugh with a plaque assuring him that "There's not a Femi-Nazi among us" (*Washington Post,* December 11, 1994), and one, Barbara Cubin of Wyoming, announced that she wanted "to be considered a contrast to [outgoing CCWI cochair] Patricia Schroeder and to the more militant-type feminists" (*USA Today,* December 17, 1994). The depths of their hostility to gender-oriented women's organizations was revealed when one of them referred to the traditionally nonpartisan League of Women Voters as the "League of Women Vipers" (*USA Today,* November 11, 1994).

These congresswomen were not the first to ignore or reject offers of caucus membership, but they were the first to work actively to undermine its influence. In the 103rd Congress, for example, support for the Violence Against Women Act had been widespread, and Republican whip Newt Gingrich had been a cosponsor. But when it came time to pay for the program in the 104th Congress, many, including outspoken first-term GOP congresswomen, demurred. A Capitol Hill staffer referred to them as the "foot soldiers recruited by the Republican leadership to roll back past progressive gains," although it was evident that the fledgling GOP women needed little prodding in that direction. Even when they agreed in principle with a CCWI-supported proposal, they often found reasons for opposing it. Said one caucus leader, these women would say something like, "We want more research on breast cancer, but we cannot support this particular bill, or too much money is being requested."

The new women distanced themselves from the caucus, in part, because they were far more interested in reflecting the revolutionary elan associated with their freshmen class than they were in calling attention to their gender. As a result, several refused to be called "congresswoman," preferring "congressman," and they took pains to avoid being associated with issues understood to affect women primarily. One veteran GOP women House member observed:

> There are women on Capitol Hill who refuse to accept the nomenclature "congresswoman." "I'm a congressman," they'll come back. They refuse to get involved in women's issues because they are so afraid to admit that they are women and that they can be strong on women's issues and still be strong on crime, balancing the budget, and tax issues.

One consequence of their behavior was a diminution of caucus credibility. For the first time the House contained a group of women who were prepared to stymie CCWI initiatives at every opportunity, and congressmen who might otherwise have supported caucus proposals grew skeptical about the extent to which the CCWI spoke for all women. Other male members now had reasons to give voice to the doubts that they had harbored all along. One CCWI leader described the changed circumstances in this way:

> Women elected in the late 80s and early 90s were joining the Caucus, were working together, and it made a terrific difference in the congressional agenda because women were speaking with one voice across party lines. That's how we got family leave, the Women's Health Equity Act and Economic Equity passed. We kept moving forward on Title IX—all of those things.
>
> But then came the 1994 election in which you get this group of women who didn't want anything to do with the Caucus, and came with an entirely different agenda. At that point, everything stops. Because when you stand up and talk about any [women's] issue, the opposition can get a woman on the floor taking the opposite side. And what happened was that people said, "Oh, the women haven't made up their minds yet, so I don't have to pay attention. I don't have to think about this until all the women make up their minds." . . . But when you're such a small minority, the only way you get a priority position—when you really get people to take what you're saying seriously, is for all the women to look like they have a consensus. So the 1994 election blew us out of the water.

Another member noted that the new Republican women "stayed away from the women stuff because they wanted to be seen as individuals, not as representatives of women." Several members of both parties commented on the new women's style. A liberal Democratic congresswoman remarked: "Some of these women are bad old girls who what to be good old boys." A Democratic colleague observed:

> You've heard the story of Rose Red and Rose White. When one of them spoke, diamonds and pearls came out of her mouth; when the other spoke toads, snakes and frogs came out. Congresswoman [name withheld] is the one with toads and snakes. Every time she opens her mouth vituperatives [sic] come out. Even the men look at each other and say, "My God, she's mean."

Some senior Republican women also commented on the harshness of the new women's style, attributing it in part to their inexperience. One said:

One of the things that surprised me about our Republican women is how harsh they are. They are worse than some of our Republican men on the welfare issue. [During the debate] they were awful. . . . Most of the moderate Republican women were trying to get their Republican male colleagues to see how important it was to pass a bill that would not harm people. But most of the new Republican women had little patience for this approach. Because they were still so new, they hadn't found their way [to seeing things in this light].

One African American congresswoman expressed an alienation from the new women that was shared by several of her black colleagues. She remarked:

This crowd of Republican women really doesn't have much in common with me, and I will not pretend that I have anything in common with them. When one of them tells me how lucky I am that I survived slavery, and when another mentions slavery whenever we are in the elevator together, then I think I have a problem with them.

The distance between black Democratic congresswomen and the new Republicans may have been fostered by Ku Klux Klan claims that the 1994 election victory of Idaho's Helen Chenoweth was a "victory for raced-based campaigns." The Klan had distributed videotapes during her campaign, some of which depicted her saying that affirmative action and other government programs made white men "an endangered species" (*New York Times,* January 11, 1996). Chenoweth subsequently disassociated herself from the Klan, but for many black colleagues the distancing was too little and too late.

The behavior that perhaps best encapsulates the policy orientation and style of the new women was reflected in their reaction to a proposal to install the "Portrait Monument" in the Capitol Rotunda. The monument is a marble sculpture featuring three nineteenth-century women suffrage leaders—Susan B. Anthony, Lucretia Mott, and Elizabeth Cady Stanton. The rendering of the three had been sculpted by Adelaide Johnson in 1920, the year the Nineteenth Amendment was passed, and donated to Congress by the National Women's Party (NWP) in 1921. Congress's Joint Committee on the Library at first refused to accept the bulky statue, but Alice Paul, NWP president, had it delivered to the Capitol anyway. After brief negotiations, it was agreed that the seven-ton Italian marble statue would remain in the Capitol Rotunda for two days, after which it would be placed among other statuary one floor below in a section of the Capitol known as "the Crypt."

During the next seventy-five years, periodic efforts by women's groups to restore the Portrait Monument to the Rotunda were unsuccessful. And then in April 1995 a group called the Women's Suffrage Statue Campaign, after receiving positive feedback from members of Congress, expressed hope that the statue would be moved by August 26, in time to mark the seventy-fifth anniversary celebration of women's suffrage. The occasion would be observed by a rededication of the statute, to be followed by a women's rights march and rally on the Mall. Proponents of the move argued that the country needed public symbols depicting women who were instrumental in nation building. They pointed out that visitors to a Rotunda housing statues of men alone were left with the impression that women played no role in the process. Said one of the celebration's planners, "It's not nice to put your forefathers in the living room and your foremothers in the basement."

Senator Ted Stevens of Alaska, chair of the Rules Committee, responded by introducing a joint resolution instructing the Architect of the Capitol, George White, to move the monument to a more prominent display site. Stevens said he was leading the way because Alaska had played an important role in the suffrage movement, and because his grandmother, Elizabeth Stevens, who had raised him, had been an active suffragist. He noted that most Rotunda statues honor presidents and that all, to date, have been men, adding: "Someday I hope the Rotunda will be graced with a statue of the first female president. Until then, it is my hope to honor the role women have played by moving the women's suffrage statue up to the place of honor it should have in the Rotunda" (Love 1995c).

The Senate passed Stevens's resolution by voice vote, but the measure ran into serious obstacles on its way to the House. Perhaps the most daunting challenge appeared in a memo written by Architect White and circulated in the House even as the Senate was approving the resolution. In it, White, a longtime opponent of the move, listed reasons why the statue should remain in the Crypt. The sculpture's massive weight would make relocation difficult and expensive, he argued. Moreover, a statue already in the Rotunda would have to be sent to the Crypt to make room for the Portrait Monument. To a proposal that the heavy marble slabs in the base be replaced by lightweight steel with a marble veneer to meet cost and logistical objections, he demurred on historic and aesthetic grounds: "It is generally not acceptable to make such changes." He made no reference to an offer by the Capitol Preservation Commission, a private organization, to fund the project (Love 1995b).

White's memo gave many House members pause, and Speaker Gingrich, already pressed to put off some appropriations bills until after the pending August recess, declined to bring the resolution to a vote in time for the August 26 rededication ceremonies. Caucus cochair Constance Morella voiced disappointment, but promised to urge the House to consider the resolution after the recess (Love 1995b). In the meantime, women's groups celebrated the occasion in the Crypt, believing, like Morella, that the proposal would receive speedy approval when Congress returned.

But they were unprepared for the strenuous opposition they encountered from first-term Republican women. When the resolution arrived on the House floor in the fall, the new congresswomen objected to the $75,000 that would be authorized to pay for the move, arguing that the government should not subsidize the project. Several suggested that if women were to be represented in the Rotunda, radicals like Anthony, Mott, and Stanton did not deserve the recognition, and that less controversial women should be considered.[2] Pat Schroeder, then in her last House term, was dismayed by these objections, wondering in an interview, "[I]s this the 1990s or the 1890s[?] What century are we in?"

The dispute led to further House-Senate negotiations, and in June 1997, after $83,000 had been collected by the Women Suffrage Statue Campaign, and after twelve hours of heavy lifting, the statue was returned to the Rotunda. During rededication ceremonies, former CCWI cochair Senator Olympia Snowe said that women members of Congress never dreamed the relocation would encounter so many obstacles. She called the experience "Tales from the Crypt," adding: "We thought it seemed like a little thing to ask. In many ways the struggle to move the statue was emblematic of women's struggle for justice and equality throughout the history of this country" (Eilperin 1997b).

The new Republican women were not the relocation's only opponents, but they played a prominent role in forcing the delay beyond the August 1995 celebration date, as well as in demanding private funding for moving the statue—a condition not normally insisted upon when Capitol statuary is shifted. That their position on the issue was consistent with that of the Capitol Architect gave their arguments considerable weight. That they succeeded in withholding public money for what they believed was an unnecessary project meant they were in synch with their class's revolutionary zeal. When Connie Morella pointed out that the sum involved was relatively small given the statue's symbolic importance, North Carolina's Sue Myrick said, "Yeah, it's not a lot of money, the way they throw money around up here. But that's what we're trying to stop (*Washington Post*, April 4, 1997).

But their opposition can also be explained in terms of gender as well. The statue issue gave the new women an opportunity to demonstrate to male colleagues that they would not associate themselves with even relatively benign women's issues, that they would aggressively oppose the legislative agenda of the CCWI, that they would not bend to the blandishments of outside women's lobbies, and that they could be as hard-nosed and tough as any of their male colleagues. And when the statue was finally rededicated, Helen Chenoweth, one of the original resolution's fiercest opponents, put the best face on the decision. She pointed out that a keystone of Susan B. Anthony's legacy was her opposition to abortion (Eilperin 1997b).

Abortion Rights Redux

The new women had many reasons for not joining the caucus, but the CCWI's pro-choice orientation was among the most important. Their arrival in the House markedly diminished the pro-choice tilt among Republican women. Before the 1994 election, ten of the twelve Republican congresswomen had been pro-choice. After the election, eight of seventeen were pro-life. Admonitions from GOP leaders to shun the CCWI almost certainly influenced the newcomers' decision, but the caucus's position on reproductive rights gave these women a reason for declining membership that would trump all others. One veteran Democratic congresswoman said she understood the newcomers' decision, but lamented it nonetheless:

> What weakened the Caucus was not so much the defunding in 1995, as much as it was the attitudes of the [Republican] women elected in 1994. They refused to join because they viewed the Caucus as being single-minded and too focused on abortion. And yet, over the years the progress made on women in the military, domestic violence, financing women's businesses and home ownership—all of that came about because of the Caucus. So what happened in 1994 was to me very disconcerting.

Several of the newcomers said they rejected invitations to join the caucus not to make a political statement, but to keep from spreading themselves too thin. But most also made clear that they found their social philosophy incompatible with the CCWI's official position on abortion rights. Sophomore Jennifer Dunn, a non-CCWI member who was pro-choice, but who opposed federal funding to pay for abortions, concurred, noting, "If they got rid of that [the official pro-choice position] I'd be happy to join" (*Washington Post,* February 15, 1995). For another Republican congresswoman, "Everything the Caucus does is in terms of bashing Republicans and advancing the abortion lobbyist's agenda. So it is really uncomfortable for me to participate."

The caucus's identification with abortion rights was strengthened by the uncompromising pro-choice agenda of its two newly elected cochairs, Nita Lowey and Constance Morella. Lowey was chair of the House Pro-Choice Task Force, a bipartisan group of both men and women. The task force was not a new House group, but after the 1994 election it raised its profile, in part to fill the gap left when the CCWI was stripped of its staff. Lowey sent packets of information to House members claiming that women's reproductive rights were being threatened in the new Congress. And when Henry W. Foster Jr., an obstetrician who had acknowledged performing legal abortions as a part of his practice, was nominated as surgeon general, Lowey called a press conference and, surrounded by other task force members, enthusiastically endorsed the nomination (*Washington Post,* February 15, 1995).

At the same time, Morella and her staff were active in the Congressional Coalition on Population and Development, a group that addressed international family planning issues and that often coordinated public relations strategy with members of the CCWI and the Pro-Choice Task Force. Consequently, distinctions between leadership of the CCWI and these other pro-choice groups were blurred, and Lowey and Morella were seen as speaking for the CCWI on reproductive rights, even when they were wearing a "different hat."

But even if the cochairs had tried to place the abortion issue on the back burner, they would have been blocked by other CCWI members. Those elected for the first time in 1992 were members of a class more liberal than many Democrats, and virtually all supported the rights of gays in the military, affirmative action, and abortion rights, positions that made some senior Democrats uncomfortable. They expected abortion rights to be an integral part of the group's mission, largely unaware that the deliberate exclusion of this issue from the CCWI agenda had been one of the caucus's initial strategic calculations. They could not have agreed more with a veteran Democrat who observed:

> It is the right to choose that gave women the freedom to develop into the wonderful human beings they are. By giving them that choice, they are able to determine everything else about their lives. If we lose that, we go back to what we used to be. We could even go so far back

that—because of the great nostalgia for the 19th century—pregnant women could not work or go to college, or, if married, they would have to leave. And I remember that. And that is my greatest fear.

Weeks into their first term, they had rallied behind the first pro-choice president in twelve years when he issued executive orders lifting restrictions on abortion and abortion counseling, and they were delighted when Clinton's comprehensive health care bill included abortion coverage, designation of obstetricians and gynecologists as primary care physicians, and preventive screening for breast cancer, cervical cancer, and other diseases. After African American Joycelyn Elders was nominated as surgeon general and conservatives attacked her position on abortion rights, sex education, and condom distribution, it was the CCWI that came to Elders's defense (*Washington Post,* February 15, 1995).

When the 1994 election produced a pro-life House, CCWI members circled the wagons, determined to hold on to gains made in the 103rd Congress. They fought every effort by the new House majority to eliminate or dilute abortion protections, and when some pro-choice Republican members of the CCWI, intoxicated with being a part of the first Republican majority in forty years, appeared to abandon the caucus, a handful of Democrats, believing the CCWI would not survive, formed a new group and began working with the Democratic Congressional Campaign Committee to recruit progressive women candidates for the House.

One sophomore Democrat, Elizabeth Furse of Oregon, did in fact resign from the CCWI, concluding it had lost its pro-choice identity. Furse felt betrayed when a pro-choice Republican member of the CCWI, Susan Molinari, appeared in her district late in the 1994 campaign and endorsed Furse's male, Republican, pro-life opponent. After she was reelected by 301 votes, Furse decided that membership in the organization had been cheapened by what she saw as Molinari's betrayal (*Washington Post,* February 15, 1995). The Staten Island Republican later acknowledged that she had endured bitter criticism from such organizations as the National Organization for Women (NOW) and the National Abortion Rights Action League (NARAL) because she campaigned for anti-choice candidates. She explained: "I refused to be a single-issue campaigner. . . . That's bad for America. Anyway, what did they want me to do? Campaign against my husband and father?" (Molinari 1998, p. 142).[3]

But Furse's decision was understandable in light of her own encounter with abortion proscriptions thirty-five years earlier. In 1961 she was a thirty-five-year-old physician's wife and mother of two. After she became pregnant again, doctors told her that there was a good chance her third child would be born with devastating disabilities, including brain damage. She and her husband considered an abortion, but rejected the option of undergoing an illegal procedure, largely because so many of them ended in permanent injury to the mother and even death. Her obstetrician advised her that an abortion could be performed only if it could be justified on "life-saving" grounds. He added that inasmuch as she had only one kidney, she could possibly persuade a hospital panel that this physical impairment would be potentially life-threatening if she carried the fetus to term. The panel granted her request, but insisted that she also undergo a hysterectomy, which would assure the panel that she would never again put her life in jeopardy by becoming pregnant. Her anguished decision was to go ahead with both procedures, a choice she believed no woman who wanted more children should have to make (*New York Times,* May 7, 2001).

Democratic doubts about the pro-choice purity of the CCWI placed enormous pressure on the cochairs, especially Morella. She was often the lone Republican attendee at caucus meetings, speaking for the slender abortion rights wing of her party. According to one staff member privy to caucus deliberations, if she had wavered in her commitment to the pro-choice position or if she had moved to drop the issue from the CCWI agenda, the Democratic women would have resigned in droves and the eighteen-year-old caucus "would have been history."

But Democratic women were not alone in keeping the abortion issue alive. Republican leaders and first-term conservatives forced the House to address abortion with exhausting regularity. According to one abortion rights lobbyist, for the first time since *Roe v. Wade* the House environment was controlled by men who were unalterably opposed to women's reproductive rights. Committee and subcommittee chairs welcomed amendments and riders to bills prohibiting abortion or embargoing the use of specified appropriated funds to underwrite their costs. During Appropriations Committee deliberations dozens of riders were introduced, and according to one committee member, "anytime it came up there was a battle."

Lowey was a member of the committee and her claims that these legislative riders did not belong in Appropriations bills were unavailing. Pro-life committee chair Bob Livingston (R–La.) allowed the proposals to come to a vote, and the pro-life position almost always prevailed. Later, Rules Committee chair Gerry Solomon (R–N.Y.), who was also strongly pro-life, structured rules allowing floor votes on anti-abortion riders, virtually all of which produced pro-life majorities.

Many attributed the House's obsession with abortion rights to the aggressiveness of CCWI members. But most committee and floor actions on the issue were initiated by anti-abortion Republicans. They capitalized on their leaders' ability to define the agenda, control the terms and forum of the debate, and determine the ground rules governing its disposition. And when critics advised CCWI members to lower their voices on the issue, exasperated congresswomen heatedly pointed out that they had no choice but to respond to the unremitting challenges launched by the new Republican majority. One staff member explained CCWI behavior in this way:

> In previous years, there had been a general feeling of support for freedom of choice. But the 104th Congress developed a strong anti-choice environment. As a result, the Caucus's focus on abortion was not a matter of congresswomen being proactive. Caucus members were responding to conservative challenges to abortion rights, and they were reacting defensively to try to head these challenges off.

Pro-choice forces almost always lost because, according to one staff member, there were now at least 221 rock-solid abortion opponents. She added:

> The new mood in the House encouraged members who had been with us 50% of the time to turn against us 90% of the time. Some Republicans were so excited about being in the majority that they went down the line with the leadership. Leaders also put pressure on some who could have gone either way on the issue. In the meantime, some male Democrats were so spooked by the 1994 election that they began to exercise greater caution on women's rights issues.

During the 104th Congress, 104 bills considered by the House Judiciary Committee had the word "abortion" in them. More than fifty roll call votes were taken on reproductive rights issues, more, calculated one staff member, than in any Congress in the preceding ten years. Pat Schroeder later observed: "It seemed the conservatives had a fast breeder anti-abortion amendment reactor that kept producing amendments prohibiting abortions on interstate highways, federal prisons or whatever else they could cook up" (Schroeder 1997, p. 112).

Pro-choice forces lost all but four abortion-related roll call votes, two in 1995, two in 1996. All four dealt with appropriations for Title X of the Public Health Service Act, a family planning measure. Because its impact was to decrease conception, and thereby decrease demand for abortions, some pro-life members supported it. In the process, feminists had to fight off an effort by Appropriations chair Bob Livingston to eviscerate Title X by transferring its funding to the states through block grants. The proposal would have given states discretion in determining how (or whether) family planning funds would be used. Livingston's critics saw it as a way of allowing the states to limit the counseling clients would receive on contraception and abortion, and Lowey and Morella worked with Republicans James Greenwood of Pennsylvania and John Porter of Illinois to revive Title X on the House floor.

Other House appropriations measures containing abortion restrictions were approved, although many failed in the Senate or were vetoed by the president. New limits on abortions were attached to the 1996 Treasury and Postal bill, and similar provisions were inserted in bills funding the Department of Defense and the District of Columbia. The Appropriations Committee prohibited federal money from being spent on biomedical research involving human embryos, and assured medical schools they would not lose Medicare funding if they chose not to teach students how to perform abortions (Wells 1995). The Hyde Amendment was once again attached to the Health and Human Services appropriations bill, and Oklahoma Republican Ernest Istook persuaded the Appropriations Committee to give states the option of withholding Medicaid funds for abortions on any grounds other than to save the life of the mother—a provision ultimately stripped from the bill on the House floor.

In the meantime, the International Relations Committee, chaired by moderate pro-choicer Benjamin Gilman of New York, failed to report out a Foreign Operations bill because it was so bitterly divided on whether to authorize funds for international family planning organizations offering abortion as an option. Rather than submit a measure that would be defeated on the floor by conservative Republicans, some of whom were prepared to oust him as chairman, Gilman chose to allow the decisions to be made in another forum. The vacuum was filled by the Appropriations Committee, which voted to cut spending to international family planning organizations that countenanced abortion counseling—whether or not resources used to underwrite the counseling were supplied by the United States. One pro-choice veteran Republican congresswoman saw the issue not as funding abortions, but as funding obstetrical and gynecological care for women. Healthy mothers, she argued, produce healthy babies. She described the agonizing decision she faced:

> Bills on international family planning should have come from Gilman's International Relations Committee, but we have not got one

for years because of the [abortion] issue. And so everything was tossed into the appropriations bill and debated on the floor. That's why these appropriations bills ended up being a disaster. You could not deal with them because they had these anti-abortion provisions in them. And yet, some of the other provisions were so good, that I wanted to vote for them. So I did, even though I didn't like the strong anti-abortion language.

There were so many votes on issues with abortion rights implications that CCWI members found themselves struggling simply to keep other priorities alive. Programs that had been around for years, such as Aid to Families with Dependent Children, Head Start, and school lunches, competed for time with the abortion fights, which was one reason the caucus did not get around to submitting Women's Health Equity and Equal Economic Opportunity bills until well into the second session.

Abortion opponents prevailed in committee and on the floor, in part, because for the first time they were able to rely on the high-profile efforts of pro-life congresswomen. Previous debates on the issue had been led largely by men, notably New Jersey's Chris Smith and Henry Hyde of Illinois. These same congressmen were prominent in 1995–1996, but they were joined by first-term Republican women who were encouraged by GOP leaders to put a "woman's face" on anti-abortion arguments. Representatives Linda Smith (Wash.), Barbara Cubin, Andrea Seastrand (Calif.), Sue Myrick, and Helen Chenoweth made speeches on the subject, and if Chris Smith, Hyde, and Charles Canady of Florida were the "stars of the show," devising winning strategies, these GOP women were an important "supporting cast," implementing tactics. They wrote "Dear Colleague" letters, lobbied other House members privately, and were as forceful in making their case as pro-choice women were in making theirs. According to a lobbyist for a pro-choice organization:

> Their role was significant every time the issue came up. They spoke out on the floor and that gave some credibility to their side that they never had when I started working on the issue 15 years ago—when there were no women on their side speaking. They make up a cadre of women who are representing Concerned Women for America, the Right-to-Life Committee, and various Christian organizations. These organizations now have women advocates when years ago they had mainly male spokesmen.

The advantages of having vocal pro-life women in the House was driven home dramatically during debate on a bill banning a late-term

abortion procedure that pro-choice partisans referred to as "intact dilation and extraction" and pro-lifers called "partial-birth abortion." The
battle centered not on whether to adopt the ban, but on whether protecting the *health* as well as the *life* of the mother should be grounds for an
exemption from the ban. Pro-life forces were hugely successful in turn-
ing the public against the procedure—principally with graphic portray-
als of how physicians abort a late-term fetus. And even members who
defined themselves as pro-choice were revolted enough to vote against
the health exemption. The demoralization of one pro-choice Republican
staffer reflected the frustrations felt by like-minded allies:

> From the day, from the instant I looked at the bill, I knew we were
> whipped. We worked with other Republican offices and with the
> Women's Caucus . . . to get outside groups to run a "big picture"
> thing, and they eventually started getting [helpful] editorials around
> the country, but we just knew we were doomed. . . . [I] was running
> this desperate battle, trying to think how I could structure [our posi-
> tion], what kind of message I could structure, and where I could run
> the message so that I could turn this thing around, knowing that it
> looked bad, and it did. It looked really bad the whole way through.

Under Lowey's leadership, the CCWI played a leading role in trying to defeat or modify the measure. The caucus held press conferences,
orchestrated floor strategies, and wrote "Dear Colleague" letters.
Women who had undergone the procedure were invited to Washington
to meet with the president, administration officials, and legislators.
They testified before committees, pointing out that some were pro-life,
that they were mothers several times over, and that the late-term abortion procedure was deemed essential by their physicians if they were
ever to have additional children.

Rosa DeLauro (D–Conn.) and Pat Schroeder were especially passionate about the issue. Schroeder's powerful pro-choice orientation
was partly due to her near-death experience during the birth of one of
her own children. She and others on the Judiciary Committee cited data
compiled by the Health and Human Services Department revealing that
one in four women encounter complications during their pregnancy and
that the maternal mortality rate was habitually underestimated. The
undercount occurred because the states applied narrow criteria to define
"maternal death." Most considered death during labor or on the delivery
table as the only circumstance under which a pregnant woman's death
could be attributed to "childbirth." In other Western countries, if a
woman dies within a year of having a baby, authorities are obligated to

explore the possibility that childbirth contributed to her death (Schroeder 1997, p. 124).

During committee debate, the Colorado Democrat offered a health exemption amendment, but it was rejected on a 13–20 party-line vote. Opponents of the ban tried to contextualize the issue as one affecting a woman's health, not her reproductive rights, but their support of a procedure seen as gruesome did not lend itself to thirty-second sound bites. Many rallied behind the Newborns and Mothers Protection Act of 1995, a measure requiring a minimum forty-eight-hour hospital stay for new mothers, but it proved to be a weak counterpoint to the massive criticism being directed against late-term abortions.

Among pro-choice Republicans, CCWI members Nancy Johnson and Jan Meyers were particularly active, speaking out during debate and button-holing members one-on-one to make their case. Johnson's description of what it is like to have lost a child was especially affecting but, in the end, unavailing. Pro-choice forces were playing against a stacked deck. Henry Hyde and Charles Canady were respectively chairs of the committee and subcommittee responsible for shaping the legislation, and rank-and-file committee members, disproportionately from the South, were solidly pro-life. One aide observed:

> [The pro-life] people controlled the debate; they controlled the hearing; controlled who spoke. It was very frustrating. [They] controlled the issue, the legislative language in the bill—everything about the bill. We played the hearings every which way. We went, participated, got frustrated. We didn't get the best press either. People kept saying, "Why did you bring this up?" *We didn't bring it up* [speaker's emphasis]. We were trying to defend late-term abortions. But when there's millions of dollars poured into a public relations effort and when you don't have the enviable grassroots resources of the right-to-life forces, you're stymied. . . . [They] portray women who have late-term abortions as frivolous, as morally depraved. . . . We were arguing for women who were pregnant and wanted to be pregnant—but for whom something went wrong. [Late-term abortions] were the only way to rectify the problem so they could become pregnant again, so their health would not be imperiled. We had a very difficult time making that argument.

The six first-term Republican congresswomen made the CCWI's task even more forbidding. They were all active in promoting the ban, and Representative Enid Waldholtz played a unique role. She was pregnant when the bill reached the floor, and the personal experience she brought to bear, an experience that her physical appearance authenticated, was telling. Her healthy pregnancy made it easier for colleagues so disposed to minimize such things as Schroeder's brush with death. Male colleagues could now infer that there were many women of childbearing age who supported the ban. Although Waldholtz was not initially prominent in debate, she later discounted arguments that the bill provided inadequate protection for women's health, suggesting, as did her male allies, that a health exception would render the ban meaningless. She later managed floor debate on the rule, and one Democratic staff member observed that "Enid's impending motherhood gave her much greater credibility on the issue." Another remarked in an interview: "[W]ith her being pregnant, here she comes, waddling down on the floor with her stomach sticking way out to talk about unborn children. I mean, on the other side of the aisle you can't attack her too much because here is this big pregnant woman."

Perhaps even more credible support for the ban came from pro-choice CCWI member Susan Molinari. The New Yorker often miffed Republican colleagues by her outspoken support for abortion rights. But after agonizing over the proposed ban, she embraced it. The sources of her ambivalence were reflected in later recollections:

> There are many people . . . who are opposed to abortion, but have no wider agenda when they advocate that women lose their right to choose. . . . There are too many who use abortion and religion to hide their misogyny, and who have an agenda that goes well beyond ending abortion. They are "pro-life" and "anti–everything else," from birth control to sex education to day care. (Molinari 1998, p. 139)

But Molinari ultimately voted for the ban because she was pregnant at the time and, as she said, "I knew that things felt different at eight months than they did at three" (Molinari 1998, p. 142). Pro-choice CCWI members had tried to persuade the New Yorker to use her position in the Republican leadership to defeat or modify the prohibition. But according to one Democratic congresswoman, Molinari responded that, *because she was in the leadership,* "she could not stray too far off the reservation."

Republican women who opposed or had doubts about the ban, like Johnson and Meyers, worked independently of the CCWI to limit its application. Aides in their offices cooperated with NARAL, Planned Parenthood, NOW, and the Center for Reproductive Law and Public Policy to ensure that pro-choice literature found its way into the offices of moderate Republicans. These groups were also advised about which

Republican House members could not be moved from the pro-life position, a prohibitively large number according to one source who added that "their phones were ringing off their hooks" with calls from abortion foes, and "even if they don't like the bill, they are going to do what their constituents tell them to do."

Under the terms of the bill, doctors performing late-term abortions could be arrested, jailed, and placed on trial before being given an opportunity to claim that the procedures they performed, or the circumstances under which the abortions were performed, were exempted from the ban. Johnson fought unsuccessfully to make the plight of doctors less daunting. Some GOP women opposing the bill worried that their party's uncompromising pro-life stance was alienating Republican women and causing them to abandon the party. One aide remarked that her boss believed that "the party was hemorrhaging internally and creating rifts between good, loyal party members." A GOP congresswoman who ultimately voted against the ban, looked back on the struggle as one of the most wrenching of her career:

> I found myself at the epicenter of the debate on abortion. I'm pro-choice. I believe in "choice" but I don't believe in willy nilly abortion. I never have. . . . In the 104th Congress leaders of my party, recognizing the district I represented, honored my right as a human being to believe what I believe and they stood 100% behind me, an act which I will never forget because there were [constituents] so vitriolic [that] it made me feel perfectly horrible. And some of these people have a hard time right now dealing with me as a human being. Some of them have never talked to me again. So it's a good thing I sit on the Republican side as a woman espousing women's interests, and especially this one particular interest. Because I don't represent the enemy, I represent a lot of women.

Pro-choice Republican Deborah Pryce, who ultimately voted in favor of the bill, nonetheless tried to soften some of its sterner features. Using her position on the Rules Committee, she succeeded in prolonging debate on whether the measure should contain a health exception, and she was the only Republican on the committee who voted to allow the full House to consider an amendment to that effect. Pryce also urged that the House be allowed to vote on a proposal permitting doctors to defend their decisions to save the life of the mother before being jailed and tried for allegedly violating the act. Her motion failed on a 6–6 committee vote (Dodson 1998).

At the end of the day, the CCWI failed to block the ban on late-term abortions, just as it failed to head off almost all other proposed abortion restrictions. Even though a presidential veto of the bill was ultimately sustained in the Senate, the measure's failure gave CCWI members little comfort. They now served in a House with a decidedly pro-life orientation. They had failed to persuade almost all new Republican women to join their organization, and claims that the caucus spoke for American women were now in doubt. For the first time, measurable numbers of Republican congresswomen were voicing pro-life opposition to what was arguably the most controversial issue directly affecting women. And senior pro-choice Republican women who worked behind the scenes to influence party leaders had little to show for their labors.

At the same time, Democratic congresswomen were demoralized, and some concluded that the CCWI was not doing enough for reproductive rights. They succeeded for the first time in placing the issue prominently in the 1996 Women's Health Equity Act, but were frustrated when the bill was delayed and ultimately ignored. Many believed that abortion was not the only (or even the central) women's concern requiring their attention, but its reappearance time and again in different contexts made it, for them, the tar baby of the 104th Congress. They expended gobs of political capital on a cause that was defeated in vote after vote, all the while losing confidence in the viability of a caucus that had already been crippled by the loss of its staff.

But perhaps most important, their preoccupation with abortion rights—a preoccupation forced on CCWI members by both hostile external forces and by internally grounded passions to keep "choice" alive—sapped energies needed to fight other feminist battles. After the 104th Congress adjourned, one senior Democratic congresswomen remarked: "There is so much we haven't done. Bladder incontinence is the number one reason women have to drop out of the military. The whole area around amenorrhea we really don't know a lot about. On eating disorders we haven't scratched the surface yet."

Given the political complexion and preoccupations of the 104th Congress, CCWI members could not realistically promote new feminist issues. But they could try to preserve past gains, which meant that the CCWI had to abandon its agenda for change, and resort to strategies of defense and incrementalism.

A Tale of Two Sessions

For the CCWI, the two sessions of the 104th Congress were starkly dissimilar. During the first session, caucus leaders fought tirelessly to defeat threats to prior feminist gains, encountering defeat after defeat, sometimes reveling not because of a victory but because they had staved off challenges to policies once thought to be secure. In the second session, they recouped earlier losses and recorded some modest victories. Overall, the 104th Congress was arguably the most challenging and difficult the organization encountered during its twenty-year history. By virtue of their newly won leverage on committees and their access to House leadership, Republican women were, for the first time since the caucus was created, more instrumental than Democratic women in securing feminist policy goals.

Caucus activities in the 104th Congress followed scripts similar to those adhered to in past years. Its leaders testified before House committees, especially the Appropriations and Rules Committees. They sent letters to committee chairs, to House conferees, to the Speaker, and to Senate leaders. They arranged for a series of one-minute speeches on selected subjects at the start of daily House sessions, and they reserved time during Special Orders for extended debate at the end of these sessions. The cochairs regularly called press conferences to help dramatize the group's policy agenda, and they scheduled a half dozen briefings on such topics as teenage pregnancy, educational equality, and reproductive rights.

At the same time, they worked closely with such organizations as the National Breast Cancer Coalition, the Osteoporosis Foundation, the Older Women's League, and Amnesty International, and they met regularly with administration cabinet officials, including the State Department's Madeline Albright, and Health and Human Services secretary Donna Shalala. Caucus leaders led forums on child care, contraception, Title IX, and women in small business, and during the closing weeks of 1996 they questioned top Army brass in secret to learn more about accusations of sexual assault and harassment of women trainees at Aberdeen Proving Grounds and other Army bases.

Reproductive rights had never been a settled issue and the persistent defeats in the first session, though unremitting and demoralizing, were predictable. More unexpected were attacks on the Equal Employment Opportunity Commission, the Violence Against Women Act (VAWA), Title IX, the Women's Educational Equity Act, the Legal Services Corporation (LSC), and affirmative action. Some crippling bills were enacted. The LSC, which provides free legal aid in divorce, custody, child support, and domestic violence cases, lost one-third of its funding for fiscal year 1996, and it was forced to close 100 offices and dismiss 20 percent of its staff. Educational Equity Act programs were cut from $4 million to zero in fiscal year 1995 budget, with only $2 million restored the following year. Portions of the VAWA were vitiated under an Anti-Terrorism Act that made it easier for immigration officials to deny entry to undocumented aliens who had been victims of domestic violence.

First-session funding cuts for the Equal Employment Opportunity Commission and Title IX were only partially restored in the second session. Without a spirited effort by Susan Molinari, Connie Morella, and Nita Lowey, among others, the bulk of promised funding for the VAWA in the first session would have been lost. The same CCWI players worked hard to defeat an attempt to shift Title X family planning programs to the states under a block grant. The caucus also contributed to rejection of what sponsors Senator Bob Dole and Representative Charles Canady called "the Equal Opportunity Act of 1995," a measure designed to end affirmative action in employment and the awarding of government contracts.

The challenges dogging CCWI leaders were summed up in the comments of a feminist interest group representative:

> What we faced [in the 104th Congress] was a climate that was so different from the 103rd and from every other Congress in my lifetime that it was very difficult for my organization and the Caucus to be truly effective. We all had to learn how to function in a climate where there was virtually no hope of getting anything positive through, of advancing our agenda at all. The only hope was to hold the line so that not a lot of damage was done to our issues. The 104th Congress reopened everything that any of us cared about and had worked on for years and years. Whether it was in the field of education, in the field of poor women, whether it was reproductive rights, health care, civil rights—everything you can think of was under attack.

According to Women's Policy Inc., only two measures of special benefit to women became law in 1995, a figure dwarfed by the thirty bills enacted in 1993. Lowey was appalled by the CCWI's record, noting, "This year has been the bleakest for women in my seven years in Congress. We have seen the rights of women rolled backward in nearly every area" (*Houston Chronicle,* March 20, 1996).

The second session witnessed a turnabout in feminist fortunes. By early 1996 the "Republican revolution" seemed to have lost much of its energy (Bader 1996, p. 203). GOP House members became more independent, and the proportion of roll call votes on which a majority of one party voted against a majority of the other dropped from 73 percent in 1995 to 56 percent in 1996 (Rae 1998, p. 111). At the same time,

Republican conservatives suffered a decline in credibility after forcing a governmental shutdown. Also important were first-termers' growing fears that they might have misread what they thought was a mandate for change—a concern acknowledged by about half of them—in the face of a looming midterm election (Barnett 1999, p. 45). Newt Gingrich's dismal public opinion ratings and increasing impatience with Congress prompted the Speaker to strike a moderate tone, pulling his party to the center (Barnett 1998, p. 194). But the second session also saw the CCWI recover its equilibrium after a year of frantically dousing one fire after another, and some of its agenda items gained acceptance as Republican congresswomen worked closely with moderate GOP men.

The most remarkable feminist gains were made in women's health. The Health Insurance Portability and Accountability (Kassebaum/ Kennedy) Act was signed in August 1996 and provided continued health care coverage for workers who changed or lost their jobs. It also narrowed the grounds under which coverage could be denied because of preexisting medical conditions. Included in the act were two WHEA provisions. One, vigorously sponsored by Morella and Molinari, prohibited insurers from discriminating against victims of domestic violence. The second, promoted by Louise Slaughter in the House and Olympia Snowe in the Senate, prevented insurers from using a person's genetic makeup as a preexisting condition or as a basis for denying insurance.

Other measures expanded insurance coverage for postpartum hospital stays, and required insurers who offered mental health coverage to set comparable coverage limits for both physical and mental ailments. Women veterans were helped by legislation requiring periodic inspection of mammography procedures at Department of Veterans Affairs facilities. Legislation barring female genital mutilation for girls under eighteen included a Schroeder-sponsored provision to direct the Immigration and Naturalization Service to advise immigrants about the legal consequences of performing the procedure in the United States. And incremental gains were made in appropriations for research on breast cancer, ovarian cancer, and osteoporosis. One GOP congresswoman attributed many of these changes to Republican weakness among women voters: "The gender gap helped promote health insurance reform in the 104th. The polls indicated that the top three issues were education, health care and the environment, and that the Republicans were failing miserably. . . . The party leaders had to do something."

The most dramatic economic victory for women during the 104th Congress was not brought about by the CCWI, although it had championed such legislation for years. Paradoxically, the engine driving the change was the new Republican majority. On the first day of the 104th Congress, the House passed a measure granting to congressional employees on-the-job civil rights protections that American workers in the private sector had enjoyed for years. Capitol Hill employees would now be covered by such laws as the 1937 Fair Labor Standards Act, the Civil Rights Act of 1964, and the two-year-old Family and Medical Leave Act.

During the second session, an additional half dozen measures that had been part of the 1996 Economic Equity Act were enacted. The minimum wage was increased to $5.15 an hour, and the limit on how much money nonworking spouses could save in a tax-deferred individual retirement account was raised from $250 to $2,000. The same legislation required that steps be taken to ensure that parties to a divorce as well as survivors of spouses entitled to annuities were made aware of their rights—before they unwittingly signed away their benefits.

The 1996 Defense Authorization Act protected military pension benefits for former spouses of military retirees who joined the civil service and rolled their military pensions into civil service pensions, a practice that had the effect of delaying distribution of benefits to spouses. An attempt by California Republican Robert Dornan to end this program altogether, and require former spouses who had already received these benefits to give the money back, was blocked by the House National Security Committee. Schroeder, a committee member, promised an all-out gender war if the measure ever got to the floor (Schroeder 1997, p. 161).

Caucus members were sharply divided on the second session's welfare reform law, but under the leadership of women on the Ways and Means Committee they coalesced effectively to help insert several key provisions. One significantly increased the amount of money states could spend to help welfare recipients and the working poor secure child care. A second strengthened the procedures by which child support payments could be collected from delinquent, noncustodial parents.

Although the new law dealt severely with legal and undocumented aliens, it nevertheless allowed battered immigrant women who would have been legal immigrants were it not for the behavior of their abusers to receive benefits to the same extent as legal immigrants. In other legislation, the Legal Services Corporation was given authority to use nonfederal funds to assist undocumented victims of domestic violence who are married to their abusers. Mindful of China's strict policy on birth control, Congress extended political asylum to victims of coercive population control policies.

Sexual assault, domestic violence, and child abuse were also addressed in the second session. Molinari, Morella, and Lowey beat back efforts to cut VAWA funding, and the antistalking provisions of the act were extended to apply to federal property—with restraining orders against stalkers automatically made effective in all states. Individuals convicted on misdemeanor charges of domestic violence were barred from owning firearms. Congress also directed the FBI to create a national database to help keep track of those convicted of sex crimes against minors, and it extended New Jersey's "Megan's law," requiring all states to inform community law enforcement agencies of the whereabouts of sex offenders after they had been released from prison. Immigration legislation added stalking, domestic violence, and child abuse to the list of crimes for which aliens could be deported.

In response to a federal court finding that sexual assault during a car-jacking did not constitute "serious bodily injury," a condition that increases the severity of the penalty for such crimes, Congress clarified existing law by placing sexual assault under the heading of "serious bodily injury." It also made it a federal offense to use a controlled substance, like Rophynol, to facilitate a violent crime, including rape. Rophynol, whose manufacture and import into the United States was illegal, had been used to drug and disarm unsuspecting women and render them vulnerable to sexual assault.

Most of these victories could not have been won without the help of Republican men. The health insurance provisions were ultimately crafted by an all-male task force led by Chief Deputy Whip Dennis Hastert. It was Harold Rogers of Kentucky to whom Morella appealed to help keep VAWA programs alive. And it was Appropriations subcommittee chair John Porter of Illinois and Pennsylvania's James Greenwood who provided much of the clout to save Title X. Commenting on the dynamic by which Republican women and men combined forces on the welfare reform measure, a Ways and Means Committee staff member observed:

> The male members were persuaded to vote for child support for political reasons. They did not feel that they had to be tough on dead-beat dads to balance toughness on females in the welfare bill. That was never a consideration. Rather, I believe the males had a certain willingness to give extra weight to what women said about issues like child care and child support—social issues. Not all males, but a major-

ity were prepared to defer to female members because they are women and therefore more sensitive to and knowledgeable about these issues.

The Erosion of Strategic Premises

The CCWI's frustrations and policy failures in the 104th Congress stemmed fundamentally from an inability to realize most of its six strategic goals. Bipartisan cooperation between Republican and Democratic women was the exception rather than the rule. Claims of inclusivity had a hollow ring when so many congresswomen either refused to join the caucus or were members in name only. The group's organizational integrity was threatened by bitter policy disputes among members and by the loss of its professional staff. It was unable to establish a close working relationship with a hostile Republican House leadership, in sharp contrast to the ready access the group had had to Democratic leaders. And while White House support never flagged, the Clinton administration was so busy blocking threats to settled policy that it had little energy remaining to promote CCWI priorities.

Elimination of the LSOs exacerbated antagonism between Republican and Democratic women. Partisan hostilities, largely latent in the past, became palpable soon after the 104th Congress convened. Democrats blamed Republican women for allowing Gingrich and company to undermine the CCWI, and Republican women began to have less to do with the caucus. One black Democratic congresswomen remarked in an interview: "Republican women are a distinct breed; they are in fact so different that sometimes I wonder where they came from and if they are truly women." Republican congresswomen, in turn, were keenly aware of Democrats' animus, and one observed: "I was stunned at the lack of [Caucus] support for any Republican legislative issues. I felt I was looked at by the Democratic women . . . as an odd person because I am a very strong Republican and fiscally conservative. . . . They wondered what I was doing in the Women's Caucus. Well I'm in the Women's Caucus because I believe in women's issues."

Antagonism between the two also grew out of predispositions shared by Democratic women first elected in 1992. They had never served with either a Republican president or a Republican House majority. During their first two years, they ignored Republican leaders and tended to treat GOP women as junior partners. Republicans had, after all, been in the minority for so long that they were not to be taken seriously. Democrats, on the other hand, had often acted as if the CCWI was an instrument to promote their own partisan and ideological objectives. In the 104th Congress, these Democratic women were overwhelmed by their loss of access and influence, and their distrust of Republicans extended to GOP women with whom they had once worked toward common goals.

Sour relations induced some Democrats and some Republicans to think about abandoning the CCWI and create separate women's caucuses. Patsy Mink, among the most liberal of CCWI Democrats, launched a "Democratic Women's Group," which began to meet on Thursdays. Its members shared the view that Republican destruction of the LSOs had so weakened the CCWI that it was pointless to continue the charade of bipartisanship. Mink stated, "The Republicans did away with our other [women's] caucus by making it very difficult to exist in a mode we had become accustomed to."

Republican women who considered breaking away concluded that since their party now controlled the House, there was no need sit at a Democratic table where they had formerly endured indignities associated with second-class membership. Said one Republican second-termer, "Being a member of a Caucus that is a small minority of the House is incompatible with being a member of the majority party, which after all sets the agenda."

Women in both parties credited Lowey and Morella with overcoming these centrifugal forces. Their close personal ties together with a determination to resist the alienation and defections of other members helped salvage the organization during its darkest hours. Morella, particularly, was credited with keeping the group alive because she had so few allies within her own party. One black congresswoman observed that even under these difficult circumstances, "the Caucus meetings fostered a sense of sisterhood for those of us who did go to the meetings and they enhanced my respect for Connie Morella because she was literally carrying the load for her entire party."

Morella's task was especially challenging because the Republican leaders were hostile to the CCWI and did whatever they could to persuade Republican women to quit. Speaker Gingrich was no fan of bipartisanship, apart from the lip service he paid it for tactical reasons, and, continuing a practice he had begun in the 103rd Congress, he met with Republican women periodically to brief them and thereby make CCWI affiliation seem superfluous. First-term GOP women were especially pleased with the arrangement. But some Republican congresswomen were unimpressed by an accessibility that declined as the 104th Congress unfolded. One veteran explained the meetings with Gingrich as an attempt by the leadership to address the gender gap, believing that congresswomen would provide the "magic formula" for closing the gap. Another skeptic referred to the meetings "as a pathetic attempt to make it seem as if women were being included [in the decisionmaking process], when, in fact, they were being co-opted." Still another doubted the effectiveness of the meetings, noting that "time after time before we knew it the new women had brought up the abortion issue and I would just think, 'Oh the hell with this. I've been here before. Just let me go home.'" Before long, meetings with the Speaker stopped.

Threats to the bipartisan character of the CCWI were compounded by the organization's difficulties in recruiting new members and in sustaining the interests of women who retained their affiliations. Six of the seven new Republican women not only refused to join the caucus but worked actively to undermine its credibility. Their attacks on the caucus were unprecedented, driven in part by a desire to gain the respect of their fellow Republican revolutionaries, and they planted doubts in the minds of male colleagues about the extent to which the CCWI spoke for American womanhood.

At the same time, the number of women who were members in name only grew. One Democratic congresswoman remarked:

> The Congressional Caucus for Women's Issues is not an organization I am active in. I belong, but I don't feel it is really useful to me. . . . I'm not sure what it is supposed to do. I know the issues that are coming up. My staff and I research them and understand them, and I understand my constituents' views on them. So I don't know what the Caucus would provide to me beyond that.

These sentiments were widely held by members of both parties, but were especially prevalent among women who came to the House after the legislative service organizations had been eliminated. First-termers in the 104th Congress had no way of knowing just how valuable the caucus's professional staff services could be. They had never had a chance to capitalize on the expertise, institutional memory, or entrepreneurial skills of in-house feminists whose sole purpose was to address the needs of CCWI members. And their indifference tended to contradict claims that congresswomen who belonged to the caucus were fully committed to its policy objectives.

Caucus efforts to balance respect for diversity with consensus building often foundered. The Republican agenda and legislative strategies had the effect of polarizing members of the two parties. Proposed welfare legislation, for example, inflamed partisan divisions and triggered disputes among Democrats as well. Differences on whether job training for recipients should be made explicit in the bill and whether assistance should come in the form of block grants to the states prevented the CCWI from presenting a united front on the measure. Democratic women were shocked when moderate Republican CCWI members asserted that many poor women did not want to get off "the dole." And they reluctantly acknowledged that the only issues on which consensus could be reached were a few dealing with women's health. A liberal Democrat remarked, "There is no way the Caucus can coalesce around almost any issue. There is such a split between Democrats and Republicans on priorities that it poisons our discussion of almost every issue."

No policy setback subverted CCWI effectiveness as much as its losing battles over reproductive rights. Because abortion debates recurred with dizzying frequency, and because CCWI leaders were forced to pour so much fruitless energy into countering attacks on *Roe v. Wade,* other priorities received less attention. At the same time, the caucus was increasingly associated with losing causes. In 1977 the CCWI had pointedly spared itself from such risks, declaring abortion to be the one issue on which the caucus would not take a position. By abandoning that strategic calculation, the CCWI left itself open to attack from a critical mass of new, pro-life members who made abortion the signature issue of their social revolution.

No structural change in the 104th Congress undermined the avowed purposes of the caucus as much as the loss of its permanent staff. The slack was picked up by staff in the offices of the CCWI cochairs, and by Women's Policy Inc. Each cochair appointed a staff member to handle communications among offices of caucus members, keep them informed about breaking developments, advise them about the agenda for CCWI meetings, and help frame actions to be taken in the name of the caucus. WPI began to prepare weekly, quarterly, and annual reports designed to keep members conversant with the scheduling and legislation bearing on caucus interests.

But these alternative arrangements did not fill the void left by the departing permanent staff. During the 103rd Congress, six professionals assisted by interns gave their undivided attention to caucus needs. Their budget topped $250,000 annually (*Washington Post,* February 15, 1995), and they used the office equipment and the furnishings and space in the Rayburn Building, much as any House member would. For years they had helped the caucus realize its objectives as catalyst, facilitator, incubator, and advocate for House feminists. Their departure meant that some of these responsibilities would be neglected.

Affected was the CCWI's ability to build consensus on key issues. The time, imagination, and expertise needed to discover and refine the ideas on which caucus members could agree—and which could conceivably attract support from nonmembers—were sharply curtailed. Caucus meetings were fewer and less purposive than they had been. Opportunities for congresswomen to raise issues unaddressed by the standing committees, float ideas, reinforce preferences, explore law-making possibilities, enlist cosponsors, and discover unintended consequences were diminished. Loss of a permanent staff also meant that task force activities were uncoordinated, and the viability of these subgroups began to deteriorate. Productive alliances with the Congressional Black Caucus, the Human Rights Caucus, and other House groups were rarely struck. Links to feminist groups outside the House were weakened. And legislative strategies were less systematically devised and implemented.

In the meantime, the product of past CCWI research, the caucus's reservoir of ideas, and its historical artifacts, now largely in the care of WPI, became less accessible in a timely way. Members and their staffs would have to rely on sources and materials no longer on Capitol Hill. Lost, too, were the subject-matter expertise, evaluative judgment, and interpretive skill of people who had spent years developing these assets. In short, the basis for the group's institutional memory was seriously eroded.

The caucus's failure to establish a good working relationship with House majority leaders in the 104th Congress was unique. From its creation, caucus cochairs had always had the ear, even if not always the support, of Democratic Speakers and floor leaders. Speakers Tip O'Neill, Jim Wright, and Tom Foley were at least approachable, and O'Neill and Foley had joined the CCWI when it opened its doors to congressmen. By contrast, Speaker Gingrich and other GOP leaders sought actively to diminish both its membership and its influence. Committee chairs did the same, and even if the Republican agenda had not crowded out other legislative initiatives, caucus priorities would have received little attention. Efforts to work through Democratic leaders were equally hopeless inasmuch as Republicans refused to consult minority party leaders on most matters.

Elevation of two GOP women, Susan Molinari and Barbara Vucanovich, to secondary leadership roles gave the caucus little comfort. Vucanovich had never been a CCWI member, and her generally conservative positions made her an unlikely conduit to GOP councils. Molinari, on the other hand, had joined the caucus the moment she arrived in Washington, but loyalties to Speaker Gingrich and other Republican House leaders, which included her husband, inhibited aggressive promotion of caucus causes. Some claimed that since women made up only about 7 percent of Republican House members (they made up 16 percent of the Democrats), feminist concerns could not be expected to claim the majority party's attention. But one Republican observer remarked that it was not the numbers that made women less influential. It was that the "thinking" of the two women chosen for leadership positions "was just like the thinking of the guys at the head of the table."

Molinari later described the dilemmas she faced as a nominal member of the leadership while trying to promote—all at once—the interests of her party, feminist issues, concerns of her urban constituents, and her own political ambitions:

> I'd become the Vice Chair of the Republican Conference . . . but that was as far as a moderate female from the northeast could go in the Republican Conference. While my input was accepted and sometimes even acted upon, I could never feel like a real player. I was a member of the leadership, but I was not, for example, a member of Newt's inner circle, the Speaker's advisory group, which is where ninety-nine percent of the decisions that are supposed to be made in leadership meetings are actually formulated. . . . Once I hit the woman wall, then how much could I really have accomplished? I was getting ahead, but I still hadn't been offered a place on any of the really important committees. The Republican Conference didn't care much about urban issues, so I couldn't accomplish as much as I would have liked for my district. The conservatives would never embrace me since I was immovable on my abortion position and bucked the party line too frequently on social policy issues they consider the *sine qua non* of trueblue conservatives. The liberals wouldn't call me one of their own because I believed fervently that the federal government was too big and unwieldy to right the wrongs of modern day America. (Molinari 1998, p. 260)

Among the strategic objectives that traditionally guided the CCWI, cultivating the support of the president was the one it came closest to achieving in the 104th Congress. For all of President Clinton's backing and sliding, he was generally firm in promoting feminist values. In his first two years, he had signed scores of measures endorsed by the caucus, and he had issued a half dozen executive orders making abortion more accessible. From the perspective of most feminist organizations, he was the most empathetic president ever to occupy the White House.

The administration continued to voice support for caucus policy goals during the second two years of the president's first term, but the humiliation Democrats suffered in the 1994 election sharply limited the extent to which he could add substantively to feminist gains. His efforts to defeat a balanced budget amendment, to head off elimination of federal agencies, and to prevent cutbacks in social programs sapped much of the administration's resources. Democrats used filibuster threats in the Senate and the president's veto power to frustrate Republican policy goals, but they were left with precious little political credit to be effectively proactive on most issues, including feminist issues.

Consequently, although the caucus maintained a healthy rapport with the president, its failure fully to achieve other strategic objectives made developments in the 104th Congress a greater threat to its organizational vitality than any encountered since the caucus was established. The two cochairs selected to lead the CCWI in the 105th Congress were mindful of the group's vulnerabilities, and they acted quickly to try to secure its future.

Notes

1. According to regulations issued by the House Oversight Committee on February 8, 1995, a CMO is "an informal organization of Members who share official resources to jointly carry out activities. . . . [It has] no separate corporate or legal identity apart from the Members who comprise it. . . . [It] is not an employing authority, and no staff may be appointed by, or in the name of a CMO. A CMO may not be assigned separate office space."

2. The matter was further complicated by the demand of Congresswoman Cynthia McKinney and other national black leaders that a statue of Sojourner Truth, a nineteenth-century black abolitionist and suffragist, also be placed in the Rotunda. They claimed that Truth's likeness had been part of the original sculpture, but was dropped prior to its completion. McKinney's objection was not acted upon (Bradley 1997).

3. Molinari was not the first congresswoman to campaign actively against another CCWI member. In 1982, Geraldine Ferraro campaigned against Margaret Heckler in a race against Barney Frank. That same year, she worked to defeat Millicent Fenwick when the New Jersey Republican ran against Bill Bradley for a Senate seat, although by then Fenwick had resigned from the CCWI (Ferraro 1985, p. 48).

6 Reclaiming the Initiative: 1997–1998

The 105th Congress served up an unprecedented challenge to the Congressional Caucus for Women's Issues. The 104th Congress had reversed past achievements, shredded its agenda, and threatened its survival. Its resiliency would be tested during the next two years. Leading the caucus were the District of Columbia's Democratic delegate Eleanor Holmes Norton and Connecticut's Nancy Johnson. The new cochairs ran unopposed, and were joined in CCWI leadership positions by New Yorkers Carolyn Maloney (D) and Sue Kelly (R) as vice chairs. Norton had served as vice chair during the 104th Congress and, even though her selection as Democratic cochair was widely expected, she campaigned actively to secure unanimous support. Her status as a nonvoting delegate had limited her influence in the House. Caucus leadership now promised increased opportunities to publicize D.C. needs, the women's agenda, and her own policy priorities in ways not normally available to a "second-class congressional citizen." As one Republican staffer remarked, "Norton has no vote in the House, she's a minority member of the minority party, and the Republican leadership is inclined to ignore her." Her role as CCWI cochair would increase her visibility, better showcase her considerable skills, and possibly offer more hope to her mainly black constituents and to women of color generally.

Johnson was the unanimous choice of Republican CCWI members, but was not at first certain she wanted the job. She was completing a two-year term as chair of the House Ethics Committee, and had been badly bruised by the panel's struggle with allegations against Speaker Newt Gingrich. The Connecticut congresswoman had been excoriated by Democrats who believed she was protecting her party leader through dilatory tactics while at the same time playing a complicit role in the decision to "reprimand" the Georgia Republican—a decision that grew out of a plea bargain with an independent counsel who was considering the more serious punishment of House censure and removal as Speaker. Many of Johnson's constituents identified her with both the protracted investigation and the tarnished Speaker, and in the 1996 election came within 1,600 votes of ousting her from a traditionally Republican seat.

Ultimately, Johnson agreed to join Norton as CCWI cochair, and she solicited the support of GOP congresswomen. The position offered a relief from the hothouse atmosphere of the Ethics Committee, and as a leader of the CCWI she could increase her personal contacts with a wide range of executive branch officials. But the most important reasons she became cochair grew out of a belief in the efficacy of the caucus, concern that the organization was in danger of being disbanded, and the realization that her seniority, her moderate political orientation, and the high regard in which she was held by Republicans and Democrats alike made her the natural if not the only choice for the job.

Norton and Johnson worked well together, exhibiting mutual respect. Both were enthusiastic, committed, and cerebral. Their styles differed markedly, but by each doing what she did best, the caucus endured. Norton worked tirelessly to promote the organization and its goals, paying close attention to detail, and ensuring that meetings and other planned events were adequately advertised and attended. She regularly followed up on the product of these events to try to reap the policy and public relations benefits implicit in their being held. Johnson, on the other hand, was less involved in day-to-day activities. Her strengths lay in persuading doubtful Republican women that caucus membership was worthwhile, in finding and defining the issues on which bipartisan consensus was more likely, in serving as a conduit between the caucus and majority party leaders, and in employing an impressive intellect and force of personality to try to secure feminist policy goals.

The cochairs' complementary skills were maximized because the two women shared a common view about how to recover credibility the CCWI had lost in the 104th Congress, and how to make the organization more relevant in the 105th. They agreed to focus on a range of issues that would not deeply offend any congresswoman, regardless of her party or ideological orientation, and that would persuade Republican leaders that the caucus should be taken seriously. They also agreed to try to strengthen Women's Policy Inc. (WPI), and to restructure the CCWI's system of task forces. They concluded that all of these goals could be achieved by adhering more steadfastly to the strategic objectives that, until the 103rd Congress, had been faithfully pursued. This meant a membership that embraced all congresswomen, bipartisanship in pursuit of collective policy goals, more steadfast sources of information and analysis, exclusion of highly controversial issues, like abortion, from its agenda, and good working relationships with House leaders and the administration. Norton and Johnson set out to address each of these goals.

Recruiting New Members

A more inclusive membership was the first objective the leaders tackled, each asking party colleagues to either retain their affiliation or join anew. Forty of the forty-nine congresswomen had belonged during the 104th Congress, and Norton and Johnson were determined to do better in the 105th. Norton had little difficulty persuading all Democrats to sign on. Few needed coaxing, although for some their membership was meaningless. She sent a memo to each highlighting the importance of the CCWI, promising committed leadership during the next two years and requesting full participation. She further proposed a special membership task force to assist with recruitment and improve the quality of participation. Two of its collateral goals would be to explore resumption of male membership and advance the prospect of drawing women Senators more fully into "our work," thereby increasing the likelihood of passing caucus priorities in both chambers.[1] The special task force was never formed, and the two related proposals never got off the drawing board.

Johnson had the more daunting task. Accordingly, she approached each Republican congresswoman individually, noting the advantages of joining forces with other women. She believed that the last Congress "had been an anomaly" and that it was important for the CCWI to be inclusive during the next two years (*Dallas Morning News,* August 24, 1997). She told wavering colleagues that "abortion" would not be a caucus priority and that their membership would neither embarrass them nor prevent them from pursuing their own legislative goals. Reproductive rights would not be raised in the name of the caucus, she said, and members could take any position they chose during committee and floor deliberations. These assurances resonated with at least one veteran Republican who had never been a member. She remarked in an interview, "I joined the Caucus because Nancy Johnson asked me to join and she said she was not going to use [the caucus] as an abortion platform—

which it has been in the past. I have nothing against joining and I like to join, but I'm not going to be an apologist for my pro-life views."

In the end, all but the two Republican first-termers, Jo Ann Emerson of Missouri and Kentucky's Ann Northup, affiliated with the CCWI. All four of the remaining conservative women first elected in 1994 signed on.[2] Johnson's effectiveness was evident in the observations of one of the four: "Nancy is an incredible woman . . . she hasn't allowed party lines to affect relationships. And she has been very instrumental in bringing women together."

These once distant Republican conservatives were not prominent caucus members during the 105th Congress, but they now had reasons for being associated with the group. They were no longer overwhelmed by the furious tempo maintained during their first two years in the House, and as sophomores they could better manage their time. One of the four was considering a Senate race and sought a higher profile on women's issues. Another regretted that conservative women had not participated in the past, leaving a policy vacuum that she believed she could now fill. Several Republican women, new and old, viewed their identification with the CCWI as a way to improve their images with female constituents and possibly help their party narrow the gender gap. None was under the illusion that she could significantly affect caucus priorities, and a few did not go out of their way to publicize their membership. But they had no regrets. One sophomore congresswoman observed: "I haven't been able to attend as often as I want to . . . but, you know, there is a lot that we women share in the way we view [women's] problems. And the camaraderie that is created in the jobs that we set out to do in representing our various constituencies means we have an awful lot in common; and its fun and comfortable to be with [other women]."

The two first-term women who declined membership attributed their decisions to the CCWI's pro-choice reputation. Northup found the caucus a "divisive" rather than a harmonious presence in the House, adding: "I'm against the politics of dividing people on teams. But that doesn't mean I don't think women are very important. There's a difference between each of us trying to walk in one another's shoes and being confrontational" (*Dallas Morning News,* August 24, 1997). She later became one of the most active proponent's of a constitutional amendment to ban late-term abortions.

Even without the two first-termers, the CCWI could now boast the largest number of women members in its twenty-year history, forty-nine, a figure that grew to fifty-three when all four of the women elected to fill vacancies created after the 105th Congress convened— Lois Capps (D–Calif.), Mary Bono (R–Calif.), Barbara Lee (D–Calif.), and Heather Wilson (R–N.Mex.)—affiliated with the group soon after they were sworn into the House. (These figures do not include nonvoting House members.) Mindful of its record numbers, the caucus seized on opportunities to call attention to itself and raise the profiles of present and former members. Norton and Johnson asked the House clerk to publish an updated edition of *Women in Congress,* a compilation of biographies and photographs of all the women who served in the House or Senate, and whose most recent edition had appeared in 1991.

Hundreds of Washington notables attended WPI's gala marking the caucus's twentieth anniversary in October 1997, and later, Jennifer Dunn and Juanita Millender-McDonald organized a Women's History Month reception honoring caucus founders Elizabeth Holtzman and Margaret Heckler, as well as others who had played a prominent role in the group's development. Norton and Johnson worked with the House staff to improve the amenities of the Lindy Boggs Reading Room to help accommodate the caucus's increased numbers. And they joined WPI and the American College of Obstetricians and Gynecologists in sponsoring a champagne reception for congresswomen filling vacancies in special elections. Their goals were to pump up the caucus's image, and to strengthen the esprit of its members.

Reinforcing Bipartisanship

Norton and Johnson next turned their attention to devising means by which Republicans and Democrats could work together more closely. Among their first acts was to eliminate the task forces initially established in 1993 and replace them with legislative "teams." The step was taken, in part, because the term "task force" was being used to describe influential ad hoc groups that party leaders had been appointing to supplement or circumvent the work of standing committees. Consequently, using the same label for CCWI policy groups was both presumptuous and misleading. Moreover, several CCWI task forces had gradually become inactive, surfacing mainly at press conferences, when members would simply announce the bills they were introducing as part of a caucus omnibus package. Some of these caucus subgroups, like the one on reproductive rights, had been associated with controversial policies, and the cochairs believed that structural change would defuse the acrimony exhibited in the past among ideologically heterogeneous congresswomen.

Perhaps most important, the "team" concept more aptly characterized the bipartisan working relationships Norton and Johnson hoped would develop among caucus members.

Team titles and jurisdictions were determined largely by Johnson in consultation with other Republican women and with Norton. The Connecticut Republican met with all GOP congresswomen, explored the policies they believed the caucus should address, and asked each to sign on as a coleader of a caucus team. Twelve of the thirteen Republicans agreed, after which Norton joined Johnson in creating fourteen teams, two of which initially possessed no Republican coleader.[3] The subject matter to be addressed by each team (e.g., women-owned businesses, women and the military) was selected not only because it had occupied past caucus interests, but also because it was likely to be taken seriously by Republican leaders. There were no teams on, for example, improving the Family and Medical Leave Act, or on family planning, reproductive rights, or equality for gays and lesbians.

Meanwhile, Norton was choosing fourteen Democratic colleagues to serve as team coleaders, selecting several junior members and a relatively large number of racial and ethnic minority women. Among the fourteen were six African Americans, two Hispanics, and one Asian. Virgin Islands delegate Donna Christian-Green, for example, was tapped to lead the team on preventive health services for women. And first-termer Loretta Sanchez, who spent much of her time fighting off a protracted challenge to her 1996 House election, was named leader of the team on the Higher Education Act. Some of Norton's choices were controversial, but they grew out of sentiments expressed in a May 7, 1997, memo she and Johnson sent to members:

> In choosing Team Leaders, we have been mindful of the fact that low participation in some Caucus activities is related to the fact that opportunities to offer leadership have not always been available. Therefore, with few exceptions, we have tried to involve Members who did not already have leadership responsibilities in other Caucuses or House activities, especially since there are only a limited number of spots.

Later, remaining caucus participants were asked to affiliate with one of the teams. Although most chose a team, the great majority became members in name only, and most teams rarely, if ever, convened. Nonetheless, team jurisdictions and responsibilities were carefully spelled out, and team leaders were encouraged to keep caucus members informed about new developments within their subject-matter areas, make formal recommendations on bills under consideration, and organize briefings. They were also expected to suggest guest speakers for CCWI Executive Committee meetings, hold press conferences, sponsor events highlighting the importance of their policy priorities, and communicate CCWI positions to House and Senate committees and to the administration. Teams' collective activities would help define the CCWI's agenda.

Throughout 1997 and 1998, most legislative teams barely met expectations. They did little more than arrange for Special Orders, circulate "Dear Colleague" letters, and hold press conferences. Some did even less than that. On the other hand, notable success was scored by the team on women-owned businesses, led by New York Republican Sue Kelly and California Democrat Juanita Millender-McDonald. During the first session, they hosted a CCWI Executive Committee meeting informing congresswomen about the issues they planned to address, and later held a hearing on opportunities available to businesswomen interested in securing government contracts. A CCWI-sponsored provision in a law passed in 1994, the Federal Acquisition Streamlining Act, asked federal agencies to earmark at least 5 percent of their contracts for women-owned firms. Three years later fewer than 2 percent of federal contracts had gone to female entrepreneurs. The hearings highlighted the shortfall, produced recommendations for reducing it, and gave Kelly and Millender-McDonald justification for introducing a "Sense of Congress" resolution calling on federal agencies to live up to the 1994 goal. "The federal contracting issue," said Kelly, "is a glaring example of a good ol' boys network" (*Roll Call,* September 25, 1997).

During the months that followed, they lobbied these agencies and distributed "Dear Colleague" letters requesting support for the measure when it came to the floor. On International Working Women's Day, they held a press conference and sponsored a Special Order celebrating Women's History Month to recognize both the achievements of businesswomen and the gender-related obstacles their companies encountered. Later the two congresswomen coordinated a Women's Business Roundtable, and Millender-McDonald subsequently introduced legislation increasing Small Business Administration funds for Women's Business Centers, then operating in thirty-six states.

The range of actions taken by Kelly and Millender-McDonald, and their periodic progress reports submitted to the caucus, were precisely what Norton and Johnson had in mind when they adopted the team concept—notwithstanding the fact that Kelly, as a subcommittee chair on the House Small Business Committee, cleared all important team activities with her committee chair, Missouri's James Talent, so that the

CCWI would not work at cross-purposes with the committee or subvert the Republican agenda.

Few other teams were as energetic and resourceful. Much depended upon the extent to which team leaders were committed to their cause, whether they were prepared to take the time to pursue team goals, and the degree to which they shared mutual respect with their coleaders. The team on job training and vocational education, for example, foundered because Republican coleader Susan Molinari resigned from the House during the first session, and because Democratic coleader Patsy Mink had earlier distanced herself from CCWI activities and was leader in name only. The team on higher education hardly got off the ground because the energies of Democratic coleader Loretta Sanchez were consumed by the Republican challenge to her 1996 House election, and because coleader Marge Roukema allocated little time to CCWI activities.

Some Republican women participated minimally, choosing to invest their time in committee and party leadership responsibilities rather than in CCWI activities. A few were hesitant to bring women's issues to the caucus because it had been led in the past by women who did not share their views, and several believed they could promote women-related goals without caucus help because they were in the majority. A number of Democratic women thought that the teams had been created without sufficient consultation. They believed that Norton's criteria for selecting team leaders had been arbitrary, and that their political and personal interests had been ignored. Nita Lowey was disappointed because the task force on reproductive rights had not been replaced by a comparable team. Louise Slaughter was displeased because she had been denied a leadership position on a team she preferred, and was assigned to head a team whose GOP coleader was a congresswoman with whom she had little in common.

Johnson and Norton irritated some socially conservative members when they later created and led a team on contraceptive technology. The caucus cochairs addressed the issue of unwanted pregnancies, called for renewed government research on contraception, and urged insurance companies to incorporate contraceptive prescription costs into health plans. These steps, they argued, would reduce the incidence of abortions. Some congresswomen did not see it that way and accused Johnson of resurrecting the issue of reproductive rights even though she had assured them the issue would be off the table when she invited them to join the caucus. One Republican remarked in an interview: "I'm having my reservations [about the CCWI]. They are doing meetings on reproductive health, which is their way of showing their [pro-choice] bias. So I'm going to share my reservations with Nancy. But I think the reproductive health meeting will be a one-time seminar and I hope they are going to move on to other things." There were no resignations, however, even after Johnson and Norton conducted a high-profile hearing on contraception.

Caucus members ultimately concluded that efforts to improve bipartisanship were generally successful, even if far from optimal. After her first year as cochair, Johnson boasted that the caucus was the only bipartisan group in Congress that met regularly "to talk about things, to coordinate and cooperate. That is very healthful in a legislative body, and women are good at that. The clear commitment to bipartisanship has enabled us to get things done" (*Washington Post,* October 22, 1997).

Sue Kelly noted that attendance at caucus meetings was "way up," and that a greater range of substantive issues was being addressed. Florida Democrat Carrie Meek saw the increased participation of Republican women as strengthening the organization "to the point where it is truly a bipartisan Caucus and we are doing some good things together, particularly in women's health." Some participants noted the marginally increasing presence of some of the newly affiliated conservative Republicans. Johnson remarked that "these women have become better integrated into the Caucus than I expected . . . and they are making positive connections with the Caucus that many Democrats are unaware of." A GOP staff member said:

> I've been at these closed-door meetings with just members and [these conservative] women have more of a common bond with other women than you might think. . . . It was easy for the Democratic women to write these right-wingers off. They believed these conservative women did not care at all. [But] now they're sitting in the same room, and they say, "Oh, congresswoman so and so supports child care funding. I had no idea." Before, it was easier to call her a right-wing gun nut.

Strengthening the Caucus Infrastructure

Weeks before the 1996 election, Norton sent a memo to Democratic congresswomen outlining the goals she would pursue if chosen CCWI coleader in the 105th Congress.[4] She began by asserting that the Democrats must retake the House and reestablish legislative service organizations (LSOs). As a congressional membership organization (CMO), Norton wrote, the CCWI was dogged by inefficiency, duplication of effort, and insufficient resources. The permanent staff, the research capabilities, and the institutional memory available to the caucus in years past had to be recaptured, she argued, and this meant restoration of LSOs.

Norton recognized, however, that the return to Democratic ascendancy was by no means ensured, and the memo stipulated steps she would take in the event that Republicans retained House control and refused to resurrect LSOs. Above all, she wrote, Women's Policy Inc. had to be strengthened. She noted that WPI's financial viability had become tenuous. It had raised $250,000 to produce its biweekly, quarterly, and annual publications during the past eighteen months but, by the end of 1996 it had less than $50,000 in the bank to fund future issues and to pay its three permanent staff members.

Only thirty female members of Congress (twenty-seven Representatives and three Senators) and thirteen male members (eleven in the House, two in the Senate) paid the $495 subscription price for WPI publications. And fewer than a dozen women's organizations were regular subscribers, a huge drop from the 7,000 groups and individuals receiving caucus newsletters before LSOs were abolished. The staff had little time to solicit contributions or market their product to women's advocacy groups, and the scarcity of resources left them without health benefits. Had it not been for the free office space provided by the American College of Obstetrics and Gynecology, WPI would have gone broke months earlier. Moreover, its usefulness to caucus members had continued to be problematic, with one senior Democrat remarking that the nonprofit organization was seriously "strapped for cash, and we have nobody we can call and ask, 'Can you get us a little research?'"

House Ethics Committee restrictions on how WPI might serve the CCWI placed a greater burden on the coleaders' staff and on the liaison staffers in members' offices. It was these staffers who largely sustained the momentum for members' initiatives and helped the caucus maintain its role as a catalyst on women's issues. They continued the practice begun in the 104th Congress of leading luncheon meetings attended by office liaisons, sharing information about pending bills, offering insights about legislative strategies, and alerting participants to new initiatives that CCWI members were considering. Members' office staffs, in turn, urged support for their bosses' priorities, and collectively constituted a network of policy specialists who came to rely upon one another to answer questions about legislation within their areas of expertise.

But staff meetings were underattended, with no more than twelve to fifteen offices represented at most, and with the number of staffers from

Democratic offices disproportionately higher than the number from Republican offices. Over time, meetings became pro forma, shorter, and less enmeshed in legislative business. WPI representatives could not always be present, many who attended were interns rather than permanent staff members, and the aide Norton had hired specifically to help her handle CCWI affairs, Erin Prangley, had to work overtime to maintain the group's viability, experimenting with different meeting times to try to increase turnout.

It was this tenuous infrastructure that had earlier led Norton to propose giving WPI more responsibility, while simultaneously bolstering its financially viability. To make it more user-friendly for members, and thereby increase the likelihood of their subscribing to WPI services, Norton proposed that it prepare reports on women's issues broken down by congressional districts and states. She also suggested that WPI distribute a weekly fax to subscribers and establish an online Internet service. Norton recommended that WPI be allowed to affiliate with a university, an affiliation that would make office facilities and equipment more accessible, give it greater recognition and prestige, and provide health and other fringe benefits to WPI employees. Increased financial support, she argued, could come from an annual fundraising lunch or dinner.

In October 1997, WPI affiliated with Mount Vernon College (which subsequently became a campus of George Washington University), and its staff gained a greater measure of financial security. Later, it compiled a report, *The Status of Women in the States,* providing state-by-state data on women's political participation, economic autonomy, employment earnings, and reproductive rights. More detailed reports on women's status in a dozen states were also published. WPI worked closely with Norton and Johnson to sponsor the twentieth-anniversary fundraiser, for which hundreds turned out to see Bill and Hillary Clinton, to hear Secretary of State Madeline Albright's keynote speech, and to reminisce with ABC commentator and gala emcee Cokie Roberts, daughter of former congresswoman and CCWI stalwart Lindy Boggs. The gala was a resounding success, bringing in enough money to keep WPI up and running for another year or two. Should a future House restore LSOs, WPI was prepared to move back to Capitol Hill.

Promoting Consensus

Among the factors impeding the CCWI in the 104th Congress was the unremitting attention it was forced to give to the abortion issue. The pro-life majority that emerged after the 1994 election forced pro-choice activists to counterattack forcefully, frequently, and ultimately in vain. Although the CCWI was not the only defender of reproductive rights, it was among the most visible, and its energies and reputation were sapped by its repeated losses to conservative majorities.

Even as the 105th Congress convened, Johnson and Norton decided to scratch abortion rights from the caucus agenda. They believed that to do otherwise would undermine their efforts to bring more congress-women into the organization, thwart what they hoped would be a resurgence of bipartisanship, and squander caucus resources that could be better invested in other, winnable policy disputes. In an interview, Johnson later observed:

> I would say the Caucus was least effective in the last [104th] Congress, the least effective it has ever been. . . . Reproductive rights was a very polarizing issue. . . . [But] women's issues are not just about abortion; they are across the board. So we consciously made that decision, and we have consciously [pursued] that issue in the Pro-Choice Caucus and not the Congresswomen's Caucus. That has made a big difference both in our ability to focus on other things and our ability to get things done.

After removing abortion from caucus consideration, the cochairs agreed to abandon their traditional reliance on omnibus bills. For years, the CCWI had put together packages of policy proposals on "economic equity" and "women's health," allowing each member to incorporate her legislative priorities into these catchall measures. Little attention was given to how proposals related to one another or even to whether they had a reasonable chance of being considered by a committee, let alone by the full House. After the bills were introduced, individual members would use their entrepreneurial skills and connections, along with the caucus imprimatur to try to pass one or more of the bills' provisions. Over time, many were adopted, especially during the 103rd Congress. But as the 105th Congress got under way, Johnson and Norton concluded that the increasingly conservative character of the House rendered dead on arrival omnibus bills loaded down with twenty or more feminist priorities.

A staff member close to the leadership observed in an interview:

> The point was to focus on things we can actually achieve in this Congress, rather than trying to do these "big blanket things" that are useful for public relations purposes but really aren't necessarily any more

effective. We may be better advised to [more narrowly] pursue some things we think we can get done. The big packages were very effective in the women's health debate in the late 1980s and early 1990s, . . . [but] we may be better off being more narrow in our scope these days.

Replacing the omnibus bills was what Norton called "a more focused approach" (*Congressional Record,* August 3, 1998, p. H6881). She and Johnson initially had a general idea of the programs deserving attention, but only gradually did they identify seven specific legislative measures whose passage they believed was feasible. Selection of the seven evolved out of the judgment and priorities of the cochairs, the activities of CCWI teams, calculations about how receptive the full House and the Senate would be to each, and the strength of bipartisan support each enjoyed among CCWI members. Norton came to call these measures the "Magnificent Seven," remarking that "for the first time the Women's Caucus . . . has chosen not a wish-list, but a real list for passage" (*Congressional Record,* July 22, 1998, p. H6076).

By most standards, almost all of the seven measures were relatively uncontroversial. They called for small (or no) expenditures, and were closely linked to legislation that Congress had already passed. One, for example, simply reauthorized the Mammography Quality Standards Act, a law first passed in 1992 but about to expire. The act required all facilities performing mammographies to meet national quality control standards in order to receive accreditation, and to undergo regular inspections. Reauthorization of the expiring Violence Against Women Act was also one of the "Magnificent Seven."

Two others included the Kelly/Millender-McDonald Resolution, expressing the sense of the House that federal agencies should make the federal procurement process more accessible to women-owned businesses, and a bill sponsored principally by Connie Morella to establish a temporary commission to study the recruitment, retention, and advancement of women in the science, engineering, and technology fields. One of the seven would bar insurance companies from using genetic testing when deciding who to insure, at what rate, and with what benefits. Separate bills sponsored by Linda Smith, Louise Slaughter, and Nita Lowey addressed the issue in different ways, and rather than choosing from among the three, CCWI leaders concluded that passage of any one would be acceptable.

The two most contentious proposals on the list urged passage of a comprehensive child care measure, and inclusion of the costs of contraceptives in coverage offered federal employees by health insurers. The first was supported vigorously by the cochairs, and by Democrat Ellen Tauscher of California, although no specific bill on the subject was endorsed by the caucus. What did receive CCWI support was a set of goals that members hoped to insert in all apposite bills considered by the House. The goals, said Norton, were to increase funding for low-income families needing child care, reduce taxes for working families and stay-at-home spouses, and raise federal and state standards when evaluating the quality of child care. The second, controversial proposal, championed primarily by Nancy Johnson and Nita Lowey, required that insurance plans underwriting health benefits for federal employees cover the full range of contraceptive drugs and devices if they covered other medication.

Caucus leaders helped promote each of the seven by staging events calculated to dramatize their urgency. Hearings, the first ever orchestrated by the CCWI,[5] were conducted on child care for preschoolers, contraceptive technology, businesswomen's access to federal contracts, and breast cancer. The first drew the largest turnout, and featured specialists from the National Institutes for Health, Head Start, state agencies, academia, and the business community. Johnson and Norton presided over the second of the four and heard testimony on the limited contraceptive options available in the United States, the factors contributing to the paucity of research on the subject, and American women's inadequate understanding of available contraceptive devices. The hearing on women-owned businesses jump-started the agenda promoted by the Kelly/Millender-McDonald team.

A final hearing examined how the drug Tamoxifen affects women at high risk of breast cancer. Participants included Surgeon General David Satcher, representatives of the Food and Drug Administration (FDA), the National Cancer Institute, and the Office of Women's Health, along with women who had used the drug. Norton and Johnson capitalized on the expert testimony, on publicity generated during National Breast Cancer Month, and on the issuance of a breast cancer prevention postage stamp to boost passage of the Mammography Quality Standards Act.

Norton maintained that each of the seven legislative objectives was an essential component of the caucus's family-friendly platform. She believed that the CCWI's performance in the 105th Congress would stand or fall on the fate of the "Magnificent Seven," and she implored her colleagues to approve them. She said: "There ought to be some bills at the end of the day that wouldn't have passed if our 50 members had not made them a priority" (*The Hill*, October 22, 1997).

By the time the 105th Congress adjourned, however, three of the seven caucus goals remained unfulfilled. Left hanging were all three measures requiring health insurers to abjure the use of genetic tests when making decisions about prospective clients. Also lost were the resolution asking federal agencies to consider awarding more contracts to women-owned businesses, and child care legislation. Norton was particularly frustrated by the failure to pass a comprehensive child care bill. She lamented:

> There is the one issue we hoped would be passed this year. This should have been the year of the child. . . . The Women's Caucus put together what we thought was a bipartisan set of principles that would produce child care in this session. Something for each side of the aisle. For Democrats who tend to be concerned about working families, more low-income certificates. . . . And then, for [Republicans] . . . we said we would accept a bill for tax relief for stay-at-home spouses, and then we would accept quality that was state imposed and the Federal Government would assist the States to bring up the quality of child care. Mr. Speaker, anybody who cannot get a bipartisan bill for our children out of that is not trying hard enough. (*Congressional Record,* October 14, 1998, p. H10882)

The caucus's four legislative victories included reauthorization of both the Violence Against Women Act and the Mammography Quality Standards Act. Congress also established a commission to promote the advancement of women and minorities in science, engineering, and technology, and after a bitter parliamentary struggle and what seemed like certain defeat, Congress required health insurance plans covering federal employees to include the costs of five different methods of contraception.

The legislative history of this last of the "Magnificent Seven" illustrates the difficulties CCWI leaders faced when they endorsed a proposal that could be construed as promoting reproductive rights. Appropriations for federal employees' health insurance are handled by the subcommittee on the Treasury and Postal Service. The subcommittee normally addresses more than its share of controversial issues, funding such agencies as the Bureau of Alcohol, Tobacco, and Firearms, the Internal Revenue Service, the Federal Elections Commission (FEC), and the Immigration and Naturalization Service. In 1998 it also considered $2.5 billion in emergency funding to help executive branch agencies address potential Y2K glitches in their computer networks, a cost-of-living salary increase for members of Congress, and a measure allowing federal agencies to use some of their money to help low-income workers pay for child care. Other proposals the subcommittee considered included one allowing 40,000 Haitian immigrants to gain permanent residence in the United States, and another placing term limits on the staff director and general counsel of the FEC. Strangely, the fate of all of these issues became linked in one way or another with the survival of Nita Lowey's language on contraceptive devices.

The subcommittee's recommendation to the full Appropriations Committee did not include Lowey's proposal, but in mid-June 1998, during full committee deliberations, the New York Democrat's amendment unexpectedly won approval, 28–26 (Taylor 1998a). The measure required companies providing health insurance for federal employees to cover women's costs for five FDA-approved contraceptive methods—birth control pills, diaphragms, interuterine devices, Depo-Provera, and Norplant. Insurance companies objecting to contraceptive devices on moral grounds were exempted from the requirement.

The Treasury/Postal Service bill then went to the House Rules Committee, which issued a rule protecting the Lowey provision and about fifty other riders from being subjected to points of order. Under House rules, language changing existing law may not be appended to funding resolutions, unless exempted by the rule governing debate, and virtually all of the riders qualified as "lawmaking" rather than as "spending." But when the rule came up for a vote, it was defeated overwhelmingly, 125–291, the victim of Republican opposition to the Lowey provision and Democratic objections to omission of administration-backed emergency funds of $2.25 billion to help prevent governmental computer shutdown on January 1, 2000. Most Democrats were not assuaged by Republican assurances that the money would be provided in a supplemental Appropriations bill.

Embarrassed by the defeat, Republican leaders returned the measure to the Rules Committee, and crafted a rule that removed protection from all but one of the legislative riders previously accepted by the Appropriations Committee—the exception being language to block an automatic cost-of-living salary increase for members of Congress. According to Republican Rules Committee member John Linder of Georgia, the new rule was designed to attract the support of conservative Republicans, who could now move to strike the Lowey language from the bill, and to bully Democrats to vote for it lest they be accused of trying to increase the size of their paychecks. The strategy seemed to work, and the rule was narrowly adopted (Gruenwald 1998a).

Soon after debate on the Appropriations bill began the next day, the legislative riders were stricken one-by-one on points of order, the Lowey amendment among them. But minutes later the New York Democrat, with the support of Norton, Johnson, and other CCWI members, outmaneuvered her opponents, introducing an amendment containing contraceptive coverage for federal employees, the language of which could be construed as "spending" rather than as "lawmaking." Her earlier proposal had imposed a requirement on health insurers to be enforced by federal officials, a legislative act. Her eleventh-hour substitute barred the use of federal funds to renew contracts with health care plans for federal employees that provided coverage for prescription drugs but not contraceptives. When asked to rule, the House Parliamentarian rejected a point of order, noting that House rules allow Appropriations measures to place limits on how money is to be spent. The new Lowey language did not, he said, "affirmatively mandate coverage" or require new determinations by "federal officials." Proponents of the amendment were triumphant when it passed 224–198 (Gruenwald 1998a).

But they had to marshal their efforts once again later in the day when New Jersey Republican Chris Smith offered an amendment to bar insurance coverage of contraceptives that induce abortion chemically. During debate he implied that any of the five methods could affect "implantation" of the fetus rather than simply preventing fertilization, upon which Lowey accused Smith of "saying to every woman who may take a birth control pill or use one of the five accepted methods of contraception that they are abortionists" (*Congressional Record,* July 16, 1998, p. H5720). Nancy Johnson insisted that all five contraceptive methods be available to women, maintaining:

> Some women cannot take the pill. It is too disruptive to them. Some women depend on intrauterine devices and other such contraceptives. When we get to the point when we have the courage to do more research in contraception, we will have many other options to offer women so that they can have safe contraception. . . . For us to imagine here tonight that it is either right or proper or possible for the gentleman [Mr. Smith] to impose his determination on others at this level is extraordinary. As a Republican who believes that government should stay out of our lives, I oppose this amendment with everything in me. (*Congressional Record,* July 16, 1998, p. H5721)

The House rejected the Smith amendment 198–222, with only seven CCWI members (six Republicans and one Democrat) supporting it. Days later, Norton took the House floor and said:

> I come to the floor today in the name of the bipartisan Women's Caucus to thank the House for the vote . . . to cover contraceptive prescriptions

for Federal employees. . . . Without contraception, of course, abortions are promoted, and some of these devices in fact lead to abortions because they are not as effective as others. That is why women need these choices, at least these choices when deciding something as central to their health as preventing abortions and deciding whether or not to bear a child. Every woman has had some contraceptive device that does not work for her. With this bill, we have passed one of the most significant women's health bills in many years. (*Congressional Record,* July 20, 1998, p. H5865)

In the meantime, Senate Appropriations Committee chair Ted Stevens of Alaska indicated he supported the Lowey amendment, and ranking Democrat Harry Reid of Nevada planned to offer it on the Senate floor if the Appropriations bill did not already contain it (Gruenwald 1998a). True to his word, Reid, together with Maine's Olympia Snowe, cosponsored the provision in the Senate. It was approved by voice vote, and the Appropriations bill passed 91–5 (Gruenwald 1998b). With both chambers agreeing to the provision, it was not surprising to find the Lowey language included in the House-Senate conference committee report.

But opponents were not ready to acquiesce. When the House met on October 10, it defeated the House Rules Committee resolution defining the ground rules under which the final version of the Appropriations measure would be debated. Conservative Republicans objected not only to the contraceptive provision, but to measures allowing 40,000 Haitians to gain permanent residence in the United States, and permitting federal agencies to use funds to help low-income federal workers pay for child care. They were joined by Democrats who protested the term limits placed on the FEC staff director and general counsel, officials who many Republicans believed spent too much time questioning election campaign practices employed by GOP-leaning organizations (Gruenwald 1998c).

Defeat of the rule forced House-Senate conferees to meet again, and House subcommittee chair Jim Kolbe (R–Ariz.) offered a compromise. He suggested that the three provisions dealing with Haitian immigrants, child care, and FEC term limits be removed from the bill, while retaining the language on contraception for federal workers. But the Democrats balked, insisting that since the FEC provision was the only one of the four that did not have bipartisan support, it should be the only one cut from the bill. Kolbe and other Republican leaders would not yield, however, and they struck all four from the bill.

Caucus members were devastated, and several spoke with unconcealed anger. Lowey noted that the leadership's arbitrary removal from the bill of a provision that passed the House and Senate and was in the conference report . . . is an extraordinary way to run the shop" (Gruenwald 1998c). Norton referred to the action as "a case study on how victory can be stolen from women." It was, she said, "a move that deserves remark for its profound anti-democratic tactics" (*Congressional Record,* October 14, 1998, p. H10882). House Democrats tried to send the bill back to conference with instructions to restore the contraceptives provision, but failed on a 202–226 vote. Moderate Republicans, in turn, blamed the Democrats, maintaining they should have swallowed the FEC proposal on term limits and adopted the compromise House rule offered by Kolbe. Nancy Johnson accused Democrats of deciding that "contraceptive coverage was expendable" in exchange for other items in the bill. Along with virtually all Republican CCWI members, she voted for final passage of the Appropriations bill. It was adopted 290–137, with almost all Democratic women opposed.

Obituaries for the Lowey amendment were already written when events in the Senate gave its proponents an unexpected opportunity for resurrection. During final debate on the Treasury/Postal Service bill, Reid objected to removal of the contraceptive provision and stalled a final vote on the measure. Whereupon it was swept up in the larger appropriations process and the rush to adjourn on the eve of the 1998 election. The unfinished Treasury/Postal Service measure, along with seven other pending appropriations bills, were lumped into an omnibus bill, and an intensive closed-door discussion began between Republican congressional leaders and a team of White House advisers. Much of the action took place in Speaker Gingrich's office, and the size of the bill together with the covert nature of the deliberations allowed members of both parties to insert hundreds of provisions promoting parochial interests (Doherty 1998).

After eight days of nonstop negotiations, participants had distributed $500 billion among the agencies funded by the eight bills, in many cases exceeding the expenditure limits that Congress had imposed only a year earlier. It was during this process that the contraception provision was added to the bill, among the last of the sticking points to be resolved (Doherty 1998). Strong support from the administration, Appropriations chair Ted Stevens, and other Senate Republicans surely helped. But there is reason to believe that Gingrich, too, threw his support behind it, in part the result of passionate prodding by Nancy Johnson. The two had a strong personal rapport, not least because Johnson's Ethics Committee had earlier recommended a reprimand for Gingrich, rather than censure, thereby saving his Speakership. The support of

House Democratic leaders was probably less important because they were denied direct access to the closed-door discussions.

On the other hand, Lowey's role was crucial. The nature of her contribution surfaced after conservatives Republicans expressed outrage when details of the omnibus package became known. They criticized their leaders for profligate spending and for caving in to the demands of a weakened president whose impeachment seemed imminent. Gingrich responded by asserting that the omnibus measure reflected many conservative goals, and cited, as an example, a modification of the Lowey language that exempted doctors with moral objections from being forced to prescribe contraceptives under the requirement that federal employees' health insurance plans cover such devices. Thus the Speaker tried to put the best face on the adoption of a contraceptive policy unacceptable to most Republicans by highlighting a change that Lowey almost certainly signed off on, but that, given the importance of the underlying issue, was relatively insignificant. Initial passage of the measure by both chambers, the rush toward adjournment, and the imminent midterm elections probably all contributed to the survival of the New Yorker's initiative. As House Democratic Caucus chair Vic Fazio remarked: "Why the Republicans would want a debate on contraception three weeks before an election is beyond my comprehension" (Taylor 1998b).

Subjects embraced by the CCWI's seven legislative priorities were not the only matters claiming the caucus's attention. The group scored what one staffer called "a huge victory" when it helped expand Medicaid coverage to annual mammograms for women over age thirty-nine, with the deductible waived. The change was part of the 1997 Balanced Budget Act, which also extended Medicare coverage to bone-density measurements for women at high risk of developing osteoporosis.

Congresswomen also succeeded in educating their colleagues and the public about legislation that was not yet ripe for full House debate. A CCWI-sponsored forum was held on the issue of lactation in the workplace, during which panelists explored the benefits of breast-feeding, discrimination and legal obstacles encountered by breast-feeding mothers, and success stories at companies that provide lactation facilities. Norton later held a "town meeting" on bills to narrow the wage gap between male and female federal employees. She explained that the "fair pay" bills did not have the level of bipartisan consensus accorded the seven "must pass" measures, adding that "the more the Women's Caucus demonstrates an ability to pass actual legislation, the greater will be our capacity in the future" to pass legislation mandating equal pay for men and women.[6]

During the 105th Congress, the CCWI addressed sexual harassment in the military services, and the integration of women in basic-training units. The issue of women in the military had claimed national attention following revelations that male drill sergeants at Maryland's Aberdeen Proving Grounds and, later, Missouri's Fort Leonard Wood, had sexually harassed female trainees under their charge. House leaders asked Indiana's Steve Buyer, chair of the Military Personnel Subcommittee of the National Security Committee, to form a task force and investigate the Aberdeen allegations. He chose Republican Tillie Fowler and Democrat Jane Harman (Calif.), ranking women on the National Security Committee, to round out the task force. The two were cochairs of the CCWI's team on women in the military, and as the inquiry progressed they and Buyer kept the caucus apprised of new developments. In the end, the task force divided on the issue of whether male and female recruits should train in integrated units. Harman and Fowler leaned toward continuation of the status quo. Buyer wanted a return to segregated training.

He was supported by recommendations of a commission set up by the Department of Defense to study the issue. The commission was led by former Republican Senators Nancy Kassebaum and Howard Baker and it urged the Army, Navy, and Air Force to adopt the segregated system employed by the Marines. Later, Secretary of Defense William Cohen rejected the proposal (*New York Times,* May 21, 1998), but the failure to produce consensus in the House drew Fowler, Harman, and the CCWI into a heated conflict with House leaders, Buyer, and a majority of the National Security Committee. The response of CCWI activists was pointed. Norton remarked:

> The bipartisan Women's Caucus disagrees that women should be separated in training. We think all you do is delay the problem. If women are separated in training, you are going to get women and men coming together for the first time when they are in fact in the field. Rather work these problems out in training, than bring them to the field. (*Congressional Record,* March 5, 1998, p. H895)

She alluded to the fight for racial integration in the military to bolster her position:

> If anybody had looked closely at the integration of blacks and whites in the services after World War II, I can tell you that there were many incidents, and that it was very hard to get southern white men under the command of black men. But in a command structure, you can do it, and we did it successfully in the military with blacks and whites,

and the Women's Caucus is going to demand it be done as well with
women and men. . . . Thus far all is quiet on the home front. I think
those who want to try to sex segregate training know that they are
going to have a fight on their hands. . . . You are going to meet a pha-
lanx of women on the floor if you try, and they are going to be Republican women and they are going to be Democratic women. (*Congressional Record,* March 5, 1998, p. H895)

But Norton and the caucus lost the fight, and the House passed a bill
calling for separate basic training for men and women in all military
services. The defeat was particularly disappointing because one of the
proposal's authors, Nancy Kassebaum, had been sympathetic to most
CCWI initiatives when she had served in the Senate. The upper chamber came to the rescue, however, and refused to include the change in
its version of the Defense appropriations bill, forcing House conferees
to back off.

Perhaps the most interesting and consequential development in the
105th Congress was not legislative in nature. It was, instead, the emergence of a new modus operandi by which the CCWI could exert legislative influence. A few of the caucus teams were led by cochairs who
were also members of House committees exercising jurisdiction over
their team's subject matter. This arrangement allowed the caucus to rely
upon congresswomen in both parties who were integral participants in
the House's established decisionmaking process. Membership of Tillie
Fowler and Jane Harman on the Military Security Committee, for example, made them major players when issues relating to women in the military surfaced. They were in a position to represent caucus perspectives
when dealing with the committee, and to represent committee perspectives when dealing with the caucus. Small Business Committee members Sue Kelly and Juanita Millender-McDonald played a similar role
when, as team cochairs, they sought to increase opportunities for female
entrepreneurs.

These dynamics were not entirely new, inasmuch as the CCWI had
always relied on men as well as women serving on relevant committees
to act as proponents of its priorities. What was new was the formation
of teams, a few of whose cochairs served on a committee commanding
jurisdiction over matters mirroring those of their teams. These circumstances could not have occurred when there were fewer women in the
House and when many House committees did not include at least one
woman in each party willing to reflect feminist values. By the end of the
105th Congress, however, caucus members were able collectively to
claim direct access to House consideration of any and all national policies

affecting women. Moreover, many of these women had acquired a level of seniority that allowed them to be more than marginal players at the committee level. Ironically, one consequence of this development has been a weakening in the ties many congresswomen have with the CCWI. As their responsibilities and influence in the House has increased, their need to work through the caucus has decreased, a consequence that will be discussed more fully in the next chapter.

Improving Rapport with House and Administration Leaders

During their two years as CCWI cochairs, Johnson and Norton attempted to improve working relations with congressional and administration leaders, or at the very least maintain reliable avenues of communication between them. Unsurprisingly, they received a warmer welcome at the White House than they did among Republican House leaders.

The caucus's reputation as a liberal redoubt was surely one reason the Republican House hierarchy held it at arm's length. Moreover, when the 105th Congress got under way, Republicans were still reeling from a 1996 election that had returned their nemesis to the White House and nibbled away at their majority. The momentum built up after the 1994 election had dissipated, and the influence Republican leaders could exert in Congress and with the public was noticeably diminished. This meant that they were unprepared to extend much magnanimity or even respect to a group for which they had harbored deep suspicion.

But CCWI leaders, too, were responsible for House leaders' neglect. Months of delay in organizing, while recruiting new members and establishing teams, slowed formulation of their agenda and postponed opportunities to reach out to the Speaker and other GOP influentials. Gingrich met with the Congressional Black Caucus two months after the new Congress convened. His first and only meeting with the CCWI, on the other hand, occurred almost eighteen months later. During discussions with members of the Congressional Black Caucus, Gingrich said he would revisit the decision to eliminate legislative service organizations (Eilperin 1997a). An early meeting with CCWI members might conceivably have strengthened that resolve, although it is difficult to believe that GOP conservatives who were already criticizing their leader for meeting with Jesse Jackson and other black Democrats before conferring with groups of black Republicans would have countenanced restoration of LSOs. In any event, the idea died aborning.

To be sure, GOP leaders were in daily contact with Republican congresswomen occupying key party and committee positions. Even before the 105th Congress convened, Speaker Gingrich had officially moved Conference vice chair Susan Molinari and Conference secretary Jennifer Dunn into his leadership circle. He said at the time that he wanted to make sure that GOP policies reflected the views of women, Americans who make up nearly half of Republican voters (*USA Today,* December 10, 1996). When Molinari later resigned her House seat, Gingrich encouraged Dunn's elevation to vice chair and the election of Deborah Pryce as secretary.

In closed leadership meetings these women sometimes chastised male colleagues for proposing ideas in language bound to frighten women voters. On one occasion Dunn interrupted a tax-cutting diatribe by Majority Leader Richard Armey, urging him to consider the impact of tax cuts on the programs many women were finding indispensable. Pryce later observed: "Perhaps we [women] are more sensitive to how deeply troubling our harsh rhetoric is to some people, especially women." Both congresswomen were acutely aware of their party's difficulty in attracting women, and Pryce founded a political action committee—VIEW PAC—to support female GOP candidates regardless of their ideology. Dunn, in the meantime, led a drive to attract more women to the Republican Party, convening a three-day conference of GOP leaders to help achieve that end (*Washington Post,* April 29, 1998).

But neither Dunn nor Pryce was prepared to serve as a conduit for CCWI priorities. Moreover, their influence as Conference officers was doubtful because they were unable to establish a thoroughly trustful working relationship with Conference chair John Boehner of Ohio. The two congresswomen wanted some control over the committee's finances and its public relations and communications strategies, and Boehner told them he did not know whether he had the authority to delegate more power to them (*Roll Call,* May 25, 1996). Other GOP women were positioned to transmit the caucus message to their party leaders, notably Deputy Whip Barbara Cubin, Sue Myrick, who was sophomore class representative on the Speaker's leadership council, and Ways and Means subcommittee chair Nancy Johnson, but with the exception of Johnson, none was predisposed to do so.

It was not until midway through the second session that CCWI leaders fully orchestrated a strategy designed to secure support for its "Magnificent Seven." On June 10, 1998, they held a press conference unveiling their seven-pronged agenda, and met the next day with Democratic minority leader Richard Gephardt. Two months later, they hosted

Newt Gingrich at an Executive Committee meeting, and once again tried to drive home the virtues of their legislative goals. Gingrich was responsive but not altogether encouraging. He advised them to ask Majority Leader Richard Armey to schedule House debate on the legislation concerning mammography and women in science, implying that these two measures would be readily adopted once they reached the floor—which is what happened. But he also indicated that bills increasing opportunities for women entrepreneurs, promoting child care, and preventing insurance company discrimination based on genetic makeup were unlikely to receive House consideration, either because hearings had not yet been held or because the Senate was unlikely to act on them before the 105th Congress adjourned.

But the bulk of the meeting was spent discussing the role of the CCWI in the House. Gingrich praised the caucus for drawing up its list of seven, must-pass legislative priorities, something no previous caucus had done, and offered two suggestions for the future. First, he advised members to develop an agenda more expeditiously, giving the House more time to consider and digest their proposals. Second, he asked the caucus to appoint one of its members to serve as a liaison to the Republican leadership to keep him informed about CCWI activities. Deborah Pryce and Jennifer Dunn were likely candidates, he said, since they already held leadership positions.[7] Caucus leaders took no action on the Speaker's second proposal, but they did contact Majority Leader Armey to urge him to speed up floor consideration of the bills addressing mammography and women in science.

Caucus relations with the president and his administration began on a strongly positive note, deteriorating only after the White House sex scandal broke in January 1998. Two months after the new Congress got under way, the president invited CCWI members to join him in the White House State Dining Room for a roundtable discussion of women's issues. Nearly fifty House and Senate women in both parties participated. Present, too, were officials from the Women's Initiatives and Outreach Office, a White House agency President Clinton had created to cultivate and respond to the needs of women's advocacy groups, the female electorate, and women lawmakers.

Caucus leaders subsequently capitalized on the rapport established with the administration, inviting almost a dozen presidential advisers—chiefly specialists in health, military training, and labor—to CCWI Executive Committee meetings. The caucus joined the White House in sponsoring a conference on child care, and Norton's "town meeting" on the wage gap between men and women and the "glass ceiling" received strong support from Labor Department officials. In his remarks at the twentieth-anniversary gala, the president noted the pivotal role the CCWI had played in securing a balanced budget agreement, and in bringing about more funding for breast cancer research and osteoporosis prevention. Moreover, the presidential couple's appearance at the event almost certainly increased the evening's take.

But CCWI members began to distance themselves from the White House after accusations about the president's affair with an intern claimed the media's undivided attention. Clinton's initial denials did little to diminish attacks from critics, and his supporters were often forced to respond with carefully hedged defenses of the president. Discussions at CCWI Executive Committee meetings consciously skirted mention of the scandal, but in extramural conversations congresswomen could scarcely avoid the topic.

Republican women found themselves in a delicate position. They wanted to attack the president for his outrageous behavior, but were inhibited by an initial GOP strategy of allowing revelations emerging from Independent Counsel Kenneth Starr's investigation to inflict the damage. Their leaders also worried that by calling attention to the president's flagrant indiscretion they would be making "marital infidelity a legitimate part of political discourse and further erode the ever-shrinking zone of privacy accorded elected officials" (Kirchoff and Cassata 1998). Instead, Republican women tried to force Democratic women to speak out against their president, and thereby head off charges of partisanship that would inevitably be leveled against their own remonstrances.

Two months after the president's affair was made public, Deborah Pryce and Senator Kay Bailey Hutchison helped organize a meeting in Speaker Gingrich's office. There, a dozen House and Senate women considered asking women's groups around the country to speak out about the sexual allegations and to pressure Democratic women in the House and Senate to be as critical of the president as many of them had been about Clarence Thomas after Anita Hill's allegations and about Senator Bob Packwood following a flood of similar accusations. "Sexual harassment is not a partisan issue," said CCWI vice chair Sue Kelly, who attended the meeting. "We'd like to see our Democratic sisters speak out on the floor . . . only everyone seems to be ducking for cover." She recalled the strident tones Democratic women had used in the Thomas and Packwood cases, noting that these women "were there then, and they're not here now, and I wonder, why the silence?" (Contiguglia and VandeHei 1998).

But not all Republican women were circumspect when prodding Democratic colleagues and attacking the president. Marge Roukema took feminist groups to task, asserting that "character [in the White House] counts, and I think the so-called feminists are conspicuous by their absence" (Kirchoff and Cassata 1998). Non-CCWI member Anne Northup denounced the president publicly and lashed out at Democratic women. The Kentucky first-termer made the rounds of television talk shows, and her views appeared in leading newspapers. "This isn't [the president's] private life," she said. "[The White House] is his work place." Northup pointed out that leaders of the women's movement ought to be "asking questions about the fact that there's a whole class of interns. . . . Do they have a chance to get a permanent job in the White House? . . . How did all the other women feel who didn't have that chance? Like maybe they should have gone around in different style clothes?" (*New York Times,* February 17, 1998).

Responses by Democratic women were either cautiously protective of the president, or directed against the Starr investigation. They maintained that the charges against the president were allegations only, that they had yet to be proved, and that Clinton had steadfastly denied them. Maxine Waters found nothing wrong with the way in which the president was confronting the issue. "There is nothing unfair in his refutations," she said. "Everyone has a right to defend themselves in a fashion they think will get people to listen" (Contiguglia and VandeHei 1998). California's Nancy Pelosi remarked: "We don't know whether it took place or not. But, if it did, it comes as a great big surprise to a great many people. I don't think for one minute there's an atmosphere of sexual harassment in the White House" (*New York Times,* February 17, 1998).

Decisions by CCWI leaders to keep the scandal out of its deliberations and by Republican women to exercise restraint permitted the group to stay on-message and maintain at least the appearance of bipartisanship. But there is little doubt that just as the parade of tawdry revelations from the Starr investigation poisoned the atmosphere in the House, they served as numbing distractions for CCWI members, impeding the group's agenda and affecting relations between Democratic and Republican women. The White House scandal was not the only distraction, however. Bitter recriminations following two close 1996 election contests—one for the Senate, the other for the House—also sapped the caucus's productive energy and further divided the group along party lines.

Two Contested Elections

All congressional elections produce a few results that are so close that initial tallies are followed by contested recounts and sometimes lawsuits.

The 1996 election was true to form, except that the two closest contests featured razor-thin victories for Democratic women over Republican men who, with the vigorous support of GOP allies, were prepared to go to unusual lengths to challenge the certified outcomes. As a result, Senate candidate Mary Landrieu of Louisiana, and California House candidate Loretta Sanchez, spent their first year in office trying desperately to hold on to small margins of victory. Their struggles became famous, and the acrimony they generated subtly affected the working relationship between Democratic and Republican members of the CCWI.

Jenkins v. Landrieu

Disputed Senate elections do not generally affect relationships within the House, and vice versa, but the 1996 contest for the upper chamber in Louisiana reverberated unmistakably in the lower chamber. The race had ended with Mary Landrieu defeating Republican Woody Jenkins by fewer than 6,000 votes out of 1.7 million cast. Jenkins vigorously contested the result, and asked the Senate not to seat Landrieu until it had investigated election-law violations he alleged had produced her margin of victory. These violations, he said, included the buying of votes, multiple voting by Landrieu partisans, phantom voting (i.e., votes cast by the dead), votes cast by persons who were either unregistered or who had registered fraudulently, and the use of voting machines that had been tampered with or that worked improperly. Landrieu was also accused of countenancing "vote hauling," that is, paying campaign workers to transport people to the polls, an illegal practice under Louisiana law. Jenkins further alleged that New Orleans gambling interests and a political organization controlled by New Orleans Democratic mayor Marc Morial, the Louisiana Independent Federation of Electors (LIFE), had illegally funneled large sums of money into Landrieu's campaign (Cook 1997).

Jenkins's charges were referred to the Senate Rules Committee, led by Republican John Warner of Virginia, and the committee appointed two lawyers, Bill Canfield, a Republican, and Bob Bauer, a Democrat, to conduct a preliminary investigation into the allegations. Both were specialists in election law, and both had helped the Senate resolve a challenge brought by California's Michael Huffington to Dianne Feinstein's narrow but ultimately insurmountable margin of victory in 1994 (Cook 1997). In the meantime, Landrieu was allowed to take her Senate seat, until such time as that body was prepared to declare an undisputed winner or call for a new election.

In April 1997 the two lawyers completed their report and recommended that the Rules Committee limit its inquiry to three allegations—that the Landrieu campaign organization had paid people to vote, that it had inspired multiple voting, and that it had benefited from fraudulent registration. The report advised the committee to focus on allegations that vans had picked up poor New Orleans residents and paid them to vote numerous times for Landrieu. It went on to propose that other charges be dismissed, including phantom voting and voting-machine tampering and malfunctioning. The report recommended that all allegations of financial improprieties be dropped, concluding that efforts to link illegal campaign contributions by gambling interests and by LIFE to vote totals would be impossible (Sheffner 1997c).

Warner, strongly influenced by conservative Rules Committee Republicans, including Majority Whip Don Nickle, Campaign Committee chair Mitch McConnell, North Carolina's Jesse Helms, and Rick Santorum of Pennsylvania, rejected that advice, and announced that his committee would look into not only the three recommended areas, but also the allegations of voting-machine error and tampering, phantom voting, and campaign finance violations. On a 9–7 party-line vote, the Rules Committee agreed in mid-April to appoint a team of investigators consisting of four attorneys, three Republicans and one Democrat, to explore the full range of Jenkins's allegations. They would be aided by agents of the FBI and the General Accounting Office, as well as by the two attorneys whose recommendations the committee had largely ignored. Warner said he expected the entire matter to be wrapped up by Memorial Day (Sheffner 1997d).

Democrats were incensed by the committee's decision to expand its inquiry beyond the three areas singled out in the preliminary report, and vowed to take whatever floor action was necessary to help Landrieu retain her seat. Veteran Democrat Robert Byrd intoned: "I take it that the majority has decided to go to war. So be it." Dianne Feinstein, citing the ongoing fight over the House seat held by Loretta Sanchez (and with her own 1994 travails against Huffington in mind), railed against the disproportionate frequency with which women were targets of contested elections. "Hell hath no fury like a man beaten by a woman," she said. When appearing before the Rules Committee, she stared directly at its Republican members, her voice rising to a shout, and said, "You have no idea how hard it is for a woman to be elected to the U.S. Senate" (Sheffner 1997d).

Feinstein vowed to use all of her power to block a Senate resolution to authorize the Rules Committee to subpoena witnesses and to allow staff members and outside consultants to take depositions (a promise she was later unable to keep). She added, "I will filibuster, I will fight it every step of the way because I think it is plain wrong" (Sheffner 1997d). Subsequent efforts by Minority Leader Tom Daschle to stall or end the inquiry were unavailing, although when the Rules Committee's Republican majority voted in July to continue the investigation, Democratic Senators began to boycott committee meetings—which Republicans said had the effect of prolonging the investigation.

The decision of the Senate Rules Committee to expand the investigation received strong support from House Republicans, however. While the committee considered whether to reject the Canfield-Bauer recommendation to limit the inquiry, five House members from Louisiana, led by the chair of the powerful Appropriations Committee, Robert Livingston, urged a full-blown investigation. In a letter to Warner, they said: "We are especially concerned that counsel refused to examine the role played by gambling interests and the political organization LIFE in the election. Thus we urge you to undertake a fully complete, fair and unlimited investigation. The very integrity of the Senate and indeed the entire Congress hinges on your action" (Sheffner 1997c). Democratic women in the House bitterly resented efforts by Livingston to unseat a Democratic women in the Senate at the same time that House Republicans were trying to do the same thing in the lower chamber. But some CCWI Democrats also resented what they saw as Livingston's thinly veiled attempt to use his Appropriations Committee chairmanship to throw his weight around among Senators who spend much of their political capital trying to increase federal expenditures within their states.

By the time Congress returned from its summer recess, the Rules Committee had learned that there was little evidence to suggest that the election result should be overturned. The General Accounting Office had found some unexplained votes, but nothing like the tens of thousands that Jenkins and Louisiana Republicans had claimed were illegally cast (Cassata 1997). Warner had by now lost his taste for the investigation and was quoted as saying, "My guys want blood—well, not my guys—but I don't care anymore" (*New York Times,* September 17, 1997). Two weeks later, the committee voted 16–0 to end the inquiry, although some Republican "aye" votes were halfhearted (*New York Times,* October 4, 1997).

Landrieu's victory was not complete, however. Her request to be reimbursed the $500,000 spent to respond to Jenkins's challenge was denied on another 9–7 party-line Rules Committee vote. This final chapter in the dispute reflected the partisan divisions within the "hard-charging Senate, where some view the divide between the majority and minority as a demilitarized zone" (Cassata 1997). The relationship between Warner and Kentucky's Wendell Ford, the ranking Democrat on his committee, was bruised, and some Senators believed the interpersonal comity normally characteristic of the institution had been threatened. But the temporary lapse in Senate civility was tame compared to the all-out war going on in the House over the 1996 election result in California's forty-sixth district.

Dornan v. Sanchez

Republican Robert Dornan had represented his Orange County, California, constituency for eighteen years. He was first elected to the House in 1976, served three terms, gave up his House seat to run unsuccessfully for the Senate, and returned to the House in 1985. During the next twelve years he was the scourge of Democrats, especially the liberal variety, and he regularly blasted them as supporters of gun control, gay rights, and abortion, tarring some opponents as communist sympathizers and draft dodgers. A former fighter pilot, his repeated endorsements of expanded American air power earned him the sobriquet "B-1 Bob," after the bomber of the same name, and his unvarnished conservatism made him a favorite of like-minded talk-show hosts, including the redoubtable Rush Limbaugh—for whom he sometimes substituted.

A combative partisan, Dornan nonetheless did not allow party loyalty to prevent him from berating GOP colleagues who were not sufficiently conservative, and he once outed a gay Republican on the House floor by referring to the "revolving door on his closet" (*New York Times,* December 18, 1996). But throughout the 1990s, Dornan's most caustic invectives were reserved for Bill Clinton. During the 1992 presidential campaign, he called Clinton a "womanizer-adulterer," a "sleazeball who can't keep his pants on," and a "disgraced draft dodger," and later accused the president of having acted as a KGB agent when visiting Russia during his days abroad as a Rhodes scholar. After Dornan gave up a brief attempt to secure his party's presidential nomination in the 1996 primaries, he announced he would seek to retain his House seat and vowed he would press for impeachment hearings against the president because of apparent campaign contributions from foreign individuals and corporations (*USA Today,* November 14, 1996). Dornan's short-lived run for the presidency diminished his treasury and postponed the start of his House campaign, but these were not seen as serious setbacks.

After all, he had been reelected by 20 percentage points in 1994, and he would be facing a political unknown in the coming contest.

The novice was a thirty-six-year-old businesswoman, Loretta Sanchez. She was one of seven children of Mexican immigrants, and had earned a bachelor's degree in economics and a master's in business administration. She worked as a financial consultant, defined herself as a fiscal conservative, and in 1992 had changed her allegiance from the Republican to the Democratic Party because she believed the GOP was wrong on most immigration and women's issues (*New York Times,* December 18, 1996). Her lone prior foray into politics occurred in 1994, when, in an at-large election, she tried to capture one of five seats on the Anaheim city council. She finished eighth among sixteen candidates. Nonetheless, two years later she won the Democratic primary for the House seat by defeating two better-known, better-financed opponents.

The forty-sixth congressional district had been politically conservative and reliably Republican over the years, not unlike virtually all of Orange County. At the same time, it was experiencing seismic demographic shifts. The 1990 census revealed that the Hispanic population had doubled in ten years, and now made up 50 percent of the district's population. Residents with Asian backgrounds increased from 6 percent to about 13 percent (*USA Today,* November 14, 1996). These changes were not expected to make a difference in the election—Dornan was a heavy favorite—but Sanchez doggedly began a house-to-house campaign talking about the minimum wage, employment, education, and crime, hoping to improve turnout among blue-collar, ethnic voters.

She was helped by the appearance on the ballot of a referendum threatening affirmative action in state hiring, contracting, and educational programs, and expected to benefit from campaign visits to the district by two of the nation's best-known Hispanics, Federico Peña, secretary of transportation, and Henry Cisneros, secretary of housing and urban development. The president also campaigned for Sanchez, savoring the prospect of shooting down "B-1 Bob," and he helped her raise part of the $600,000 she used to finance her campaign and outspend her opponent. Dornan, in the meantime, was claiming that Sanchez's pro-choice position made her "anti-Catholic" and a "pretend Hispanic." He called her a "champion of homosexuals" and alleged that she was a "carpetbagger." Days before the election, one of his grown sons tried to make a "citizen's arrest" of Sanchez's husband as he was posting "Sanchez" signs (*New York Times,* December 18, 1996).

On election night, it appeared as if Dornan had narrowly prevailed, holding a 233-vote lead. But when mail-in ballots were counted in the days that followed, Sanchez forged ahead, ultimately winning the race by 984 votes and pulling off one of the biggest upsets of the decade. Dornan refused to concede, however, characteristically reviling his opponent as "an inarticulate, flaky, non-qualified person." He demanded a recount, charging that the margin of victory was a product of fraudulent registrations and illegally cast ballots (*USA Today,* November 14, 1996). He accused Sanchez of having used illegal aliens to stuff ballot boxes, and asserted that pro-Sandinista communist interlopers organized "motivation troops" to send Sanchez voters to the polls in low-turnout neighborhoods (*New York Times,* December 18, 1996). A recount did not change the result. Sanchez was sworn in with the new cohort of House first-termers and assigned to the Education and Workforce Committee.

Undaunted, Dornan continued to press his case, alleging that an immigrant-rights group, Hermandad Mexicana Nacional (HMN), had induced Hispanic immigrants to register and vote before they were legally eligible. Over the years, HMN had received $35 million in state and federal government funds to conduct classes for immigrants, help them understand naturalization procedures, tutor them for citizenship tests, and prepare them to take advantage of their rights as Americans, registering and voting among them (Sheffner 1997a). Dornan claimed that its leaders had conspired against him, and that the absentee ballots of more than 100 people had been illegally submitted by a third party. In early February, his lawyer announced that 1,789 illegal votes had been identified, adding, "We are frankly astounded by the magnitude of the voter fraud and irregularities uncovered . . . at this early date," whereupon Dornan called upon Sanchez to resign her House seat and join him in calling for a new election—a request she ignored (Sheffner 1997a).

Dornan lodged his complaints with the House, and they were referred to the Oversight Committee, chaired by California Republican Bill Thomas. The committee, in turn, chose a task force of two Republicans and a Democrat to investigate the charges. It was chaired by Michigan Republican Vern Ehlers. The inquiry dragged on for more than a year, with the California secretary of state, the Orange County District Attorney's Office, and the Immigration and Naturalization Service (INS) ultimately drawn into the controversy. At issue was how many illegal voters had participated in the House contest, how many had been encouraged to do so by HMN and other organizations, and how many had voted for each of the two candidates. The last question could never be confidently answered, given the secrecy of the vote. But answers to even the first two questions were difficult to nail down because of uncertainties that arose when trying to match INS worksheets of Orange County residents who were *possibly* noncitizens with registration and turnout records for the forty-sixth district.

The unreliability of whatever findings would emerge, together with the intensely political character of the issue, poisoned the atmosphere in the House and exacerbated the already strained relations between the two parties. Republicans, particularly those from California, rallied to Dornan's side. Five GOP members from Orange County wrote to the chair of the Government Reform and Oversight Committee asking him to investigate the charges against HMN. At the same time, they encouraged the California secretary of state, Republican Bill Jones, to conduct investigations into possible criminal wrongdoing by HMN and any other group that might have been complicit in fraudulently adding to Sanchez's vote count (Sheffner 1997a).

The chair of Sanchez's Education subcommittee, another California Republican, was loath to give her presence in Congress public exposure, and reneged on a promise to allow her to hold field hearings in her district on postsecondary education. According to disappointed Education Committee Democrats, the change was made because of the ongoing contested election (Sheffner 1997b). Republicans responded that a hearing had already been held in California and that the committee could support no more than one field hearing in each state. When Democrats pointed out that two hearings had been conducted in Pennsylvania and Indiana, their objections were explained away.

Bill Thomas was among the most unrelenting supporters of Dornan's cause, partly because the election occurred in a California district, and partly because memory of a previous election dispute in which he was a frustrated major player continued to haunt him. In 1984 he was the lone Republican on a three-member subcommittee investigating a close election in what came to be called Indiana's "bloody eighth district." In spite of the fact that the Indiana secretary of state certified the victory of GOP candidate Richard McIntyre over Democrat Frank McCloskey, McCloskey was seated after a protracted recount—during which subcommittee members painstakingly examined individual ballots. The decision outraged Republicans and became a rallying cry when important partisan disputes arose in ensuing years.

Consequently, when some Republicans began to lose interest in the Sanchez investigation—largely because definitive proof of fraud was hard to come by—Thomas refused to close down the inquiry (Greenblatt 1997). Even after it was reported that the Orange County district attorney would not prosecute HMN and that its leader, Nativo Lopez, had never been a target of the investigation, Thomas and a majority of the task force decided to subpoena Lopez anyway. The California Republican referred to HMN as a gang of "criminals," asserting that "this organization is not a mom-and-pop struggling local organization. For half a century, they have laundered federal funds," adding that "we are trying to find out the extent of their activity" (Van Dongen 1997c).

When Dornan's challenge was finally rejected, Thomas accepted the decision reluctantly. In fact, some Californians vowed to take retribution on their own colleagues. Orange County conservative Dana Rohrbacher said: "We placed our faith in our leaders to have the courage and energy to do what is right. It appears they did not." Rohrbacher went on to predict that future Republican candidates would pay a political price for House leaders' failure to back the Dornan challenge. He warned that "whoever comes to California, either looking for money or support, who has permitted an election to be stolen by the Democrats, is going to have trouble gaining the trust of the California Republican party" (Van Dongen 1998a).

But Dornan's own behavior probably preordained the outcome. After the House's August 1997 recess, he came to Washington to plead his cause directly. As a former congressman, he was allowed access to the House floor, a privilege granted under House rules as long as those claiming it did not have any direct personal or pecuniary interest in legislative matters then pending before the chamber. Democrats cried foul, arguing that the election dispute had not yet been resolved and that Dornan's lobbying on the House floor violated the spirit if not the letter of the rules. The California Republican denied he was using the House floor to lobby former colleagues, but critics were unconvinced and New Jersey Democrat Robert Menendez introduced legislation to prohibit all former members from lobbying on the House floor on their own behalf. Days later he was approached by Dornan on the floor and asked whether he thought the Californian was "stupid enough" to violate House rules. According to Menendez, Dornan "came after me. He verbally accosted me," uttered a profanity, and "called me anti-Catholic and a liar." He then taunted the New Jersey Democrat to take "the fight outside" by calling him a "coward" (Van Dongen 1997b).

Dornan vigorously denied this account, calling it a "foul lie," maintaining that he had told Menendez that the spin Democrats were putting on the election probe was "vile, disgusting, and anti-Christian and is itself racist." Menendez later offered a privileged resolution requiring the House sergeant at arms to bar Dornan from the floor until the House Oversight Committee completed its investigation (Van Dongen 1997b).

The next day the House, in an unprecedented action, banished Dornan from the floor by a vote of 289 to 65, with 111 Republicans, including most GOP leaders, voting "aye" (Carney 1997).

This rebuff signaled the beginning of the end for Dornan. The Oversight Committee continued its probe, but leaders of both parties were working behind the scenes to bring closure and allow Sanchez to retain her seat. Nonetheless, Dornan believed he would prevail and continued to raise funds for the special election he believed would be called after the House voted to throw out the 1996 result and declare Sanchez's seat vacant (Van Dongen 1997f). (Although the Federal Election Commission had written Dornan advising him that he could not lawfully raise funds for a 1997 special election that was not expected to take place, he continued to prepare for it.) Later, he denounced his party's leaders, asserting, "I'm as angry at my country's government as I've ever been in my life." He declared that he would challenge Sanchez in the November 1998 election, dedicating his campaign to the patron saint of Mexico, Our Lady of Guadalupe. He said he would take Sanchez to task for being "flaky" and "pro-abortion," and that he would attack her for being the poster-child for voter fraud (Van Dongen 1998c).

The unremitting assault on Sanchez by Dornan and conservative colleagues was countered at every turn by Democrats, especially Minority Leader Dick Gephardt and Menendez, with salvos from antagonists on both sides of the aisle further eroding the rapport between the two parties. When Sanchez was denied the opportunity to hold a hearing in her district, Gephardt issued a statement calling it an outrage. He added:

> The conduct of the Republican leadership . . . and the Education Committee in this matter has been vindictive and mean-spirited. . . . Although many on the other side of the aisle may like to pretend that Bob Dornan is still a Member of Congress, the reality is that Loretta Sanchez was elected and should be allowed to fulfill her responsibilities without interference. (Sheffner 1997b)

As the inquiry dragged on, Gephardt threatened to "shut the House down" by employing such dilatory tactics as demanding roll call votes on innocuous matters and offering motions to adjourn. "If they continue this immoral pursuit," he said, he would do whatever he could to end the investigation (Bradley and Van Dongen 1997a). During debate on legislative branch spending, Democrats charged Republicans with targeting Sanchez because she was Hispanic, and denounced the use of INS immigration lists to identify illegal voters as an invasion of an ethnic minority's privacy. The lone Democrat on the three-member task force, Maryland's Steny Hoyer, declared that "this is the first time in history the INS has been asked to compare the names of voters to lists. Think of the message this is sending to the Americans, Americans I stress, of Hispanic background." Republicans shot back that the Democrats were "waving the bloody shirt of ethnicity" and called them "racist" for even raising the issue (Bradley and Van Dongen 1997a).

Democrats began what Gephardt called "guerrilla warfare" in the weeks leading up to adjournment, introducing privileged resolutions calling for an immediate end to the election probe. Gephardt's motion in late October failed on a nearly party-line vote, 204–222, but that did not stop other Democrats from offering more than forty similar resolutions, which forced the Republican leadership to take the highly unusual step of changing House rules by prohibiting anyone but the majority and minority leaders from submitting privileged resolutions for the remainder of the legislative session (Bradley and Van Dongen 1997b).

In the meantime, Democratic Hispanic members met with such organizations as La Raza, the Puerto Rican Legal Defense Fund, and the Hispanic Bar Association to mobilize national support for Sanchez. Republicans with relatively large numbers of Hispanic constituents, including GOP leaders Richard Army and Tom DeLay, were put on notice that protests and press conferences would be held in their districts (Van Dongen 1997a). Sanchez sympathizers began to wear "Free Sanchez" orange ribbons, and when Republicans later decided to delegate the nuts and bolts of the recount to California secretary of state Bill Jones, Hoyer and other Democratic leaders vigorously objected (Van Dongen 1997a). In time, Democrats began to condemn the "prohibitive cost" of the investigation, which at summer's end they estimated to be $300,000 and climbing (*Los Angeles Times,* September 30, 1997). When the investigation was completed, Republicans announced that it had cost $254,000. Democrats claimed that the figure was more like $1 million. These figures do not include legal fees incurred by Sanchez and Dornan, which may have together exceeded $1 million (Van Dongen 1998b).

In the end, the task force unanimously recommended shutting down the inquiry, the Oversight Committee accepted the recommendation, 8 to 1, and the House voted 378 to 33 to reject Dornan's challenge. For most Republicans, the fourteen-month investigation produced too few possibly fraudulent votes to overcome Sanchez's 984-vote margin. The task force had identified 748 illegal votes, which its chair indicated was not enough to call for a new election, but more than enough to prove that Dornan's claim of fraud was not frivolous and that his party had not unfairly targeted Hispanics (Koszczuk 1998). The protracted character of the investigation, said Republicans, as well as its inconclusiveness (many believed more illegal voters could have been discovered), were largely due to Democratic foot-dragging and insufficient cooperation from the INS and the Justice Department (Van Dongen 1998a).

For Democrats, even the 748 figure was an exaggeration. They pointed out that the task force had produced no evidence that these voters had not been citizens at the time they cast ballots, that there was no way of knowing for whom they had voted (or that they had even made a choice for the House, as distinct from votes cast for president and other offices), and that almost 40 percent were not registered Democrats (Van Dongen 1997d, Koszczuk 1998). They also accused Republicans of trying to intimidate Hispanic voters, with Gephardt stating:

> The actions of Republicans on this issue have been shameful. [The investigation] was the largest waste of congressional time and money I have seen. . . . They impugned the integrity and standing of Loretta Sanchez's victory—and then cast aspersions about the political participation of Latinos who exercised their constitutional rights in the 1996 election. (Van Dongen 1998a)

The ferocity of the partisan struggle over Sanchez's House seat affected the relationship between CCWI Democrats and Republicans. Few references to the dispute surfaced at caucus meetings, with women in both parties inclined to avoid discussion of so fractious a topic. But Democratic women were incensed by the assault on Sanchez. They viewed the attack as sexist as well as racist. One Representative from New York remarked: "We [the CCWI] don't even call the press conferences we used to. We're all very much concerned right now with Loretta Sanchez. We see the challenge as a women's issue. Certainly had she been a man this would never have happened."

A Florida CCWI member attributed much of the divisiveness in the House to the Sanchez investigation. "There is so much anger," she said. And just as Republican women were disturbed by the silence of Democratic women after revelations of the Clinton affair with Monica Lewinsky, Democratic women were critical of Republican women's failure to support Sanchez. Said one, "It's hard for some of us to believe that Republican women won't stand up for other women in a case like this." This criticism was not entirely justified. Nine of fourteen GOP congresswomen voted against tabling the motion to deny Dornan access to the floor, and ten voted with most GOP leaders to banish him from the floor until his challenge to Sanchez was resolved.

Democratic women worked collectively as well as individually to support Sanchez's cause. Just before the August recess, more than a score spoke during Special Orders demanding that the cloud cast over her election be removed. Many later participated in a joint press conference with Senate women to denounce investigations of both the Sanchez and Landrieu elections and urged the Senate Rules Committee and the House Oversight Committee to reject claims of fraud in both disputes (Van Dongen 1997e).

As their frustration grew, Democratic women coordinated radio and newspaper interviews with media outlets in California, Florida, and Texas, defending Sanchez before heavily Hispanic audiences (*Los Angeles Times,* September 30, 1997). Some of the same women were driven to meet collectively with Newt Gingrich to request an immediate end to the probe. Although placated by a promise of greater expeditiousness, they were not encouraged by the Speaker's subsequent statement that "[t]his investigation will not end until all the facts have been uncovered and a fair, impartial review of all the evidence has taken place" (Bradley and Van Dongen 1997b). Among the Democrats introducing privileged resolutions calling a halt to the investigation, twenty-two were members of the CCWI. A Republican motion to adjourn effectively nipped them in the bud, and a subsequent rules change prohibited their reintroduction later in the session (Bradley and Van Dongen 1997b).

Barbara Kennelly was among Sanchez's most sympathetic supporters. In the process of preparing a campaign for governor, the veteran Connecticut Democrat nevertheless took Sanchez under her wing. She invited Sanchez to move into her apartment as a roommate, an invitation the embattled Californian accepted, and she was one of many who demanded that the election challenge be rejected. Kennelly declared: "Since the polls closed in November, one of our colleagues—Loretta Sanchez—has been subjected to unprecedented harassment. It's time for it to stop" (Bradley and Van Dongen 1997a). Later, she defended Sanchez against Dornan's attempts to belittle and trivialize the new member. "You don't get to Congress as a woman," Kennelly said, "unless you are successful in other areas" (*New York Times,* October 5, 1997). In the meantime, women Democrats, especially Hispanics and Californians, conducted a fundraising drive to help raise money for Sanchez's legal expenses.

The anger among Democratic congresswomen was reflected in the comments of the usually restrained Zoe Lofgren of California. She addressed the House, saying: "Mr. Speaker, I am known here in the

House as someone who is not a ranter and raver. But I find myself unable to remain silent any longer about the Sanchez race. . . . I think there is something wrong with an investigation that produces nothing, but continues in what looks to be a plan to consume the entire term of the person's office" (Van Dongen 1997e).

The pervasive bitterness unleashed by Sanchez's election can be understood as a product of the narrow majority Republicans held in the House and by partisan enmity. But it can be explained in terms of differences in gender orientations as well. California Republicans had long held a monopoly on congressional seats in Orange County. Robert Dornan had become a fixture in the forty-sixth district, territory he had easily reclaimed after he had relinquished it to run for another office in 1982. His hard-right, conservative politics were emblematic of the county delegation's ideological orientation, and when he narrowly lost in 1996, neither he nor his like-minded colleagues were prepared to accept the outcome. They had good reason to believe that some votes were cast by ineligible residents, and they were convinced that the number clearly exceeded the margin Sanchez purportedly compiled. According to a Sanchez staffer, "That a Democrat had broken the Republican hammerlock on the County was a shock. That the Democrat was Hispanic and a woman was an insult."

Aided by Californians in key committee positions, Dornan allies were able to drag out the investigation for fourteen months. They hoped the fraud would be widespread enough to force a special election. Failing that, they expected the inquiry to sow doubts about the outcome, doubts that were compelling enough to make Sanchez vulnerable in her race for reelection. They were sorely disappointed. In a 1998 rematch, Sanchez defeated Dornan by 16 percentage points.

The clashing gender orientations of the two candidates aggravated the already tense battle they were waging. The two had very different understandings about the role and responsibilities of a House member. Dornan said that Sanchez was "probably the least effective Congressman [*sic*] in the entire U.S. House of Representatives. . . . Her idea of work is to go home to read to grade-school children" (Van Dongen 1998c). That many congressional and even presidential candidates meet with school children and read to them was clearly beyond Dornan's ken. It seems fair to infer that the priorities of "B-1 Bob" resided in making military and defense policy, and in vouchsafing law and order at home and abroad. His characterization of Sanchez as principally interested in educating and nurturing children introduced a traditional gender distinction from which he believed he would profit. But by doing so, he gave voters in the forty-sixth district a choice not only between competing parties and ideologies but also between two people who had very different ideas about what constitutes legitimate public service.

Assessing the Caucus in the 105th Congress

The White House scandal and the contested elections, especially the protracted investigation of Sanchez's victory, drained some of the CCWI's productive energy. The distractions did not seriously strain relations between the cochairs, but they threatened the fragile bipartisan spirit the leaders were trying to nourish and reduced the amount of time and emotional commitment members were able to invest in the group's legislative and public relations efforts.

Even so, the CCWI's track record during the 105th Congress was not seriously affected by these events, although by most standards it was inauspicious. The caucus could point to several legislative successes, but its inability to move forward on most feminist priorities was, for some, demoralizing. In the closing days of the 105th Congress, Norton, believing women had lost the fight over insurance coverage for contraceptives, was bitterly disappointed with her group's performance. On the eve of adjournment, she said:

> Whatever we do, including the must-pass victories of the Women's Caucus, will be overwhelmed when the gavel goes down in this Congress. As delighted as I am by passage of three of our seven priorities, we of the Women's Caucus of the 105th Congress will have to answer the question: "What did you do for women in the 105th?" The answer from American women will be: Not much. (*Congressional Record*, October 14, 1998, p. H10882)

In the eyes of some, she was being too hard on herself, on her cochair, and on CCWI activists. After all, four of the caucus's seven legislative priorities had been adopted, and some high-profile measures—extending Medicaid benefits, promoting research on women's health, enforcing child support, among them—had also passed. The caucus had failed to stop the House from segregating women in military basic training, but its vehement opposition had helped spur the Senate to reject the proposal. And some members chose to emphasize structural improvements rather than legislative gains when evaluating the CCWI's performance. In an interview, Johnson remarked: "It has really been fun to see people's gratification at rebuilding [the CCWI]. Eleanor and I have really made a lot of changes and done things in a way that include people, and it is fun to see all that coming back and around."

Most important, the caucus revived a commitment to its initial strategic objectives and would begin the 106th Congress with more confidence and vitality than it began the 105th. Its membership had ballooned to fifty-six, almost four times the number who had inaugurated the caucus twenty years earlier, and virtually all congresswomen were now affiliated. Creation of teams had fostered the bipartisan spirit Norton and Johnson sought to engender, and even though many teams did not live up to expectations and some existed on paper only, a structural framework had been established to accommodate future cooperation between Democrats and Republicans.

In the meantime, Women's Policy Inc. had been given a financial shot in the arm, and although its subscriber list remained small, it was now better poised to provide research and public relations support, in short supply ever since LSOs had been eliminated. Decisions to shun such contentious issues as reproductive rights, and to concentrate on consensus building, promised to make the caucus a more credible player in House politics. Its more mainstream positions, together with its numbers and bipartisan cast, now made it more difficult for the Republican majority to write it off.

But perhaps the most promising development was the emergence of several teams led by Republicans and Democrats who also served on the standing committees whose jurisdiction embraced their teams' subject matter. Caucus priorities could now be defined by team leaders who had direct access to the committee councils in which national policy received formative consideration. The two perspectives these leaders brought to bear—that of the caucus and that of the committee—provided them with greater opportunities to discover public policy innovations likely to be acceptable to each. Of course, much depended on team leaders' endorsement of feminist goals. But even in the event of a tepid commitment, and even if teams were undependable and the system of teams was unstable, as it proved to be, Norton and Johnson had nonetheless established a blueprint to guide ever-changing cohorts of future congresswomen on how to address women's issues in ways that could make a difference. All of these developments meant that the future of the CCWI was secure, at least in the short term.

Notes

1. These proposals appear in two memos, dated September 10, 1996, and January 7, 1997, sent by Norton to Democratic congresswomen.

2. The other two, Andrea Seastrand and Enid Greene Waldholtz, were not returned to the 105th Congress. Seastrand was defeated in the 1996 election. Waldholtz declined to run again, following reports of financial improprieties in the 1994 election.

3. Only Idaho's Helen Chenoweth refused to head a team. Constance Morella and Sue Kelly agreed to lead two.

4. The goals appear in a memo Norton sent on September 10, 1996.

5. Technically, the CCWI is not permitted to hold hearings. Its leaders disguised the breach in House rules by calling their hearings "briefings."

6. Norton's remarks appear in a letter to the National Committee on Pay Equity dated August 18, 1998.

7. A description of the meeting with the Speaker appears in a memo from Johnson and Norton to CCWI members dated September 11, 1998.

7 Congresswomen and the New Millennium: The Future of the Caucus

Congressional caucuses are not immortal. Unlike congressional committees, they are easily created and regularly abandoned. They may disappear because the issues spawning them lose their salience, or because a standing committee co-opts their mission and message. Sometimes caucus members find that their group is no longer useful and they disaffiliate. And occasionally, a shift in the political and policy context out of which a caucus emerged makes it irrelevant (Hammond 1998, pp. 62–63). Among the approximately 150 caucuses operating in both the Senate and the House in 1993, ten had been disbanded by 1995. Another two dozen remained in place but were dormant (Hammond 1998, p. 21).

The Congressional Caucus for Women's Issues, which celebrated its twenty-fifth anniversary in 2002, is among the more long-lived informal groups in the House. Its robust size, its elastic agenda, its faithful membership, and its attentive constituency suggest that the organization will probably carry on for a while. But nothing is certain in these uncertain times, and the future of the caucus will depend on how well it manages a half dozen challenges. They include ensuring a reliable supply of cochairs from each party, continuing to recruit as members a critical mass of committed congresswomen from both parties, and reconfiguring an organizational structure whose value has been impaired by the caucus's increasing size and shifting legislative objectives.

The CCWI's agenda-setting process is also a matter of concern, especially in light of the new claims being made on the federal government's attention span and resources by wars and terrorism. And finally, the caucus's working relationship with the White House and with party and committee leaders in Congress will have to be addressed.

Recruiting Feminist Cochairs

The CCWI could not have lasted as long as it has if members of each party had been unable to recruit compatible cochairs committed to feminist goals. At first, cochairs were largely self-selected and served as long as they remained in the House. Elizabeth Holtzman, Margaret Heckler, Olympia Snowe, and Pat Schroeder were arguably the members most interested in sustaining the caucus and among the most willing to be the group's public voice. For each, the position presented little or no political risk. Since 1995, CCWI leaders have been limited to a single two-year term, although they may run for cochair again after at least a one-term hiatus.

Producing a cochair from each party gives the organization its credibility as a bipartisan voice for women, and therein lies an important challenge to the caucus's survival. Whereas Democrats have had no difficulty identifying would-be leaders, sometimes choosing from among several aspirants, Republicans have had to work hard to find willing colleagues. The number of Republican congresswomen has been fewer than one-half the number of Democrats in recent years, leaving the former with a correspondingly smaller pool of potential candidates from which to choose.

Moreover, ambitious GOP women who seek influence within their own party, more than Democratic women, risk alienating male colleagues who have little sympathy for feminist causes. For a Republican woman to accept the cochair position, not only must she have a more than passing interest in women's issues, even if not the passionate commitment possessed by such early leaders as Margaret Heckler and Olympia Snowe, but she must also be confident that a high-profile identification with the caucus will not damage later efforts to exercise influence within her party.

To date, able and willing Republican women have answered the call, but some did so only after lingering doubts were put to rest by GOP predecessors. Almost a year before Sue Kelly was to step down as cochair in 2000, she recruited first-term congresswoman Judy Biggert of Illinois to replace her in 2001. After the 2000 election, Biggert succeeded in persuading first-termer Shelley Moore Capito of West Virginia to become CCWI vice chair and the Illinois Republican's replacement in 2003. Capito, in turn, recruited newly elected Ginny Brown-Waite (R–Fla.) to serve as vice chair in the 108th Congress.

Some caucus-watchers argue that senior rather than junior members should assume future leadership roles, because the veterans' electoral security, their broader experience with House workways, and their memories of just how effective the caucus once was are likely to be more conducive to group maintenance. Democrat Louise Slaughter's selection as cochair in 2003 is their model. But most senior members are unwilling to take on caucus tasks because of weightier committee and party responsibilities. And, as one Republican insider put it, "Even if you work hard as a co-chair, you get little credit in your district. You get no extra staff and you get lots of hassles."

The system of making vice chairs in one Congress cochairs in the next has generally worked well. But vice chairs have typically assumed no more than nominal responsibilities, and the process has not necessarily made it easier for GOP caucus leaders to recruit successors. Texan Kay Granger served as vice chair in 1999 and 2000, with the understanding that GOP women would have to find someone else to be chair in 2001. Decisions by Capito and Brown-Waite to accept the vice chair positions in the 107th and 108th Congresses were influenced by their electoral vulnerability. Both won close contests to gain House seats and they and their mentors concluded that a CCWI leadership position and identification with selected women's issues would raise their profiles in districts previously held by Democrats. Only a sharp increase in the number of Republican congresswomen and/or the emergence of a Democratic majority in the House are likely to make selection of committed GOP cochairs less problematic. The first development would, of course, increase the size of the pool from which Republican leaders could be drawn. The second would decrease the incidence of House leadership opportunities available to Republican women and perhaps induce more of them to use the CCWI to achieve personal and political goals.

Differences in the styles of cochairs have occasionally dogged the caucus, but never for very long. Sometimes these differences strengthened the group. In the 105th Congress, for example, Nancy Johnson often pressured Republican leaders behind the scenes, complementing Eleanor Holmes Norton's public articulation of CCWI priorities. A similar dynamic emerged in 2001, when the caucus was led by a cautious, deliberate Republican, Judy Biggert, and a spontaneous, expansive Democrat, Juanita Millender-McDonald. The caucus can be well served by cochairs with ideological and stylistic differences as long as they exhibit mutual respect.

Leadership recruitment may never have become a concern had the caucus not begun the practice of mandatory cochair rotation. The strongest advocate for change, California's Maxine Waters, believed that diversity among Democratic women was not being sufficiently reflected by cochairs whose tenure was indeterminate. Term limits have since illuminated that diversity, and the biannual change has allowed more women to hone and display their leadership skills, while validating perspectives and ideas that had formerly been given less emphasis. African American women Eleanor Holmes Norton and Juanita Millender-McDonald rotated to the Democratic cochair position in 1997 and 2001, respectively, and Hilda Solis, Democratic vice chair in the 108th Congress, is in place to become the first Hispanic cochair in 2005. On the other hand, with each new Congress, discontinuities in leadership and staff delay, often for many months, emergence of the CCWI as an effective presence on Capitol Hill. Membership mobilization and agenda-setting suffer as inexperienced cochairs and their staffs try to get up to speed. Consequently, reliable, expeditious recruitment of committed leaders is essential if the caucus is to be sustained.

Attracting Committed Congresswomen

Persuading a critical mass of women in both parties to join the CCWI has never been difficult. Even when six first-term Republicans declined to affiliate in 1995, two-thirds of their GOP colleagues and virtually all Democrats were members. Apparently most congresswomen have believed it is in their interest to join the group, and those who thought otherwise were pressured by the cochairs to change their minds. Between 1995 and 2002, Connie Morella, Nancy Johnson, Sue Kelly, and Judy Biggert worked assiduously to corral Republicans, while Nita Lowey, Eleanor Holmes Norton, Carolyn Maloney, and Juanita Millender-McDonald had an easier time recruiting all Democrats. In 2003, Slaughter and Capito as cochairs chose to assume that all congresswomen were CCWI members unless they explicitly opted out. JoAnn Davis (R–Va.) and Anne Northup did so. Some congresswomen have been tentative about their membership, acknowledging affiliation under some circumstances and keeping their distance from the caucus when it seemed prudent. But the staffs of women who are not members are regularly kept up-to-date on caucus activities.

The blurring of membership boundaries is unlikely to be a positive development for the CCWI. If affiliation is devalued by congresswomen, by other Representatives, and by advocacy groups, the reputation and integrity of the group are threatened, as is the relevance of its message. On the other hand, a more fundamental challenge confronting the caucus is not simply to attract women, but to encourage members to contribute actively to their group's collective mission. This means that CCWI affiliation must continue to satisfy members' political, professional, and personal needs. It also means that congresswomen must continue to believe that circumstances impinge on the lives of women differently than they affect men, that they do so in a way that puts women at a disadvantage, and that a women's caucus in the House is a powerful instrument for invoking the authority of the federal government to level the playing field.

The cochairs have their work cut out for them. Republican leaders must persuade colleagues who tend to be uncomfortable with many caucus initiatives that an investment of time and energy is personally and politically worthwhile. These leaders cannot readily count on their followers' sense of sororital solidarity. As one senior GOP staffer remarked: "Republican women do not see the Caucus as having as much value as Democratic women. . . . Republican women are not much interested in the sisterhood aspect of the Caucus."

At the same time, Democratic women, although more favorably disposed to the idea of a women's caucus, are impatient with the progress the CCWI has made in recent years, and critical of the policy compromises Democratic cochairs have had to make to retain the organization's bipartisan character. Their frustrations were especially apparent after their party lost its majority in the House in the 1994 election. Since then, several have considered the possibility of starting a Democratic women's caucus, one that would showcase mostly liberal policies and allow them to promote abortion rights. Toward this end, a score or more of Democratic women have convened unofficially about once every two months (Republican women have found no reason to meet even irregularly).

Caucus unity and bipartisanship have been threatened further by the growing disaffection of black congresswomen with a White House whose Republican occupant, they believe, won the state of Florida in the 2000 election only after the votes of tens of thousands of African Americans were wrongfully invalidated. California's Maxine Waters said she was personally offended by Speaker Hastert's remarks in January 2001 urging members of both parties to "get over" the bitterness of the presidential election dispute. She responded: "This attempt to send a message that despite what happened that everyone will lock arms and have a love fest, it's not real. Some of us will not 'get over it'" (Foerstel and Ota 2001).

If the caucus is to survive in anything like its traditional form, Democrats will have to continue to believe that bipartisan pursuit of a limited set of feminist goals is preferable to disaffiliation or fomenting a schism. And rank-and-file Republican women will have to continue to believe that there are at least some feminist issues—women's health, violence against women, women-led business enterprises—that make joining the caucus worthwhile. In the spring of 2003, these thresholds were met when women in both parties found common cause in persuading the Defense Department and private contractors that women entrepreneurs should receive a larger share of federal contracts—in keeping with a 1994 statute that authorized federal agencies to earmark at least 5 percent of their contracts for women-owned businesses. On this affirmative action issue, at least, CCWI-led negotiations held out the potential for a bipartisan success story.

Changing the Caucus's Structure

Assuming the CCWI continues to recruit willing leaders and followers in both parties, its next challenge is to adapt its structure to its increased size and shifting agenda. Whereas there was once a time when the cochairs, assisted by a permanent staff, could use Executive Committee meetings as an instrument for building consensus, this is no longer the case. The permanent staff is gone, and the number of meetings, having fallen to fewer than a dozen in recent Congresses, has plummeted to zero in 2003. Declining attendance and the difficulties of finding a consensus on which issues to address, drove cochairs to conclude that most plenary CCWI meetings were a waste of time. In 2001, for example, it met on only three occasions, the last of which featured a discursive discussion of the role the caucus could play in a Congress struggling to find responses to the September 11 terrorist attack.

But even if the caucus resumes regularly scheduled meetings and even if attendance becomes more robust, it is doubtful that, in the absence of extensive, preliminary staff work, this highly diverse group of threescore women, each with her own political and personal priorities, will be able to rally around a set of mutually acceptable feminist objectives. The cochairs meet often, as do their staffs, but a membershipwide Executive Committee is too large and too diverse to be an efficient vehicle for defining and driving the caucus agenda. Its use as a forum for invited administration policymakers has also atrophied. Invitations to these officials dropped sharply during the tail end of the Clinton administration and fell into virtual disuse after George W. Bush took office.

Decline in the Executive Committee's efficacy was anticipated as early as 1993, when twenty-two first-term women joined the group and increased its membership to forty-eight. Realizing that this was too large a number to deal efficiently with women's concerns, the caucus created five task forces, each having jurisdiction over specified subject matter—a rudimentary division of labor, but not unlike Congress's committee system. Task force members were expected to generate ideas for legislation and public relations events, submit proposals to the cochairs and, through them, to the full caucus, and do whatever was needed to promote their initiatives.

In 1995, Nancy Johnson and Eleanor Holmes Norton as cochairs dropped the "task force" designation and established "teams" instead. Their immediate successors retained this format, even though the number of such units declined. The division and specialization of labor embodied by the "team" framework was expected to give the CCWI the structural arrangement needed to organize the energies of a large number of overburdened women—women who were forced to give only limited attention to the caucus, but whose collective efforts were expected to increase the likelihood of achieving a wide range of feminist objectives.

Between 1999 and 2002, most of the teams existed on paper only. Caucus cochairs prodded team leaders to press their legislative priorities, but no team meetings were ever convened, and coleader contacts to devise an agenda and plan strategy were infrequent. Some meetings were held at the staff level, but few ideas emerging from them got much further. With some exceptions, notably the team on women and business in 1999–2000, few teams held briefings for advocacy groups, or promoted policies beyond announcing support for them.

Staff who worked for CCWI cochairs tried to fill the vacuum left by team inaction, but they were already overworked and they lacked the authority of the congresswomen on whose behalf they were prepared to act. When attending the few Executive Committee meetings called by the cochairs, they had the daunting task of trying to distill member preferences from the jumble of overlapping, sometimes contradictory proposals offered by congresswomen, some of whom came to the meeting late, left early, and were indisposed to follow an agenda. In 2001 both cochairs lost their principal caucus aides, and it took months for replacements to settle in. Weekly meetings with representatives of members' office staffs were of little use. Attendance rarely rose beyond twenty-five participants. Almost all who came were from Democratic offices, and most were junior staff or interns. More helpful were e-mail messages alerting congresswomen to pending events and keeping their staffs informed about CCWI priorities.

In the end, apart from the issues promoted by the cochairs themselves, few team-generated initiatives found their way onto the legislative agenda. As a result, House attention given to most women's issues could not be attributed principally to the efforts of the caucus's subunits. One CCWI insider remarked in the spring of 2002: "The teams do not work well. They virtually do not exist. They have done nothing. There has been no progress on any issue other than the ones advanced by the co-chairs." It is no wonder then, that Capito and Slaughter as cochairs decided not to establish teams when they took over in 2003. Even the once weekly meetings of staff have become bimonthly events.

Failure to breathe life into a team or task force system could undermine the caucus's effectiveness. It has grown too large to operate efficiently without a structure facilitating division of responsibilities among its members. And most teams have not worked well because their members and even the coleaders have not had the time and the incentive to make them work well. Hope for their revitalization may rest on selection of coleaders for each team who serve on a House standing committee having jurisdiction over subject matter similar to that of the team they lead. The role played in 1997–1998 by the coleaders of the team on women and the military, Jane Harmon and Tillie Fowler, could be a model. Both women served on the House Armed Services Committee. They were familiar with feminist issues arising out of national defense policies, they were trusted by committee members and caucus colleagues alike, and they had access to the decisionmaking councils addressing these policies.

Although Harman and Fowler lost the battle in the House to preserve integration of men and women in military basic-training units, they helped win the war when a Senate-House conference committee later decided that resegregation was not the way to address sexual harassment of female recruits by male drill instructors. Fowler and Harman were doing the work of the caucus and their committee simultaneously, economizing on their available resources. Now that no House committee is without at least one woman in each party, a set of teams roughly paralleling selected standing committees could help restore and energize something like the team system.

Finally, the CCWI's mission might be better served if the staff of its vice chairs were integrated earlier and more fully into group activities than has been the case since vice chair positions were created. Much of caucus life is affected by cochair aides. Turnover of cochairs every two years has meant that the staff of their replacements have had to negotiate a steep learning curve to minister effectively to the group's needs.

By allowing them to begin their apprenticeship two years earlier, when the members for whom they work are vice chairs, the discontinuity in caucus leadership mandated by term limits could be mitigated— although high turnover of House staff may limit the usefulness of this proposal.

Finding a Usable Agenda

Congressional caucuses come into being when concerns believed by their putative members to be important are receiving insufficient attention. These groups then try to influence the national agenda by increasing the saliency of their issues and by lifting these issues to the level of committee consideration and policy formulation (Hammond 1998, p. 81). Toward that end, they also set out to educate colleagues and the public, reflect and reinforce the values of friendly advocacy groups, and serve as a catalyst to mobilize the energies of other congressional forces.

The CCWI has generally followed this developmental pattern and it, too, has sought above all to infuse the legislative agenda with its own, feminist objectives. To be sure, it has been an active educational, representative, and catalytic agency as well, but all of these activities have been employed in the service of its agenda-setting mission. When it uses Special Orders to highlight the incidence of breast cancer, or when it cosponsors a briefing on retirement security for women led by Women's Policy Inc. (WPI), or when its members testify before an Appropriations subcommittee to increase funding for the Women, Infants, and Children Act, the caucus is employing time-honored congressional rituals designed to educate, represent, and catalyze. But its primary goal is to realize the objectives on its legislative agenda.

Given this overriding mission, it is incumbent on the caucus to streamline its agenda-setting process at the start of each Congress, a challenge as significant as any it will encounter in the coming years. Loss of a permanent staff and rotation of cochairs every two years since 1995 have made formulating an agenda problematic. Priorities of each set of new cochairs differ from those of their predecessors, and their staffs must invest scarce resources redundantly while determining which objectives of previous caucuses are viable. The increasing size and diversity of the CCWI make the search for a consensus that much more complex with each new Congress.

Descriptions of agenda-setting CCWI meetings held early in the 106th Congress illustrate the difficulties the caucus has faced when determining just which causes to adopt. One congressional aide observed: "We tried to set up an agenda at the first meeting, but it was a free for all. We tried to get the members to agree on a list of top ten issues but it was like pulling teeth and the meeting was a disaster. And some congresswomen had unkind words for one another." A staff member placed some of the blame on what she called the "floating attendance": "Two members would arrive late at the same time that three left. One more would come and two would leave. When the meeting was over, it was not clear what, if anything had been agreed on." In time, the task of determining the caucus agenda for the 106th Congress was left to the staff, who had to "figure out what had taken place at that first meeting." But they knew that whatever legislative priorities they settled upon, there would be some caucus members (especially those who did not attend the meeting or who had left early) who would complain that they had not been fully consulted.

Delay in defining the agenda, along with its uncertain support and its questionable provenance, has limited the caucus's effectiveness. One longtime observer of the caucus said in an interview: "Women have come such a long way in the last 25 years. But the incremental gains we have made during the last five years seem insignificant compared with gains made before 1995. The comparison makes it seem as if the Caucus is not doing nearly as much as it could be doing." And a top staff member of a former cochair remarked: "We have done some good things but I sometimes wonder if the return had been great enough to justify all the energy we poured into the Caucus. Legislative achievements have been skimpy. The Caucus claims credit for passing women-friendly bills that would have passed anyway."

Caucus leaders often have a better sense of which issues they may not address than they do about which initiatives to undertake. What they may not do is pursue feminist goals that could fracture the often fragile bipartisan coalition that helps define the CCWI. This means that proposals touching on reproductive rights, even if only tangentially, would almost certainly be denied support by either the Republican or the Democratic cochair, or both. Other measures likely to receive the same treatment are proposals to spend truly large amounts of money to achieve feminist objectives or to cut large sums from women-friendly programs already in place. Accordingly, the caucus must continue to encourage its members to champion their own, individual policy goals without implicating the group as a whole, while at the same time relying on its arm's-length relationship with WPI, the CCWI's institutional memory. WPI, led by Cindy Hall, formerly an aide to Connie Morella, supervises a small professional staff who are able to identify approaches to issues that resonate with the feminist community and, at least potentially, with the House of Representatives. In these ways, once controversial feminist proposals may become a part of the discourse that precedes and sometimes triggers congressional action.

Adjusting to Competing Claims on National Resources

The CCWI's effectiveness depends on more than overcoming obstacles that have traditionally stalled feminist goals. The search for a usable agenda has been complicated by profoundly important developments occurring at the start of the twenty-first century. Decline in the state of the economy, loss of confidence in the business community, and the aggravation of seemingly intractable international conflicts have fundamentally changed the environment in which the caucus is accustomed to pursuing its goals.

Congresswomen have been able to hold their own in times of peace, prosperity, and trust in the capitalist system. In the 1990s the United States was unencumbered by Cold War threats, while at the same time enjoying the longest uninterrupted period of economic growth in the country's history. Not coincidently, the CCWI was able during this time to claim significant legislative successes in the fields of education, health, spousal and sexual abuse, military service, employment and business opportunities, and family planning. These advances occurred because lawmakers were prepared to approve new domestic programs, create agencies to administer them, appropriate tens of millions of dollars to fund them, and encourage (or coerce) state and local governments to do the same. The CCWI, much like other congressional caucuses, thrives when government distributes resources to underwrite its agenda.

In the years since 2001, however, the economy has faltered, the budget surplus has evaporated, corporate managers have been found to have violated the public trust, and a pervasive campaign against terror has been launched. These developments have changed the political and policy context within which Congress and its caucuses must operate, and lawmakers have had to alter the frame of reference within which they define and respond to national imperatives. As a result, the CCWI can no longer assume that feminist initiatives considered viable in the past will be given sympathetic treatment in the future. Its most daunting challenge may well be to couch its agenda items in language that squares with legislative initiatives to improve domestic security, restore economic confidence, and foster international tranquillity. Even if it is able to adapt well to a changing political context, the caucus may have to be satisfied with progress at the margins for the foreseeable future.

The wars in Afghanistan and Iraq may also have the effect of inhibiting growth in the number of women elected to the House. Wars produce military veterans who are overwhelmingly male, and who go on to capitalize politically on the sacrifices they made while serving their country. Disproportionately large numbers of men who served in Congress after the Civil War, World War I, and World War II were veterans, and the Vietnam War produced its share of congressmen as well. Inasmuch as the vast majority of women seeking national office will be unable to speak of military experience (and the attendant willingness to risk life and limb) among the qualities they offer to voters, they are likely to be at a disadvantage. As a consequence, for a time the caucus may have to pursue its objectives with modest (or no) increases in the size of its membership.

Connecting with the President and Congressional Leaders

Just how much progress the CCWI is likely to make depends in some measure on the rapport it establishes with political leaders in Washington. The group achieved its most significant legislative successes when it had ready access to the White House and to congressional leaders. Its influence was palpable when President Clinton and his staff listened to caucus concerns, and when Speakers Thomas "Tip" O'Neill and Tom Foley were themselves auxiliary CCWI members. Consequently, the group's future will turn on how well its members, particularly its co-chairs, can exert influence in high places.

During the Clinton years, congresswomen were regularly invited to the White House, and their staffs were continually in touch with the White House Office on Women's Initiatives and Outreach. Caucus policy priorities were received sympathetically because Clinton was arguably the most feminist of presidents and because he could not have been elected without the double-digit advantage he enjoyed among women voters. Accordingly, he established cordial, empathetic, and productive relations with most congresswomen. The president's sexual improprieties, together with the impeachment that followed, strained the relationship, although White House and cabinet aides continued to lean over backward to support the caucus, notably while helping to renew the Violence Against Women Act in 2000.

Caucus relations with the George W. Bush White House have been distant. The president has not met with the group as of this writing, and one of his first acts was to eliminate the Office on Women's Initiatives and Outreach. The large number of influential women in the White House, the president's staff argued, made the office unnecessary. President Bush also considered eliminating the Defense Advisory Committee on Women in the Services (DACOWITS), ten regional offices of the Labor Department's Women's Bureau, the Department of Veteran Affairs' Advisory Committee on Women Veterans, among other women-centered administrative agencies. Vacancies on these panels remained unfilled well into 2002, and some scheduled meetings were canceled. A former military director of DACOWITS, Barbara Brehm, observed that "the failure to continue such advisory groups showed a significant lack of interest in addressing women's issues" (*New York Times,* December 19, 2001). Most of these offices were retained, however, in part because of pressure brought to bear by women veterans, other women's advocacy groups, and CCWI members.

Although CCWI members have been summoned to the Bush White House several times, they came not to share their policy concerns with presidential aides but to serve as a conspicuous audience for orchestrated events to promote administration policy. They attended a briefing by the president's Commission to Strengthen Social Security, listening to former Senator Daniel Patrick Moynihan and others announce recommendations for change—including partial privatization of the program. They were invited to the White House and the Pentagon as well, to be briefed by Secretary of State Colin Powell and Defense Department officials on the progress of the war in Afghanistan. Later, the cochairs stood behind the president when he signed the Afghan Women and Children Relief Act. Much of the impetus to pass the bill came from the White House, however. The president's staff had asked Representative Deborah Pryce and Senator Kay Bailey Hutchison to introduce the measure, assuring Speaker Hastert and the cochairs that, if it passed, the president would readily sign it.

In the meantime, the State Department asked such feminist groups as the Feminist Majority to address the plight of Taliban women. Some observers saw the outreach as a way for the president to improve his standing among women voters (*New York Times,* November 19, 2001), but vice presidential aide Mary Matalin insisted that the campaign to highlight Taliban oppression of women was "a justice issue, not a women's issue" (*Newsweek,* November 26, 2001). By framing the issue in these terms, Matalin put the CCWI on notice that it had a long way to go before it could induce the White House to pay attention to its feminist priorities.

In the House of Representatives, the CCWI's principal challenge is to persuade leaders, especially majority party leaders, that the group warrants inclusion in the coalitions they build. The CCWI has to make clear that although it has an agenda of its own, it is not an incipient threat to those who run the House, and its members are prepared to work with party leaders when they can. At the same time, caucus cochairs should expect to be consulted and insist that its legislative initiatives be given a hearing.

The strength of this reciprocal relationship has varied over the years, but it has never been fatally impaired. Democratic leaders have generally been more aware of the caucus's presence than Republican leaders, but even GOP Speakers Newt Gingrich and Dennis Hastert listened to CCWI voices—Gingrich by relying primarily on Republican congresswomen, Hastert by scheduling meetings with the full membership and by conferring from time to time with Republican cochairs Sue Kelly and Judy Biggert.[1] That Biggert represents a district abutting Hastert's in Illinois probably increased the influence they were able to exert on one another. The Speaker has not met with the caucus in the 108th Congress, but he confers with Capito from time to time and has visited her district for a fundraiser.

The fine line Republican women must walk when trying to advance the CCWI's agenda while at the same time keeping party leaders happy was dramatized in 2003 when officials at the Department of Education, at the urging of college athletic directors, decided to reconsider the way Title IX was being implemented. Critics claimed that interpretations of guidelines designed to end discrimination based on sex in college athletics had had the effect of forcing colleges to eliminate such low-profile sports as wrestling and gymnastics.

The Republican House leadership and the administration generally supported reconsideration of the criteria Title IX mandated for determining when a school is in compliance. But the CCWI cochairs, along with most congresswomen, declared that no change was needed. Louise Slaughter introduced a House resolution to block guideline changes, but discovered that almost all GOP women would not cosponsor the measure or publicly declare their support for it, even though they felt as strongly about the issue as she did (Nancy Johnson was a prominent exception and signed on as a cosponsor). Some stayed on the sidelines because they did not want to offend Speaker Hastert, a onetime wrestling coach and a proponent of change. Others, including a former

CCWI cochair, worked behind the scenes, making their views known privately to combatants on both sides.

John Boehner, chair of the Education and Workforce Committee, refused to hold hearings on the Slaughter resolution, and the House never had a chance to act on it. But neither did it have the opportunity to change Title IX, not least because of the public outrage of Democratic women and the adamancy of Republican women who quietly cheered on their caucus colleagues. Both groups helped mobilize the lobbying efforts of a vast array of interest groups representing women and girls, and they arranged for the appearance on the Hill of celebrated women athletes, soccer star Mia Hamm among them, who urged Congress to leave Title IX alone. In this way, most Republican CCWI members realized personal and political objectives without publicly embarrassing their party leaders.

In the 1980s and 1990s, House leaders saw fit to institutionalize their relationship with the caucus by helping to elevate congresswomen to leadership positions, and subsequently relying upon them for advice on women's issues. Speaker O'Neill pointedly tapped at least one CCWI member to fill an at-large position on the Democratic Steering and Policy Committee. After her election as vice chair of the Democratic Caucus, Barbara Kennelly was regularly consulted by Speaker Foley and other party leaders. She was frequently asked, "Does the Caucus have a position on this bill?"

Speaker Gingrich encouraged the successful candidacies of Jennifer Dunn, Deborah Pryce, and Tillie Fowler for Republican leadership posts, and after Democrat Rosa DeLauro lost her battle for Democratic Caucus vice chair in 1998, Minority Leader Gephardt created a new party post, "assistant to the leader," and installed DeLauro as its first occupant. He also established a five-member Leadership Council, to consist of representatives of the CCWI, the Congressional Black and Hispanic Caucuses, and two moderate Democratic congressional membership organizations to meet with him each week on pending party and policy matters (*Roll Call*, January 7, 1999).

The beginning of the twenty-first century has witnessed even more impressive achievements for congresswomen. Two Republican women, Deborah Pryce and Barbara Cubin, were elected vice chair and secretary, respectively, of their party's conference. Pryce was chosen chair of the Republican Conference in the 108th Congress. In the meantime, Democrat Nita Lowey headed her party's campaign committee, a responsibility whose importance is difficult to overestimate given the narrow margin separating the parties and the heated election contests that biannually determine House control. But by far the greatest accomplishment recorded by a CCWI member was Nancy Pelosi's election as Democratic whip in 2002 and as leader of the minority party the next year.

At the same time, CCWI members have risen to key committee positions, with seven of the twenty-one Republicans chairing and eighteen of the thirty-eight Democrats serving as ranking members of subcommittees in the 108th Congress. Women's progress may best be illustrated by comparing the current proportion of women assigned to four highly coveted House committees with the share of seats women held on these panels twenty years earlier. In 1981, no woman served on the Ways and Means Committee; in 2003, three congresswomen served on that panel, constituting 7 percent of the committee. Women's composition on the Appropriations Committee has risen from 4 percent to 14 percent, on the Rules Committee from 6 percent to 23 percent, and on the Energy and Commerce Committee from 5 percent to 16 percent.

All of these developments suggest that the CCWI's rapport with influential House members is bound to improve, inasmuch as caucus activists and House leaders are, in increasing numbers, becoming one and the same. There have been few more committed caucus members than Lowey and Pelosi, for example, and it is hard to imagine that they checked their feminist orientations at the door when they entered the leadership inner sanctum. (The first public speech delivered by Pelosi after she became Democratic whip was before the National Abortion and Reproductive Action League at its annual *Roe v. Wade* dinner on the anniversary of that court decision [Foerstel 2002].) As a result, feminist priorities not yet in the mainstream, along with those that have already gained widespread acceptance, may yet become a part of the country's received wisdom. Just as economic equity, educational equality, family and medical leave, and improved health and retirement benefits for women were moved by congresswomen from the unthinkable to the plausible, proposals to provide more government-supported child care, to fund federal anti-rape programs, to help shatter the "glass ceiling," and to pay wages to mothers and fathers on family and medical leave could one day move from the periphery to center stage.

In short, the growing number of women elected to the House, their increasing seniority (Gertzog 2002, p. 111), and their selection for key party and committee positions will almost certainly help validate an expanded feminist agenda—even in the face of new and important national priorities. According to Congresswoman Maxine Waters, the face of women's issues continues to evolve: "I really do believe that women's issues enjoy a better focus today than they have in the past and this will continue." D.C. delegate Eleanor Holmes Norton concurs, observing that "there is no question there has been an exponential rise in the focus on women's issues" as more women have been elected. "The issues become more irresistible the more of us there are" (*The Hill*, April 15, 1998). As a consequence, "the women's point of view" has come to permeate the halls of Congress.

But this doesn't mean that the CCWI as an informal House group will benefit from these developments. It may, in time, atrophy, a victim partly of its own success as well as that of its members. The CCWI was created to bring more attention to the inequities women experience because of their gender, and to use its members' collective energies to persuade the federal government to remedy this condition. At the time, the group was too small to serve as an effective voting block, and none of its members occupied influential party or committee positions. As a result, congresswomen were forced to rely on "clueless," often unsympathetic male colleagues to realize their objectives.

Progress was agonizingly slow, but palpable all the same, and beginning in the 1990s a rush of successes made the effort seem worthwhile. Owing in part to elimination of legislative service organizations, the diminution of CCWI resources, less sympathetic House leaders, and later, economic decline and a campaign against terror, policy triumphs since 1995 have been more limited. Nonetheless, the beginning of the twenty-first century finds a nearly sixty-member CCWI that need no longer rely quite as much on the goodwill of male colleagues who are often otherwise engaged. Congresswomen are a far more formidable voting block than they were in 1977, they tend to vote the same way on selected equity and women's health issues, they share the House with many male colleagues who are positively oriented toward feminist concerns, and they can claim credit for scores of legislative achievements. Moreover, issues that at one time did not seem to have important implications for women are currently understood within a feminist perspective.

These developments, together with the rise of CCWI members to positions of power in the House, mean that the conditions that gave rise to the group's creation are not nearly as compelling today as they were in the 1970s. A larger percentage of congresswomen than was once the case find that they need not be committed CCWI members to achieve their feminist goals, while more senior congresswomen are unable to be active in the caucus because they have taken on key leadership and committee responsibilities. Consequently, one of the challenges the caucus must address is how to retain its identity, if not its integrity, in the face of a less committed membership, a record of accomplishments that has diminished its raison d'être, the rise to power of many of its members, and the increasing number of congressmen whose feminist perspective needs relatively little tweaking. It seems ironic that despite the increase in the number of women in the House, their rise to more powerful positions, the realization of some feminist goals, and a House environment generally more receptive to CCWI priorities, the role of the Congressional Caucus for Women's Issues as an informal House group has been diluted.

That role may continue to ebb, and when congresswomen make up 40 or 50 percent of the House membership, as they almost certainly will before the end of the twenty-first century, the need for a women's caucus may be just as compelling as the need for a men's caucus.

Note

1. Leaders' meetings with the CCWI have not always turned out as well as cochairs had anticipated. In the 106th Congress, Hastert's appearance before the caucus occurred while roll call votes were being cast on the floor, and few congresswomen were present. A larger turnout greeted Minority Leader Richard Gephardt, but only two Republican congresswomen attended.

List of Interviewees

Congresswomen

Helen D. Bentley
Corrine Brown
Leslie Byrne
Maria Cantwell
Helen Chenoweth
Eva Clayton
Barbara-Rose Collins
Cardiss Collins
Pat Danner
Rosa DeLauro
Jennifer Dunn
Karen English
Anna Eshoo
Tillie Fowler

Elizabeth Furse
Eddie Bernice Johnson
Nancy Johnson
Marcy Kaptur
Sue Kelly
Barbara Kennelly
Marilyn Lloyd
Nita Lowey
Carolyn Maloney
Marjorie Margolies-Mezvinsky
Cynthia McKinney
Jan Meyers
Patsy Mink
Susan Molinari

Constance Morella
Eleanor Holmes Norton
Lynn Rivers
Ileana Ros-Lehtinen
Marge Roukema
Lucille Roybal-Allard
Pat Schroeder
Karen Shepherd
Louise Slaughter
Olympia Snowe
Karen Thurman
Jolene Unsoeld
Barbara Vucanovich
Lynn Woolsey

Congressional Staff

Thomas Bantle
Ross Brown
Andrea Camp
Lillie Coney
Cynthia Dailard
Val Dolcini
Laura Efurd

Cynthia Hall
Kathleen Havey
Gretchen Hitchner
Kirra Jarrett
Roberta Jeanquart
James John
Maryanne Leary

Peter Muller
Libby Mullin
Jennifer Parzmark
Kathryn Pearson
Cindy Pellegrini
Craig Powers
Erin Prangley

Genet Garamendi

Michael Gerber

Don Green

Nicholas Gwynn

Kira Haas

Sharon Levin

Jason Mahler

Terri McCullough

Carole McGeehan

Lynsey Morris

Gail Ravnitzky

Krista Sheets

Conwell Smith

Howard Wolfson

Bibliography

Angle, Martha. 1994. "Women and Minorities Enjoy a Power Surge." *Congressional Quarterly Weekly Report,* May 21.

Avid, Rachel, Dena Levy, and Charles Tien. 1997. "Why Differences Matter: The Impact of Women in Congress." Paper delivered at the ninety-third annual meeting of the American Political Science Association, Washington, D.C., August 28–31.

Bader, James. 1996. *Taking the Initiative: Leadership Agendas in Congress and the Contract with America.* Washington, D.C.: Georgetown University Press.

Barnett, Timothy J. 1999. *Legislative Learning: The 104th Republican Freshmen in the House.* New York: Garland.

Bradley, Jennifer. 1997. "Suffragist Statue Finally Heading to New Home in Capitol Rotunda." *Roll Call,* January 30.

Bradley, Jennifer, and Rachel Van Dongen. 1997a. "Democrats Blast GOP for Probe of Sanchez." *Roll Call,* July 28.

———. 1997b. "House Shuts Down Effort to Shut Down Floor over California Probe." *Roll Call,* November 10.

Burger, Timothy J. 1993. "Republicans Urged to Get Out of DSG." *Roll Call,* December 9.

Carney, Don. 1997. "Dornan Barred From Floor After Verbal Altercation." *Congressional Quarterly Weekly Report,* September 20.

Cassata, Donna. 1997. "Landrieu Election Probe Yields Little Besides Partisan Animosity." *Congressional Quarterly Weekly Report,* September 27.

Chappie, Damon. 1996. "Race for Frosh Presidency Reflects Division in Class." *Roll Call,* February 1.

Clemmitt, Marcia, Lesley Primmer, and Marjorie Sims. 1996. *The Record: Gains and Losses for Women and Families in the 104th Congress (1995–1996).* Washington, D.C.: Women's Policy Inc.

Contiguglia, Francesca, and Jim VandeHei. 1998. "GOP Women Urge 'Democratic Sisters' to Stop Ducking for Cover on Clinton." *Roll Call,* March 19.

Conway, Kevin J., and Christine DeGregorio. 1998. "Republican Newcomers to the U.S. House of Representatives: A Resource to Party Leaders?" Paper delivered at the ninety-fourth annual meeting of the American Political Science Association, Boston, September 3–6.

Cook, Charles E. 1996. "Lack of Leadership, Followership Produces House GOP Paralysis." *Roll Call,* March 11.

———. 1997. "After Countless Claims, Report Due Soon in Contested La. Seat." *Roll Call,* March 24.

Congressional Caucus for Women's Issues. 1983–1994. *Update on Women and Family Issues in Congress.*

Congressional Record. 1977–2002. Washington, D.C.: U.S. Government Printing Office.

Curren, Tim. 1995. "97 Percent Solution: GOP Frosh Stay with the Program." *Roll Call,* June 5.

Dodson, Debra. 1998. "Speaking for Women? Gendered Voices in the Debate: The Partial Birth Abortion Act of 1995." Paper delivered at the annual meeting of the Midwest Political Science Association, Chicago, April 23–26.

Doherty, Carroll J. 1998. "Riding the Omnibus Off into the Sunset." *Congressional Quarterly Weekly Report,* October 17.

Doherty, Carroll J., and Jeffrey L. Katz. 1998. "Firebrand GOP Class of '94 Warms to Life on the Inside." *Congressional Quarterly Weekly Report,* January 24.

Donovan, Beth. 1992. "Freshmen Throw Weight Around, Make Their Parties Listen." *Congressional Quarterly Weekly Report,* December 12.

———. 1994. "Freshmen Toed Party Line but Helped Cut Spending." With Thomas H. Moore. *Congressional Quarterly Weekly Report,* January 15.

Drew, Elizabeth. 1996. *Showdown: The Struggle Between the Gingrich Congress and the Clinton White House.* New York: Simon and Schuster.

Duncan, Phil. 1992. "Quietly Assertive Freshmen Arrive for Orientation." *Congressional Quarterly Weekly Report,* December 5.

Eilperin, Juliet. 1997a. "Gingrich Meets with Black Caucus, Says He'll Consider Reviving LSOs." *Roll Call*, March 24.

———. 1997b. "'It Seemed Like a Little Thing to Ask': Seventy-six Years Later, Women Celebrate Move Upstairs of Suffragists Statue." *Roll Call*, June 30.

———. 1998. "Sanchez Wins, Fight Still Rages." *Roll Call*, February 19.

Fenno, Richard F., Jr. 1997. *Learning to Govern: An Institutional View of the 104th Congress.* Washington, D.C.: Brookings Institution.

Ferraro, Geraldine A. 1985. *Ferraro: My Story.* With Linda Bird Franke. New York: Bantam Books.

Foerstel, Karen. 1994. "Women Democrats Won't Sign Protest Letter to Stark." *Roll Call*, March 21.

———. 2002. "Pelosi Plans Quiet Move to History-Making Post." *Congressional Quarterly Weekly Report*, January 12.

Foerstel, Karen, and Alan K. Ota. 2001. "Early Grief for GOP Leaders in New Committee Rules." *Congressional Quarterly Weekly Report*, January 6.

Gertzog, Irwin N. 1995. *Congressional Women: Their Recruitment, Integration, and Behavior.* 2nd ed., revised and updated. Westport, Conn.: Praeger.

———. 2002. "Widows, Elites, and Strategic Politicians: Women's Pathways to the U.S. House of Representatives." In Cindy Simon Rosenthal, ed., *Women Transforming Congress.* Norman: University of Oklahoma Press.

Glasser, Susan B. 1993. "Women's Caucus Is Now Pro-Choice." *Roll Call*, January 14.

Greenblatt, Alan. 1997. "Dornan Election Challenge Drags On." *Congressional Quarterly Weekly Report*, September 27.

Gruenwald, Juliana. 1998a. "House Members Shoot Holes in Treasury-Postal Bill." *Congressional Quarterly Weekly Report*, July 18.

———. 1998b. "Senate Passes Treasury-Postal Bill After GOP Postpones Debate on Term Limits." *Congressional Quarterly Weekly Report*, September 5.

———. 1998c. "Treasury-Postal Bill Stalls Even After Second Conference Yanks Disputed Provision." *Congressional Quarterly Weekly Report*, October 10.

Hammond, Susan Webb. 1998. *Congressional Caucuses in National Policymaking.* Baltimore: Johns Hopkins University Press.

Jacoby, Mary. 1993a. "Energy Institute Illustrates Tricky Link Between LSOs and Their Foundations." *Roll Call*, July 8.

————. 1993b. "Former Selects Bid to Return as LSOs." *Roll Call,* October 7.

————. 1993c. "In a Twist, Nigeria's Abiola a Center of House Debate." *Roll Call,* November 22.

————. 1993d. "Raucous House Administration Meeting Leaves New LSO Rules Stalled, Some in 'Kleczka Gulch.'" *Roll Call,* August 9.

————. 1994a. "Flying Under the House's Radar." *Roll Call,* June 27.

————. 1994b. "House Republicans Threatening to Boycott Harvard Portion of Freshmen Orientation." *Roll Call,* June 23.

————. 1994c. "LSOs to CMOs." *Roll Call,* December 1.

————. 1994d. "A Shopper's Guide to House LSOs." *Roll Call,* January 24.

————. 1994e. "Three 'LSO' Hopefuls Rejected." *Roll Call,* July 11.

Kahn, Gabriel. 1995. "Remnants of DSG Will Go to Caucus." *Roll Call,* May 29.

Kingdon, John W. 1995. *Agendas, Alternatives, and Public Policies.* 2nd ed. New York: HarperCollins College Publishers.

Kirchoff, Sue, and Donna Cassata. 1998. "Long List of Its Own Trespasses Tempers Congress' Judgment." *Congressional Quarterly Weekly Report,* January 31.

Koszczuk, Jackie. 1998. "Proof of Illegal Votes Falls Short, Keeping Sanchez in House." *Congressional Quarterly Weekly Report,* February 7.

Love, Alice A. 1994. "LSO Money: Where Will It Go?" *Roll Call,* December 8.

————. 1995a. "Black Caucus Foundations' Request for Grant Gets Flak." *Roll Call,* June 1.

————. 1995b. "House Skips Its Chance to Relocate Women's Suffrage Statue; Architect's Memo Is Blamed." *Roll Call,* August 10.

————. 1995c. "'Ladies in the Bathtub' Headed for the Rotunda." *Roll Call,* July 20.

————. 1995d. "LSO Foundations Take Financial Hit." *Roll Call,* April 27.

————. 1995e. "Money That Once Went to LSOs Is Windfall for Members' Offices." *Roll Call,* March 20.

Maloney, Carolyn B. 2000. *The Status of Women: Wins During the 106th Congress,* October 17.

Mansbridge, Jane J. 1986. *Why We Lost the ERA.* Chicago: University of Chicago Press.

Molinari, Susan. 1998. *Representative Mom: Balancing Budgets, Bill, and Baby in the U.S. Congress.* With Elinor Burkett. New York:

Doubleday.

Owens, John E. 1996. "Gingrich's House Has Something in Common with British Parliament." *Roll Call,* January 29.

Rae, Nicol C. 1998. *Conservative Reformers: The Republican Freshmen and the Lessons of the 104th Congress.* Armonk, N.Y.: M. E. Sharpe.

Roll Call. 1993. "LSOs: Less Loose." Editorial, July 29.

―――. 1997. "Morning Business: Women's Work." September 25.

―――. 1998. "Morning Business: More Power." May 25.

―――. 1999. "Morning Business: Leadership Expansion." January 7.

Schroeder, Pat. 1997. *24 Years of House Work . . . and the Place Is Still a Mess: My Life in Politics.* Kansas City, Mo.: Andrews McMeel.

Sheffner, Benjamin. 1997a. "California Official Vows Jail Time if Voter Fraud Proven in Calif. 46." *Roll Call,* February 17.

―――. 1997b. "Republicans Nix Sanchez Field Hearing, Citing Election Challenge in Her District." *Roll Call,* May 19.

―――. 1997c. "Republicans Want Broader Probe of Louisiana State Election Case." *Roll Call,* April 14.

―――. 1997d. "Rules Panel Approves Unlimited La. Probe." *Roll Call,* April 21.

Taylor, Andrew. 1998a. "Fiscal Hawks Fight Effort to Skirt Budget Caps for Year 2000 Computer Fix." *Congressional Quarterly Weekly Report,* June 20.

―――. 1998b. "This Year's Surplus-Spending Binge Will Compound Next Year's Headaches." *Congressional Quarterly Weekly Report,* October 17.

Van Dongen, Rachel. 1997a. "Congressional Investigators to Hand Sanchez Election Probe Back to State." *Roll Call,* October 23.

―――. 1997b. "Democrat Moves to Ban Dornan from House Floor." *Roll Call,* September 18.

―――. 1997c. "Democrats Again Demand End to Probe of Sanchez." *Roll Call,* October 13.

―――. 1997d. "Democrats Dismiss Report on California Election." *Roll Call,* December 15.

―――. 1997e. "Democrats Make Sanchez an Hispanic Cause Celebre." *Roll Call,* July 31.

―――. 1997f. "To Get His Honor Back Dornan Declares He Will Run Against Sanchez Once Again." *Roll Call,* October 20.

―――. 1998a. "Dornan Election Case Dismissed." *Roll Call,* February 9.

―――. 1998b. "House Votes Down Dornan Case and Horn Legislation." *Roll Call,* February 16.

―――. 1998c. "Seething Dornan Wants Rematch with Sanchez. *Roll*

Call, February 12.

Wells, Robert Marshall. 1995. "Bill's Abortion Funding Limits Attest to GOP Control." *Congressional Quarterly Weekly Report,* July 22.

Women's Policy Inc. 1996. *The Women's Health Equity Act of 1996: Legislative Summary and Overview,* July 12.

———. 1997a. *Quarterly Update: Women and Family Issues in the 105th Congress,* Summer.

———. 1997b. *Quarterly Update: Women and Family Issues in the 105th Congress,* Winter.

———. 1998. *Quarterly Update on Women's Issues in Congress,* Winter.

———. 1999. *Quarterly Update on Women's Issues in Congress,* Winter.

———. 2000. *Quarterly Update on Women's Issues in Congress,* Winter.

———. 2001. *Quarterly Update on Women's Issues in Congress,* Winter.

Index

Aberdeen Proving Grounds, 137
Abortion: change, coping with
  (1995–1996), 92–103, 112; future
  of the CCWI, 176; late-term,
  98–103; origin/early years
  (1977–1981), 11, 13, 17; partial-
  birth, 98–103; pill (RU-486), 32,
  52; reclaiming the initiative
  (1997–1998), 119–120, 127–128;
  before the Republican revolution
  (1993–1994), 39, 50–53;
  transformation/growth
  (1982–1992), 27, 30, 31
Abuse, child, 108. *See also* Domestic
  abuse/violence; Legislation,
  Violence Against Women Act;
  Sexual abuse/assault/harassment
Abzug, Bella, 7
Administration Committee, 69
Affirmative action, 4, 26, 105, 148
Afghanistan, 172, 173
African American congresswomen,
  36–37, 55, 63, 89, 165
Agenda, and future of CCWI,
  169–171
Agriculture Committee, 61
Aid to Families with Dependent
  Children, 21, 98
Albright, Madeline, 104, 127
Alexander, Lamar, 73, 74
American College of Obstetricians
  and Gynecologists, 79, 121
Amnesty International, 104

Anthony, Susan B., 16, 89, 91
Antigovernment bias of GOP
  freshman, 75–76
Appropriations Committee, 38,
  95–97, 104, 108, 132–136, 146,
  176
Armed Services Committee, 168
Armey, Richard, 77–78, 140, 141,
  153
Asian Caucus, 3
Athletics, women and college,
  174–175
Automotive Caucus, 78

Baker, Howard, 137
Banking, Currency, and Urban
  Affairs Committee, 63
Banking and Financial Services
  Committee, 63
Bank scandal, House, 36, 68
Bauer, Bob, 144–146
Bennett, William, 74
Biggert, Judy, 162–164, 174
Bipartisanship: change, coping with
  (1995–1996), 109–112; future of
  the CCWI, 165–166; origin/early
  years (1977–1981), 9–10, 21;
  reclaiming the initiative
  (1997–1998), 121–125;
  Republicans take control
  (1995–1996), 53–56;
  transformation/growth
  (1982–1992), 29–30

Boehner, John, 140, 175
Boggs, Lindy, 20, 127
Bone-density measurements, 136
Bradley, Bill, 115
Breast cancer, 130
Breast-feeding, 136
Brown-Waite, Ginny, 162, 163
Budget Committee, 38
Bureau of Alcohol, Tobacco, and
　Firearms (ATF), 131
Burke, Yvonne B., 10
Bush, George H. W., 4, 14, 25,
　28–29, 32, 45, 50, 51
Bush, George W., 14, 165, 166, 173
Buyer, Steve, 137
Byron, Beverly, 20

Canady, Charles, 98, 100, 105
Canfield, Bill, 144–146
Capito, Shelley M., 162–164, 174
Capps, Lois, 121
Carter, Jimmy, 12, 14, 20, 31–32
CCWI. *See* Congressional Caucus for
　Women's Issues
Census questions, 27
Center for Reproductive Law and
　Public Policy, 101
Change, coping with (1995–1996):
　abortion rights redux, 92–103;
　congressional membership
　organization, 77–86; erosion of
　strategic premises, 109–115; new
　women, 86–92; two sessions,
　103–108
Chenoweth, Helen, 89, 92, 98
Child abuse, 108. *See also* Domestic
　abuse/violence; Legislation,
　Violence Against Women Act;
　Sexual abuse/assault/harassment
Child care, 28, 130–132, 141, 176
Child support, 28, 49
China, 107
Chisholm, Shirley, 10
Chowder and Marching Society, 3
Christian-Green, Donna, 122
Cisneros, Henry, 148
Civil Rights Commission, 26
Civil rights protections for
　congressional employees, 107
Clayton, Eva, 37, 54
Clinton, Bill, 4, 14, 36–38, 45,

51–52, 94, 109, 114–115, 127,
　142–143, 147, 154, 166, 172
Clinton, Hillary, 4, 38, 52, 54, 127
Coalition on Population and
　Development, 93
Cochairs, future of CCWI and
　recruiting feminist, 162–164
Cohen, William, 137
Collegiality, Gingrich/GOP freshman
　rejecting norm of, 66
Collins, Barbara Rose, 63
Congressional Black Caucus, 3, 4,
　11, 67–69, 78, 80, 83, 85, 113, 139
Congressional Black Caucus
　Foundation, 69
Committee on Committees, 60
Congressional Caucus for Women's
　Issues (CCWI): catalyst/facilitator
　role, 11; Executive Committee's
　efficacy, 166–167; goals, strategic,
　109–115, 118–119, 158;
　infrastructure, 125–127, 166–169;
　leaders/power structure, 12, 14, 20,
　31–32, 113, 139–143, 172–178;
　"Magnificent Seven" (legislative
　measures), 129–131, 140–141;
　men, 23–25, 33, 82; overview of,
　1, 3–5; recruiting feminist
　cochairs, 162–164; staff, 80–81,
　86, 109, 113, 166, 169; task forces,
　39, 82, 113, 118, 167, 168; team
　concept, 122–124, 158, 167–168;
　twentieth anniversary, 121; vice
　chair positions, 168–169. *See also*
　Change, coping with (1995–1996);
　Future of the CCWI; Origin/early
　years (1977–1981); Reclaiming the
　initiative (1997–1998);
　Transformation/growth
　(1982–1992)
Congressional membership
　organizations (CMOs), 3, 4, 67,
　77–86, 125–126
Congressional Quarterly, Inc., 4, 78
Congresswomen's Caucus. *See*
　Congressional Caucus for
　Women's Issues
Conservative Action Team, 76
Conservative Opportunity Society, 3
Contested elections: *Dornan v.*
　Sanchez, 147–157; *Jenkins v.*

Landrieu, 144–147; overview, 143–144
Contraception, 47, 124–125, 129–136
Contracting issue, federal, 123
Contract with America, 2, 4, 58, 61, 64, 74–76, 86
Court cases: *Grove City v. Bell* (1983), 26–27; *Planned Parenthood v. Casey* (1992), 50; *Roe v. Wade,* 17, 50, 51, 95, 112, 176; *Webster v. Reproductive Health Services* (1989), 50
Cubin, Barbara, 87, 98, 140, 175

Danner, Pat, 56
Daschle, Tom, 146
Defense Advisory Committee on Women in the Services (DACOWITS), 173
Defense Department, U.S. (DOD), 46–47
DeLauro, Rosa, 99, 175
DeLay, Tom, 153
Democratic influence in the House, and Gingrich/GOP freshman, 62–66
Democratic Study Group (DSG), 2–4, 70, 77–78
Democratic Women's Group, 110
District of Columbia Committee, 63
Division and specialization of labor, 33
Dole, Bob, 105
Domestic abuse/violence, 47–48, 106–108, 171
Dooley, Betty, 20
Dornan, Robert, 107, 147–157
DSG. *See* Democratic Study Group
Dunn, Jennifer, 43, 56, 84, 92–93, 121, 140, 141, 175

Economic and Educational Opportunity Committee, 63
Economic equity, promoting, 48–50
Education, Department of, 174
Education, equality for women in, 26–27, 48, 171. *See also* Legislation, Title IX of the Education Amendments of 1972
Education and Labor Committee, 63
Education and Workforce Committee, 149, 175
EEOC. *See* Equal Employment Opportunity Commission
Ehlers, Vern, 149
Elders, Joycelyn, 94
Emerson, Jo Ann, 120
Energy and Commerce Committee, 38, 176
Environmental and Energy Study Conference, 4, 77
Equal Employment Opportunity Commission (EEOC), 26, 104, 105
Equal employment programs, 26
Equal Rights Amendment (ERA), 8, 16–19, 21
Ethics Committee, 78–80, 118, 126, 135

Family-oriented agenda, 44, 47. *See also* Feminist agenda, promoting a
Family planning, 27, 28, 52, 93, 96–97, 105, 171
Family Research Council, 73
Fazio, Vic, 136
FEC. *See* Federal Elections Commission
Federal Communications Commission (FCC), 26
Federal Elections Commission (FEC), 131–132, 134, 135
Feinstein, Dianne, 144–146
Feldstein, Martin, 73
Feminist agenda, promoting a, 4, 15–16, 43–50, 176–177
Fenwick, Millicent, 115
Ferraro, Geraldine, 20, 115
Fetal tissue research, 32
Financial abuses, legislative service organizations and, 3, 67–69
Foley, Tom, 40, 113, 172
Food stamps, 21
Fort Leonard Wood, 137
Foster, Henry W., Jr., 93
Fowler, Tillie, 54, 137, 138, 168, 175
Frank, Barney, 115
Free Congress Foundation, 73
Furse, Elizabeth, 94–95
Future of the CCWI: agenda, 169–171; committed congresswomen, 164–166; creation and abandonment of caucuses,

161; increases in number/power of women, 177–178; leaders/power structure, 172–178; overview, 161; recruiting feminist cochairs, 162–164; resources, adjusting to competing claims on, 171–172; structure, 166–169

Gag rule, 27, 31
Galbraith, John K., 73
General Accounting Office (GAO), 46, 69, 146
Genetic tests, 131
Genital mutilation, 106
George Washington University, 127
Gephardt, Richard, 44, 65, 79, 140, 152, 154, 175
Gilman, Benjamin, 97
Gingrich, Newt, 2, 4, 57–62, 65–68, 71–73, 84, 87, 91, 106, 109, 110, 113, 117–118, 136, 139–141, 155, 174
Girl Scouts of America, 18
Glass ceiling, 141–142, 176
Government Reform and Oversight Committee, 149
Government shutdown and decline in Republican credibility, 106
Granger, Kay, 163
Green, Edith, 7–9
Greenwood, James, 97, 108
Grove City College, 26–27
Gulf War, 68

Haitian immigrants, 132, 134
Hall, Cindy, 80, 170–171
Hamilton, Lee, 73
Hamm, Mia, 175
Hansen, Julia B., 7–9
Harman, Jane, 137, 138, 168
Harvard University, 73–74
Hastert, Dennis, 108, 165, 174–175
Hate crimes, 47–48
Head Start, 48, 50, 75, 98, 130
Health, women's: abortion, 97–103; consensus in, 112; disappointments in, 28–29; gains made in 104th Congress, 106, 108; "Magnificent Seven" (legislative measures), 129–131; mammograms, 136; omnibus bills, bundling proposals,

15; reproductive, 124–125. *See also* Abortion; Contraception; Family planning; Legislation
Health and Human Services, U.S. Department of (HHS), 27, 99
Healy, Bernadine, 32
Heckler, Margaret, 7, 9–11, 13, 18, 20, 21, 115, 121, 162
Helms, Jesse, 145
Heritage Foundation, 73, 74
Hermandad Mexicana Nacional (HMN), 149, 150–151
HHS. *See* Health and Human Services, U.S. Department of
Hill, Anita, 143
Hispanic Bar Association, 153
Hispanic Caucus, 4, 69, 78, 80, 85. *See also* Sanchez, Loretta
Hispanic Caucus Institute, 69
Historical background on CCWI. *See* Origin/early years (1977–1981)
HMN. *See* Hermandad Mexicana Nacional
Holt, Marjorie, 20
Holtzman, Elizabeth, 9–11, 13, 17, 18, 20, 21, 121, 162
House Finance Office (HFO), 69
Hoyer, Steny, 153
Huffington, Michael, 144
Human Rights Caucus, 68, 85, 113
Human Rights Foundation, 68
Hunger Caucus, 77, 85
Hutchison, Kay B., 143, 173
Hyde, Henry, 61, 98, 100
Hyde Amendment, 52, 97

Immigration and Naturalization Service (INS), 106, 131, 149, 152–153
Inclusiveness, 10, 20, 22, 109, 119, 127–139
Individual retirement accounts (IRAs), 107
Infertility research centers, 47
Infrastructure, CCWI strengthening its, 125–127, 166–169
INS. *See* Immigration and Naturalization Service
Insurance, health, 106, 108, 129, 131–136
Intact dilation and extraction, 98–103

Internal Revenue Service (IRS), 131
International Working Women's Day, 123
Iraq, 172
Istook, Ernest, 97

Jackson, Jesse, 139
Jenkins, Woody, 144–147
Johnson, Adelaide, 89
Johnson, Nancy, 43, 53, 54, 56, 83, 84, 100, 101, 117–119, 121, 122, 124, 125, 128, 130, 133, 135, 139, 140, 157, 158, 163, 164, 167, 174
Jones, Bill, 150, 153
Judiciary Committee, 18, 96, 99

Kassebaum, Nancy, 137, 138
Kelly, Sue, 87, 117, 123, 125, 129, 130, 138, 143, 162, 164, 174
Kemp, Jack, 74
Kennedy School of Government (Harvard), 73–74
Kennelly, Barbara, 40, 43, 54–55, 155, 175
Kirkpatrick, Jeane, 74
Kolbe, Jim, 134, 135
Ku Klux Klan, 89

Landrieu, Mary, 144–147
La Raza, 153
Leaders/power structure, CCWI relations with, 12, 14, 20, 31–32, 113, 139–143, 172–178
League of Women Voters, 87
Lee, Barbara, 121
Legal Services Corporation (LSC), 104, 107
Legislation: Afghan Women and Children Relief Act, 173; Balanced Budget Act of 1997, 136; Bankruptcy Reform Act, 49; Centers for Disease Control Breast and Cervical Cancer Mortality Prevention Act of 1990, 46; Civil Rights Act of 1964, 107; Civil Rights Act of 1991, 27, 28; Congressional Employees Fairness Act, 49; Crime Control Act, 47–48; Defense Authorization Act of 1996, 107; Economic Equity Act of 1996, 49, 107; Educational Equity Act, 104–105; Elementary and Secondary Education Act of 1994, 48; Equal Pay Act of 1963, 7–8; Fair Labor Standards Act of 1937, 107; Family and Medical Leave Act (FMLA) of 1993, 28–29, 38, 45–46, 50, 107, 176; Federal Acquisition Streamlining Act of 1994, 123; Freedom of Access to Clinic Entrances Act, 52; Goals 2000: Educate America Act, 48; Health Insurance Portability and Accountability Act, 106; Mammography Quality Standards Act of 1992, 129–131; National Institutes of Health Revitalization Act of 1993, 46; Newborns and Mothers Protection Act of 1995, 100; Safe and Drug-Free Schools Act, 48; School to Work Opportunities Act, 48; Title IX of the Education Amendments of 1972, 7–8, 15, 26, 104, 105, 174–175; Title X of Public Health Service Act, 96–97, 108; Violence Against Women Act (VAWA), 47, 87, 104, 105, 108, 129, 131, 172; Women's Economic Equity Act, 86, 87, 106; Women's Educational Equity Act, 104; Women's Health Equity Act, 32, 85–86, 103
Legislative service organizations (LSOs), 1–4, 23, 67–71, 109, 125–126, 139, 177. *See also* Congressional membership organizations
Levin, Sharon, 80
Lewinsky, Monica, 154
Lewis, Jerry, 72
Limbaugh, Rush, 74, 87, 147
Linder, John, 132
Lindy Boggs Reading Room, 12, 121
Livingston, Robert, 59, 97, 146
Lloyd, Marilyn, 20, 39
Lofgren, Zoe, 155–156
Lopez, Nativo, 150–151
Louisiana Independent Federation of Electors (LIFE), 144
Lowey, Nita, 39, 51–53, 55, 71, 80, 93, 95, 97, 99, 105, 108, 110, 124, 129, 130, 132–136, 164, 175

Maloney, Carolyn, 117, 164
Mammograms, 46, 106, 129–131, 136
Matalin, Mary, 173–174
McCloskey, Frank, 150
McConnell, Mitch, 145
McIntyre, Richard, 150
McKinney, Cynthia, 37, 115
Medicaid, 21, 47, 52, 97, 157
Medicare, 136
Meek, Carrie, 38, 125
Megan's Law, 108
Men, opening up CCWI to, 23–25, 33, 82
Menendez, Robert, 152
Mental health insurance coverage, 106
Merchant Marine and Fisheries Committee, 8, 62–63
"Mexico City policy," 27, 31
Meyers, Jan, 69, 83, 84, 100, 101
Midwives, nurse, 47
Mikulski, Barbara, 10, 14–15, 18
Military, women in the, 46–47, 49, 104, 106, 107, 137–138, 168, 171–173
Millender-McDonald, Juanita, 121, 123, 129, 130, 138, 163, 164
Mink, Patsy, 7, 39, 110, 124
Molinari, Guy, 40
Molinari, Susan, 40–43, 53, 54, 74–75, 83, 84, 94, 101, 106, 108, 113–115, 124, 140
Moorhead, Carlos, 59
Morella, Constance, 39, 55, 79, 80, 83, 91, 93, 95, 97, 106, 108, 110, 129, 164
Morial, Marc, 144
Motor vehicle bureaus, confidentiality of information, 48
Mott, Lucretia, 89, 91
Mount Vernon College, 127
Moynihan, Daniel Patrick, 173
Myers, John, 59
Myrick, Sue, 91, 98, 140

National Abortion Rights Action League (NARAL), 94, 101, 176
National Breast Cancer Coalition, 104
National Cancer Institute, 130
National Center for Education Statistics, 48

National Institute on Aging, 46
National Institutes of Health (NIH), 130
National Organization for Women (NOW), 18, 94, 101
National Security Committee, 137
National Women's History Week, 28
National Women's Party, 89
National Women's Political Caucus, 18
Native Americans, 47
New Federalists, 76
Nickle, Don, 145
Nigeria, 68–69
Nonprofit foundations and legislative service organizations, 68–69
Northup, Anne, 120, 143, 164
Norton, Eleanor H., 49, 56, 117–119, 121, 122, 124–130, 133, 135, 137–139, 141, 158, 163, 164, 167, 177
Novello, Antonia, 32
NOW. *See* National Organization for Women

Obey, David, 70
Office of Educational Research and Information, 48
Office of Management and Budget (OMB), 27
Office of Research on Women's Health, 28
Office of Women's Business Ownership, 49
Office of Women's Health, 130
Office on Women's Initiatives and Outreach, 172, 173
Older Women's League, 104
Omnibus bills, bundling proposals, 15–16, 30–31, 128–129, 136
O'Neill, Thomas "Tip," 10, 12, 24, 113, 172, 175
Orange County District Attorney's Office, 149
Orientation seminars for new House members, 73–74
Origin/early years (1977–1981): doubts about value of a women's group, 8–9; Equal Rights Amendment, 16–19; goals, policy, 14–16; goals, strategic, 9–13; organizational strains, 19–22;

recruiting members, 7–9;
workways, 13–14
Osteoporosis Foundation, 104
Oversight Committee, 149, 151–152

Packwood, Bob, 142
Paul, Alice, 28, 89
Paxon, Bill, 41
Pay equity for women working on
Capitol Hill, 49
Pelosi, Nancy, 43, 143, 176
Peña, Federico, 148
Pettis, Shirley, 10
Planned Parenthood, 27, 101
Population control polices, asylum to
victims of coercive, 107
Porter, John, 108
Portrait Monument, 89–92
Post Office and Civil Service
Committee, 63
Post Office scandal, House, 36, 68
Powell, Colin, 173
Primmer, Lesley, 79
Pro-Choice Task Force, 93
Proxy voting, 64–65
Pryce, Deborah, 54, 56, 102, 141,
143, 173, 175
Puerto Rico Legal Defense, 153

Quarterly Update, 79

Radanovich, George, 76
Rankin, Jeannette, 28
Rape, 108, 176
Reagan, Nancy, 32, 38
Reagan, Ronald, 4, 14, 21–22,
25–28, 32, 50, 51
Reclaiming the initiative
(1997–1998): assessing the caucus
in the 105th Congress, 157–158;
bipartisanship, 121–125;
consensus, 127–139; contested
elections, 143–157; infrastructure,
125–127; leaders/power structure,
139–143; overview, 117–119;
recruiting new members, 119–121
Reed, Ralph, 74
Reich, Robert, 73
Reid, Harry, 134
Republican Conference, 77
Republican congresswomen:

abortion, 92–103; contested
elections, 144, 154–157;
disengagement from CCWI,
83–85; future of the CCWI,
164–166; Gingrich strengthening
his rapport with, 84; and government's role, 85; 1993 CCWI
membership, 30; 1994 elections,
86–92; Portrait Monument, 89–92;
reclaiming the initiative, CCWI's
attempts at, 119–125; recruiting
feminist cochairs, 162; relations
between Democratic and, 109–112;
and the Republican Party, 140;
Title IX of the Education
Amendments of 1972, 174–175
Republican Digest, 78
Republican revolution, before the
(1993–1994): abortion issue,
50–53; bipartisanship, 53–56;
economic equity, 48–50; feminist
agenda, 43–50; leverage, gaining,
37–39; power in the House, 40–43;
social agenda, 45–48. *See also*
Transformation/growth
(1982–1992)
Republicans take control
(1995–1996): consolidating power,
58–66; Contract with America and
the role of government, 74–76;
legislative service organizations,
abolishing, 67–71; overview, 1–5,
57–58; the revolutionaries, 71–74
Republican Study Committee, 3, 77,
78
Rice, Condoleezza, 73
Riders attached to appropriation bills,
62, 95, 132–133
Roberts, Cokie, 127
Roberts, Pat, 67, 70
Rogers, Harold, 108
Rohrbacher, Dana, 151
Rophynol, 108
Rose, Charlie, 67–69
Roukema, Marge, 44–45, 83, 124,
142–143
Rules, Gingrich/GOP freshman
altering House and party, 59–65,
76, 95
Rules Committee, 40, 61–62, 95,
102, 104, 132, 134, 144–146, 155

Sanchez, Loretta, 122, 124, 144, 145, 148–157
Santorum, Rick, 145
Satcher, David, 130
SBA. *See* Small Business Administration
Scanlan, Susan, 20
School lunches, 98
Schroeder, Pat, 16, 18, 21, 24, 29, 32, 36, 38, 39, 44, 45, 54, 55, 70–71, 87, 91, 96, 99, 101, 106, 107, 162
Seastrand, Andrea, 98
Seniority system, Gingrich/GOP freshman altering, 59–61
September 11 terrorist attack, 166
Sex scandal, President Clinton, 142–143, 154
Sexual abuse/assault/harassment, 48, 50, 104, 108, 137–138, 142–143, 171. *See also* Legislation, Violence Against Women Act
Shaddegg, Steven, 76
Shalala, Donna, 104
Slaughter, Louise, 39, 40, 43, 51, 106, 124, 129, 163, 164, 175
Small Business Administration (SBA), 28, 49, 123
Small Business Committee, 123, 138
Smith, Ann Charnley, 20
Smith, Chris, 98, 133
Smith, Linda, 98, 129
Smith, Virginia, 20
Snowe, Olympia, 20, 29, 44, 55, 83, 91, 106, 162
Social policy/agenda of CCWI, 45–48, 74–75
Social Security, 21
Social support and affiliation with CCWI, 33–34
Solis, Hilda, 164
Solomon, Gerry, 95
Source, The, 79, 82
Speaker's Advisory Group (SAG), 61
Specialization and division of labor, 33
Spellman, Gladys, 18
Sportsmen's Caucus, 3
Staff, CCWI's loss of professional,

80–81, 86, 109, 113, 166, 169
Staff support, Gingrich/GOP freshman and loss of Democratic, 63
Stalking, legislation dealing with, 108
Standing committees, 59–60
Stanton, Elizabeth C., 89, 91
Stark, Pete, 53–54
Starr, Kenneth, 142, 143
Status of Women in the States, 127
Stearns, Cliff, 42
Steering Committee, Republican, 60
Stenholm, Charles, 73
Stevens, Ted, 90–91, 134, 135
Sullivan, Leonor, 7–9
Sullivan, Louis, 32
Supreme Court. *See* Court cases; Legislation

Talent, James, 123
Taliban women, 173
Tamoxifen, 130
Task forces, 39, 82, 113, 118, 167, 168
Tauscher, Ellen, 130
Team concept at CCWI, 122–124, 158, 167–168
Theme Team, 76
Thomas, Clarence, 143
Thomas, William, 67, 78, 79, 149–151
Time period on House floor and voting, 65
Training, job, 111–112, 124
Transformation/growth (1982–1992): increases in number of women serving in Congress, 35–37; membership change, 23–25; Reagan-Bush agenda, 25–29; viability, caucus, 29–34. *See also* Republican revolution, before the (1993–1994)
Treasury and Postal Service, subcommittee on the, 131–136

Unanimity rule, 10–11, 20, 22
United Nations Fund for Population Activities, 52
Update, 20, 23, 24, 31, 33

Vaccines, 47

Veterans Affairs, Department of, 47, 106, 173
Vice chair positions, 168–169
VIEW PAC, 140
Vocational education, 124
Vucanovich, Barbara, 113

Wage gap between men and women, 49, 141–142
Waldholtz, Enid, 59, 100–101
Warner, John, 144–146
Waters, Maxine, 39, 55, 143, 163–165, 176–177
Ways and Means Committee, 38, 53, 63, 108, 176
Welfare reform, 107, 108, 111
White, George, 90–91
WIC. *See* Women, Infants, and Children program
Wilson, Heather, 121

Women, Infants, and Children (WIC) program, 21–22, 49, 75
Women in Congress, 121
Women-owned businesses, 123, 129, 130, 138, 171
Women's Business Centers, 123
Women's Economic Equity Act, 86, 87, 106
Women's groups in members' constituencies, 33
Women's History Month, 123
Women's Policy, Inc. (WPI), 79–80, 105, 112, 118, 121, 126, 158, 169, 170–171
Woolsey, Lynn, 36, 38
WPI. *See* Women's Policy, Inc.
Wright, Jim, 113

Young Women's Christian Association, 18

About the Book

The Congressional Caucus for Women's Issues (CCWI) was the most effective bipartisan organization in the House—until changes wrought by the "Republican revolution" of 1994 threatened its very survival. Irwin Gertzog analyzes the origin, development, and influence of the CCWI and explores how the women associated with it have emerged from near oblivion to reassert their role in the legislative process.

Assessing the caucus within the contexts of legislative decision-making, competing policy agendas, partisan politics, and legislative-presidential relations, Gertzog demonstrates that it has evolved and survived despite substantial challenges to its integrity and mission. Although the definition of "women's issues" has changed significantly since 1977, he concludes, the CCWI continues to coalesce around strategic policy goals, thus ensuring its enduring niche in the legislative power structure.

Irwin N. Gertzog is emeritus professor of political science at Allegheny College and adjunct professor of political science at Columbia and Rutgers Universities. His publications include *Congressional Women: Their Recruitment, Integration, and Behavior.*